STAYING PUT:
Adapting the Places
Instead of the People

Edited by:

Susan Lanspery
Heller School, Brandeis University

Joan Hyde
Gerontology Institute, University of Massachusetts, Boston

Society and Aging Series
Jon Hendricks: Series Editor

BAYWOOD PUBLISHING COMPANY, INC.
Amityville, New York

Copyright © 1997 by Baywood Publishing Company, Inc., Amityville, New
York. All rights reserved. Printed in the United States of America on acid-free,
recycled paper.

Library of Congress Catalog Number: 95-51473
ISBN: 0-89503-133-7 (cloth)

Library of Congress Cataloging-in-Publication Data

Staying put : adapting the places instead of the people / edited by
   Susan Lanspery, Joan Hyde.
        p.   cm. - - (Society and aging series)
    Includes bibliographical references and index.
    ISBN 0-89503-133-7 (cloth : acid-free paper)
    1. Aged- -Dwellings- -United States.   2. Architecture and the aged-
-United States.   3. Architecture- -Environmental aspects- -United
States.   I. Lanspery, Susan. II. Hyde, Joan.   III. Series.
NA7195.A4S7   1996
728'.043- -dc20   95-51473
                                                                        CIP

Preface

M. Powell Lawton

This volume constitutes a first effort to assemble contributions providing a comprehensive treatment of a topic that has been within at least marginal awareness of the gerontological community for well over a decade [1, 2]. Publication of the book, in turn, might help to motivate a long-overdue national effort to use better the precious resource represented by the ordinary homes occupied by individuals of all ages who have disabilities or impairments. Among people sixty-five and over, an estimated 89 percent own or rent such ordinary homes. These dwellings have usually been chosen by their occupants. Despite the availability of newer housing types such as retirement communities, senior citizen housing, or purpose-built residences for the handicapped, the overwhelming majority of people sixty and over wish to remain where they are [3].

Staying put is contingent on the livability of the dwelling unit. Attaining such livability by means of changes in the physical character of the dwelling unit represents an attractive goal for two reasons. First, it is probably easier (and is often preferable) to change physical housing than to change the frail user. Second, the principles of achieving livability are applicable to all levels of housing. As indicated in Chapter 11 of this book, adaptation of planned housing originally built for healthy elders is a very attainable goal. One could imagine applying similar principles to new construction of planned housing, re-use housing, or naturally occurring retirement communities (NORCs—housing that evolves in an unplanned manner over time to serve older users).

Examining the content of the diverse chapters from a longer perspective may afford an integrated picture of the separate chapters' messages. A model of adapted housing and its implementation must begin, as always, with the intricate system that represents person-in-environment. This system is itself embedded in a larger context, composed of six elements: the consumer context, the family context, the commercial housing context, the technology context, the service agency context, and the legal context. The complex interactions among the person-environment system and its multiple contexts in turn have outcomes in housing policy and practice. Each of the chapters in this book may be located in terms of its emphasis on one or more of these components. As a whole they provide a moving (and advancing) target to guide policy and program development in the future.

The *person* is, for convenience, discussed separately from the residential environment, despite the basic inseparability of the two. Asserting the common cause of the frail elders and people with disabilities (see especially Zola's Chapter 2) is a major strength of the editors' conception of their task. On the other hand, the content emphasizes throughout the idea that the single solution is impossible. Individual needs are always the beginning point.

The *dwelling unit* is a co-equal in the person-environment system. Regnier and Pynoos (Chapter 3) provide the best possible illustration of the oneness of person and environment in their articulation of twelve principles linking characteristics of the person to the ability of the residence to support. Similar reasoning underlies the approach of Connell and Sanford (Chapter 7). Person-environment congruence is the end goal.

The *consumer context* represents users in the aggregate. Ohta and Ohta (Chapter 5) provide an excellent model for comprehending how consumer acceptance may become enhanced. Although consumer activism is mentioned at various points in the book, the possibilities for advancing further by collective action in the model of the disabilities constituency requires further attention.

The *family context* is another arena for activity that is noted but not elaborated. Future study of home adaptations would do well to examine the process by which family assistance, by both household members and non-resident relatives, is made most effective. Many changes are the joint result of the user and the family member. The family member is also a potential member of the consumer constituency. Chapter 6 takes a step in this direction with respect to caregivers for people with Alzheimer's disease. Further examination of the processes of knowledge diffusion and product awareness among family members would be rewarding.

The *commercial housing context* includes diverse actors such as developers, builders, owners, rental agents, and others. The Robert Wood Johnson study reported by Lanspery (Chapter 11) deals with this context. The motivation to benefit the needy user is not sufficient for the commercial context. Cost guidelines must be developed for all degrees of intervention in this area, including better estimates of the benefits derived from increased user satisfaction and improved property upkeep.

The *technology context's* most evident members are the architects and professional designers responsible for many decisions regarding the form of modifications (see Chapter 3 by Regnier and Pynoos, Chapter 4 by Grayson, and Chapter 7 by Connell and Sanford). Such high-level expertise is only the beginning, however. Increased involvement by product designers, engineers, and human-factors psychologists will be needed. A less technical level of expertise will also be needed, such as that possessed by home modifications craftsmen or in-home service aides. Everyday practice clearly cannot afford to utilize only the highest-level expertise.

The *service agency context* may provide the second tier of expertise in housing modification. Several chapters (particularly Chapter 9 by Pynoos and colleagues and Chapter 10 by Hereford) seek to analyze how social agencies have dealt with some housing-related needs of their clients. The service agency is particularly problematic. Traditionally, social agencies lack expertise in housing, and housing agencies lack expertise in social needs and service delivery. On a local level, the delivery of home modification services may be a good starting point for the integration of such perspectives.

The staff of local agencies should be the beneficiaries of the expertise of the technology context. In-service training can provide an increment in usable knowledge about housing user needs, basic design principles, how to "diagnose" a dwelling unit on a walk-through, and how to enlist the occupant in an environmental problem-solving effort. Sensitization to the concept of need-relevant design is the primary goal. The secondary goal is to learn to distinguish between major tasks requiring professional expertise and less complex tasks that are within the realm of aging expertise. The last goal is to develop a repertory of suggested solutions to the set of relatively minor home modification problems.

The *legal context* is crucial to the implementation model. For the first time, this book presents the background and present status of the national legislative acts designed to help equalize environmental usability by diverse consumers (Chapters 12 by Talbert and colleagues and Chapter 13 by Newman and Mezrich). Continued collection of experience with local laws, ordinances, and codes is also required in order to build up "how-to" procedural manuals for local action. The political entities (city councils, planning commissions, and so on) represent another side of the legal context.

The book is exemplary also by virtue of its integration of research into the treatment of home modifications. Chapters 7 (Silverstein and Hyde), 8 (Mutschler), 9 (Pynoos and colleagues), and 11 (Lanspery) document empirical attempts to provide knowledge regarding the consumer as well as the workings of agency programs. The recent research of Manton, Corder, and Stallard raises the intriguing question as to whether the person-level outcomes of adapted housing may have a measurable impact on impaired function [4]. We need focused research to test such hypotheses. The concluding Chapter 14 (Sloan, Hyde, and Lanspery) calls clearly for such continued investment of resources in search of empirical knowledge.

The concept of practice thus does not involve only the agency that delivers the service. That agency depends on the confluence of all other contexts, beginning with the person-environment system. Similarly, we clearly do not have a simplistic society in which a policy is formulated, then followed by implemented practice and linear effects of the policy on each of the contexts. In our highly complicated system, the policy evolves through contributions from all systems and continually changing feedback from policy to context and among combinations of contexts.

It seems to this writer that such a process involving the contexts of home adaptation policies and practices has been in operation long enough for a major articulation of a planful policy to evolve. As both the opening and closing chapters of this book indicate, policy has heretofore been implicit. The book's publication will help to make policy issues overt. Simultaneously, the larger issues surrounding practice should be exposed to broader debate. A key issue is the continued bifurcation of activity into housing on the one hand and welfare on the other. This artificial division still, after thirty-five years, begins with the U.S. Department of Housing and Urban Development's standing firm on the side of housing development ("hard services") and the U.S. Department of Health and Human Services on the side of welfare ("soft services"). The same division works its way through state and local levels, putting major obstacles into the path of local agencies that wish to integrate the hard and soft services. This writer's optimistic view is that this book can argue persuasively at each of these levels in favor of the indivisibility of housing, welfare, persons, and environments.

REFERENCES

1. E. Steinfeld, Residential Repair and Renovation, in *Handbook of Human Services for Older Persons,* M. B. Holmes and D. Holmes (eds.), Human Science Press, New York, pp. 145-181, 1979.
2. E. Steinfeld, The Scope of Residential Repair and Renovation Services and Models of Service Delivery, in *Community Housing Choices for Older Americans,* M. P. Lawton and S. L. Hoover (eds.), Springer, New York, pp. 201-220, 1981.
3. American Association of Retired Persons, *Understanding Senior Housing for the 1990s,* AARP, Washington, D.C., 1993.
4. K. Manton, L. Corder, and E. Stallard, Changes in the Use of Personal Assistance and Special Equipment from 1982 to 1989: Results from the 1982 and 1989 NLTCS, *The Gerontologist, 33*:2, pp. 168-176, 1993.

Acknowledgments

We dedicate this book to five people who have inspired our philosophy.

Elaine Ostroff has, sometimes singlehandedly, made the world pay attention to home adaptations. Executive Director of the Adaptive Environments Center in Boston, she provided the original impetus for this book in 1989.

Gunnar Dybwad's and the late *Rosemary Dybwad's* unwavering, lifelong fight for dignity, power, and normalcy for people with disabilities has motivated countless others to hold fast. Gunnar continues to define the cutting edge in consumer influence.

We also want to honor two of our authors who, in a tragic coincidence, died untimely deaths in the same month—December 1994.

Irv Zola's death has left a leadership void that no one can fill. His bridging of the worlds of academia and advocacy was unique, his compassion and warmth legendary, and his intellectual strength unequaled.

Judith Miller, relatively new to the field of home adaptation, had made her mark in public health as a staunch advocate of consumer education and research that makes a difference. She even voluntarily helped to copy-edit an earlier draft of this book.

Elaine, Gunnar, Rosemary, Irv, and Judith have made a profound difference in the world. We hope that this book, in some small way, reflects and adds to that difference.

The editors also thank the authors for their distinguished contributions, commitment, and matchless patience. Despite delays, the book still breaks new ground, and we are grateful for the opportunity to have collaborated with such an outstanding group.

Last but not least, we also thank Jim O'Brien, Derwin Hyde, Judith Miller, and Jim Callahan for copy-editing assistance above and beyond the call of duty; Jon Hendricks for thoughtful reviews and judicious nudging; and Diane Hines for fleet-fingered word processing and tolerant editorial assistance.

Table of Contents

Chapter 1   Introduction: Staying Put   1
Susan Lanspery, James J. Callahan, Jr.,
Judith R. Miller, and Joan Hyde

PART I
REFRAMING HOUSING ADAPTATIONS **23**

Chapter 2   Living at Home: The Convergence of Aging
and Disability   25
Irving Kenneth Zola

Chapter 3   Design Directives in Home Adaptation   41
Jon Pynoos and Victor Regnier

Chapter 4   Technology and Home Adaptations   55
Paul John Grayson

PART II
USERS' PERSPECTIVES IN HOME ADAPTATION **75**

Chapter 5   The Elderly Consumer's Decision to Accept or Reject
Home Adaptations: Issues and Perspectives   79
Russell J. Ohta and Brenda M. Ohta

Chapter 6   The Importance of a Consumer Perspective in
Home Adaptation of Alzheimer's Households   91
Nina M. Silverstein and Joan Hyde

Chapter 7   Individualizing Home Modification Recommendations
to Facilitate Performance of Routine Activities   113
Bettye Rose Connell and Jon A. Sanford

Chapter 8   The Effects of Income on Home Modification:
Can They Afford to Stay Put?   149
Phyllis H. Mutschler

PART III
IMPLEMENTING HOUSING ADAPTATION PROGRAMS 169

Chapter 9   The Delivery of Home Modification and
Repair Services 171
Jon Pynoos, Phoebe Liebig, Julie Overton,
and Emily Calvert

Chapter 10   Establishing Home Modification, Maintenance, and
Repair Programs in Community-Based Agencies   193
Russell W. Hereford

Chapter 11   Adapting Subsidized Housing: The Experience of the
Supportive Services Program in Senior Housing 207
Susan C. Lanspery

PART IV
HOUSING ADAPTATION POLICY 221

Chapter 12   Fostering Adaptive Housing: An Overview of
Funding Sources, Laws, and Policies 223
Joan Hyde, Robin Talbert, and Paul John Grayson

Chapter 13   Implications of the 1988 Fair Housing Act for
the Frail Elderly 237
Sandra J. Newman and Molli N. Mezrich

Chapter 14   Research, Policy, and Practice in Housing Adaptation:
Future Directions 253
Katrinka Smith Sloan, Joan Hyde, and Susan Lanspery

Epilogue   Report on the First National Invitational Conference
on Home Modification 263
Mary Ann Wilner

Contributors   273

Index   279

CHAPTER
1

Introduction:
Staying Put

*Susan Lanspery, James J. Callahan, Jr.,
Judith R. Miller, and Joan Hyde*

For most of us, the word "home" evokes powerful emotions and images. It is no accident that realtors sell homes, not houses, that home plate is not fourth base, and that Dorothy chooses the familiarity of Kansas over the enhancement of Oz. Rented or owned, private or shared, single-family or multi-unit, attractive or dilapidated, safe or dangerous, disheveled or tidy, accessible or inaccessible, in a prime or mediocre location, with or without good neighbors—home is a place to take one's ease, a refuge, a center, a treasure chest of memories and of valued (if not valuable) belongings, and an extension and reflection of oneself.

Neither growing older nor having a disability makes the idea of "home" any less compelling. Most older people and people with disabilities want to remain in their homes, even if disabilities worsen, safety and independence are compromised, and these residences become outmoded or in ill repair. Housing adaptations and repairs can often help them to remain, and may even reduce the need for, or increase the effectiveness of, caregivers. As a result, they may save money as they enhance independence.

More and more people are making modifications [1]. Many modifications cost relatively little, can be installed easily, and require low maintenance—in one study, the most important and effective modifications were completed for an average of about $1,500 [2]. Moreover, many older people have the potential to

1

tap the equity in their homes to help pay for modifications and repairs [3, 4]. At the same time, as Mrs. R[1] tells us, obstacles still exist:

> They told me I should be thankful because I'm house-rich. Sure, I said. The railing just about holds my parakeet if he doesn't put all his weight down, and the wall cabinets and stove knobs might as well be in the next county. I haven't gotten all the way into the tub since they remodeled the Statue of Liberty. I want to say in my home, but I'm eighty-five years old, I have arthritis, and my hammer swing ain't what it used to be. The bank won't lend me money because my income is so low, and the carpenter won't take my checks if all my bank statement says is that I'm house-rich.

The relatively modest home adaptations and repairs to which Mrs. R refers would enhance her safety and independence while helping her to remain in her home. Finding the funds and the workers to fix the problems, or even locating a knowledgeable person to help one through the process, however, is easier said than done.

Placing home modifications in context and addressing such challenges are the purposes of this book. In compiling some of the leading work in the field, *Staying Put* brings together issues and state-of-the-art theory and practice in home adaptations. It advocates considering adaptations and repairs before relocation, increasing their availability and affordability, and promoting flexible, individualized choices among adaptations and in-home services to satisfy consumer preferences and accommodate changing needs.

Throughout the book, the words *housing* and *home* are used interchangeably, as are *adaptations* and *modifications*. *Adaptations* and *repairs* are not synonymous, but disentangling the two topics is difficult. Structurally sound housing that meets minimum standards for heat, light, ventilation, plumbing, and cooking facilities is a prerequisite for effective adaptations as well as for quality of life [5, 6]. Older people are more likely than younger people to live in older homes, which tend to be larger, worth less, and more in need of updating, repairs, and accessibility modifications [7, p. 198]. Additionally, more than 8 percent of the twenty million housing units occupied by elderly householders in 1987 had moderate to severe structural or other physical problems not correctable by relatively minor repairs [8]. Thus, the topic of repair deserves to be, and is, included.

The remainder of this chapter is an introduction to and an overview of the book. After a background discussion, it is organized, as the book is, into four main parts: reframing housing adaptation, users' perspectives in home adaptation, implementing housing adaptation programs, and housing adaptation policy.

---

[1] Mrs. R is a fictitious person based on a number of thoughtful and candid consumers known by the editors. She appears occasionally throughout the book to highlight the personal perspective in home adaptations.

BACKGROUND

Why Modify?

Advocates for housing modifications have long argued that environments, not people, are "disabled," and that independence-promoting environments improve the level of functional ability. A recent study offers important evidence for both assertions. According to Manton and his colleagues [1], although the total number of people over sixty-five, and therefore the total *number* of people with disabilities, has increased, the *prevalence* of disability among this group dropped by 7 percent. This decrease is partially due to improvements in health care (such as cataract surgery and hip replacements) that can arrest or reverse the course of certain disabilities. But another important explanation is the increased use of assistive devices and housing adaptations. Mr. Swanson's experience is a good example:

> Swanson, now 80, had been living alone for 25 years in Cambridge. But last fall, he fell and broke a shoulder. The doctors put in steel pins and tried to fix him up, but the bad shoulder still limits his mobility, he says, "because it hurts if I move the wrong way. The pain is pretty bad."
>
> Without his shoulder and arm for balance, it is "dangerous for me to go down and back up" the three flights of stairs to the front door, and he's afraid to rely on a buzzer system for fear of blindly buzzing in strangers instead of people delivering hot meals to his apartment.
>
> When ElderLink (a home repair and adaptation agency) suggested an intercom, Swanson agreed. Delighted, he said, "Now I can ask who it is, and the only ones I let in are people whose voices I recognize" [9, p. 8].

Other research findings suggest that home adaptation not only supports the independent functioning of people with disabilities, but can also be cost-effective. Many of the most frequently needed adaptations are those with the lowest costs, such as grab bars. A study of respirator users at a London hospital found that housing modifications and home care services were 40 percent less costly than hospitalization. A study of three communities in Sweden found that 4 to 30 percent of the moves to nursing homes could have been avoided by accessible housing. Three other studies found that accessible housing could have saved moves from the community to sheltered housing by 12 to 30 percent [10]. Several other studies estimate low costs and project valuable benefits for building barrier-free new construction or modifying existing buildings [2, 11-14].

Appropriate environments not only enable people with some health problems or limitations to function more independently, they are also helpful throughout the lifespan. Some years ago, for example, a manufacturer developed a washing machine and dryer for use by the elderly and disabled. Large, easy-to-read dials were placed in front where they could be reached by people using wheelchairs or with mobility or visual impairments. After a slow start, sales took off: in addition to people with disabilities, working parents whose children help with the laundry were buying the machines.

Who Needs Help and Why?

Estimates of the magnitude of need for home adaptation suggest that up to 12 percent, or over two million elderly households, require home adaptations to support the needs of a member with a health or mobility problem [15-17]. According to the findings of a Robert Wood Johnson Foundation project (see Chapter 10), up to 30 percent of elderly households desire dwelling-related repair and/or modification services. These numbers are expected to rise as the population continues to age. The need is greater for persons over seventy-five, for women, for people of color, and for those with few financial resources.

How did so many elders end up in housing that needs modifications? Three important reasons are mistaken design assumptions, tax policies, and—ironically—housing policies.

First, during and since the post-World War II boom period, most homes were built for young, active people with (or expecting) children. Most of these homes—often called "Peter Pan" homes, for those who never grow old—are designed with stairs, door handles, counter heights, and fixtures that are convenient for "average" young adults [6]. Designers and developers seemed to assume that older people, if they lived long enough, would move to other settings after their children moved out or health problems developed. As noted earlier, most older people neither move nor want to move. Even if they do, they often encounter "retirement" housing that, until recently, was built under similar assumptions: the designers and developers did not expect retirees to live long after retirement, understood retirees' probable health and functional status changes poorly, and hoped to attract younger, healthier retirees by avoiding any design suggestion that residents were frail.

Second, tax policies encouraging home ownership[2]—primarily income tax deductions for mortgage interest and property taxes and federal mortgage insurance programs—reflect the value placed on home ownership in the United States [21]. In fact, such policies cost the federal government far more than programs providing rent, multi-unit construction, and other subsidies for low-income people [17, 22]. Homeowners are seen as stable, independent citizens [23] and home-ownership as good for the economy [17, p. 59]. These policies have been remarkably successful: the single-family detached dwelling is the dominant form of housing in the United States [17]. Not surprisingly, most older people own their own homes.

---

[2] For more information on tax policy and housing, see [18-22].

Finally, housing policies—both in urban renewal and public housing—have contributed to the need for modifications. Despite their intent, urban renewal programs[3] have done little to decrease the number of people living in substandard housing. Moreover, as already noted, substandard housing creates safety and health problems and inhibits the effectiveness of housing modifications. One might expect the results of public housing policy to be more positive with respect to modifications: public housing often replaces unsafe structures and, since the 1950s, many units have been built for older people. But public (and other government-subsidized) housing, although often assumed to be fully accessible and service-rich, is largely designed for independent, mobile people. Its nearly two million older residents have increasing adaptation and service needs (see Chapter 11).

Why Are Modifications on the Rise?

The number of people modifying their homes through major and minor physical and behavioral adaptations is probably increasing, however. Currently, according to the 1992 American Association of Retired Persons housing survey:

> Over half (53%) of older Americans performed a home modification. The most common are additional lighting (23%), confining living quarters to one floor to avoid stairs (18%), using lever faucets in place of knobs (18%), and installing additional hand rails or grab bars (17%). Modifications used less frequently are emergency response systems (9%), replacing door knobs with level handles (5%), replacing stairs with ramps (4%), and widening doorways (4%) [26, pp. 30-31].

Awareness of the need for and effectiveness of home adaptations has been slow to evolve: until relatively recently, people who had difficulty functioning in their homes were usually considered disabled, while their environments were scarcely considered. As a result, the historical tendency has been to focus on relocating or providing services to the people rather than modifying the environment. Applying this concept to environments outside the home helps to underscore its shortcomings: for example, we recognize that space vehicles, not astronauts, need modifications so that humans can function in them [27]. Sheehan submits that articulate people have an "impairment" in an environment where no one speaks their language [28, p. 10].

Such environmental awareness is increasing, however, as researchers begin to document a decrease in disability associated with the presence of modifications [1]. Research has identified modifications that help individuals to function better (see Chapter 7) and has explored how modifications can enhance caregivers'

---

[3] For further information, see [17, 20, 21, 24, and 25].

efforts or reduce the number of helpers needed [17, 29-31]. Policymakers, researchers, practitioners, and entrepreneurs in many fields are more and more interested in how the built environment can support people and promote health [15, 32-34].

This increase in interest is driven by theoretical, demographic, market, and other considerations. Its theoretical roots are in the evolution of appreciation for "person-environment fit." With respect to demography, elders' high homeownership rates, increasing numbers, improved economic status, and preferences to "age in place" are now well known. In the market, homebuilders show increasing awareness of these demographic imperatives as well as the declining role of new construction. Finally, several events and trends in the 1980s helped to push modifications toward the forefront of housing concerns.

Theoretical Roots

Simply put, the idea of "person-environment fit" is that a poor fit causes problems in daily functioning, while a good fit supports an individual's abilities, even if they are diminished. Kurt Lewin pioneered the concept of "continuous interaction between the internal environment of the human organism and the external environment" as early as 1936 [35, p. 279]. A 1946 booklet on purchasing homes recommended looking for bath bars [36]. Kleemeier's ecological model of aging suggests that home modifications create a prosthetic environment, assisting an individual to function better, in the same way that a hearing aid assists in replacing natural hearing [37]. Building on these precedents, Lawton and his associates launched a new appreciation of the influence of person-environment fit on successful aging [38, 39]. Poorly designed environments are increasingly understood as factors that themselves cause disability by making it impossible for all but the most robust people to function independently. This is supported by evidence that housing adaptations and assistive devices actually lower the rate of disability [1, 9].

Demographic Imperative

Meanwhile, both the numbers and resources of consumers are increasing. By the year 2040, 23 percent of the U.S. population will be over sixty-five, compared to 12 percent in 1990. The number of people over seventy-five, the group most likely to need assistance with activities of daily living, is increasing even more rapidly [7, 40]. The number of younger people with disabilities is also increasing (see Chapter 3). As the numbers increase, so apparently do elders' preferences to stay in their homes: in a 1992 national survey, 85 percent of older Americans said they wanted to stay in their present homes as they age, compared to 78 percent in 1986 [18]. Surveys and reports since at least the early 1950s have yielded similar findings [41, 42]. These strong preferences derive both from satisfaction with the status quo (such as social contacts and access to familiar stores and services) and from resistance to the emotional and financial costs of moving, which seem to be greater for elderly than younger homeowners [43]. Even if older people consider moving, new residential construction still tends toward single-family homes for younger families, and the current economic climate seems unlikely to inspire the range of housing alternatives that might entice elders to move before they need so much support that their only option is an institution.

Elders' economic status has also improved since the 1970s, giving them more options than they used to have, including making housing modifications. Indeed, such improvements have encouraged older people to live apart from their children. It is important to note, however, that elders' resources are often exaggerated. In fact, "more than a fourth of the elderly have incomes and other economic resources below or just barely over the poverty level" [7, p. 38], and the oldest elderly—those most likely to need modifications—have the lowest incomes. Thus, while some elders have the resources to make modifications, others will not be able to afford the whole cost, even if they use the equity in their homes (see Chapter 8).

Market-Driven Interest

Builders' interest in home modifications arises in part from the demographics and in part from a need for new markets: new construction has been declining [44]. The American Institute of Architects estimated that 99 percent of the housing that will be in use in the year 2000 existed in 1985 [45]. As a result, many builders and contractors have attended programs on housing, aging, and home modifications sponsored by the American Society on Aging, the National Council on the Aging, the National Association for Home Builders (NAHB), and other aging and housing groups [46]. ITT Hartford Insurance Group, in cooperation with the American Association of Retired Persons, developed the Hartford House, a traveling exhibit with over a hundred examples of home modifications [47]. A builder (Lewis Homes of California) joined with the National Council on the Aging and the Southern California Gas Company to produce the "Friendly Home," a Chino, California tract home remodeled to illustrate "a range of effective, efficient, aesthetic ideas for adapting a home" [48]. The first National Conference on Home Modifications Policy was held in 1993 in conjunction with the NAHB Remodelers' Show (see the Epilogue). The number of contractors knowledgeable about modifications, although still small, has grown. So has the number of agencies assisting with housing modifications: despite the lack of a national home modification and repair policy or program, 600 local programs were identified in a recent study, suggesting considerable recognition of the importance of these activities (see Chapter 9). Centers providing technical assistance and resources concerning adaptations are also increasing in number and scope [49].

Events and Trends in the 1980s

During the early 1980s, as the Department of Housing and Urban Development (HUD) budget was cut by more than 33 percent [20], the number of new units of all HUD housing was sharply reduced and rehabilitation funds dwindled. At the same time, the costs of nursing home care rose dramatically. The reduction in housing options for lower-income elders, along with economic interest in preventing or postponing institutionalization, moved housing modifications further up on the housing agenda [50, 51].

At the same time, individuals with disabilities gained recognition in the 1980s in what has become known as the independent living movement. Although the movement's leaders are mostly younger people, one of their priorities is to show how housing modifications promote independent living for people with disabilities, regardless of age. Their efforts have enhanced awareness of architectural and other barriers to independent living, helped to generate standards, provided prototypes, opened up markets for designs and products [10, 52], and led directly to the passage of the Americans with Disabilities Act (see Chapter 12).

Moreover, the potential for home modifications to prevent disability and increase residents' ability to remain socially active is also naturally linked to recent trends in promoting physical and mental health [53, 54]. Finally, in the 1980s, as awareness of cognitive impairments such as Alzheimer's disease rose sharply, the search intensified for effective interventions, including home adaptations, to help people with such impairments to remain at home as safely and autonomously as possible ([30, 31, 55] see also Chapter 6).

REFRAMING HOUSING ADAPTATIONS

As if approaching a house to be renovated, those studying and working in new fields of endeavor must look closely at the existing site and structure and discuss common goals in order to draw up a blueprint for the work to be done. This is the case with home adaptation. As professionals' and consumers' interest and needs increase, the time is right to formulate such a shared vision. In Section I, several leading authorities explore the issues in the field to that end. The challenge is particularly keen since so many disciplines must be brought to bear on the discussion.

First, analogous to evaluating a building site, we need to assess the context. In Chapter 2, Zola discusses two crucial links: the link between older and younger consumers with disabilities and the link between personal assistance and home modifications. The well-recognized and dramatic aging of the population, especially among the oldest old, is an important part of what drives the need to "reframe" housing adaptations. Other contributing factors, equally important but often unrecognized, include 1) the overall increase in the number of people with disabilities, as medical science increases our ability to survive serious diseases and injuries; and 2) the striking fluctuations and increasing number of secondary disabilities experienced by people with supposedly "stable" chronic conditions. According to one estimate, people younger than sixty-five now comprise one-third of those requiring long-term care services [56]. Most younger as well as older people with disabilities prefer to remain at home. This growing population of people who would benefit from housing modifications is diverse, however [6, 34]. Some people would benefit greatly from specific—often simple—modifications that accommodate disability, while others want and need repairs, and still others require both personal assistance and housing modifications. The situation is complicated by the fact that several factors—such as the number of women in the workforce and the trend toward smaller families—increasingly limit the availability of informal care.

Second, since modifications do not necessarily preclude a need for in-home services, and since not even combining adaptations and in-home services can solve all functional problems, understanding home adaptation requires appreciating its interface with the array of services and housing options available. The following summary of in-home care and housing alternatives offers background material for later presentations.

In-Home Care

Services such as meal preparation, housekeeping, personal care, transportation, and shopping assistance help people with disabilities to perform the physical and instrumental activities of daily living within the preferred setting of the home.[4] Five major factors have boosted the availability of in-home services since the late 1960s (the first 3 factors affect younger as well as older people):

- the establishment of "Medicaid waivers" allowing states to use Medicaid funds for in-home rather than institutional care
- states' efforts to organize in-home services as a component of long-term care systems
- passage of the Americans with Disabilities Act, emphasizing the right of people with disabilities to live and work independently
- a gradual expansion of Medicare-supported home health services
- the passage and reauthorization of the Older Americans Act and the strengthening of and innovations initiated by state units on aging and area agencies on aging

---

[4] Technology has also made it possible to provide some intensive medical care at home, but this is crucial for only a relatively small percentage of people.

Despite this growth, however, in-home services are often characterized by fragmentation and inefficiency:

> Most states have no mechanism to integrate the eligibility determinations and service provisions of their various programs to produce a system capable of delivering information and non-duplicative long-term care [57, p. 36].

National long-term care reform may promote improvement in this area.

Housing Alternatives

When a residence does not offer a good fit, a person may consider housing alternatives involving adaptations or relocation or both.

One type of alternative combines independent housing with assistance. *Accessory apartments*, created within existing dwellings, offer homeowners rental income and sometimes assistance and companionship from tenants. *Elder cottage housing opportunities (ECHO housing)*, prefabricated, inexpensive "cottages," are constructed on a caregiver's lot and moved, if desired, when the occupant dies or relocates. *Home sharing* often matches an older homeowner with extra space with a housemate who pays little or no rent in exchange for providing needed assistance (e.g., with heavy chores). *Another independent dwelling* may enable an older person to be more independent, secure, and active if the move is, for example, from a two-story, isolated, high-maintenance home to a one-story, low-maintenance condominium near supermarkets, drugstores, and health services.

Another alternative is specialized housing, offering more support than independent housing but less medically oriented than nursing homes. *Congregate housing* usually offers private bedrooms, private or shared baths, community space (such as kitchens and living rooms), social and recreational activities, and supportive services (such as meals and housekeeping). *Assisted living facilities* typically house frail residents who require supervision or personal care, but not skilled nursing care. *Foster care* programs place people who are older or have disabilities with individuals or families who provide room, board, and assistance. *Continuing care retirement communities (CCRCs)* frequently offer independent and assisted living units, a skilled nursing facility, and in-home services on one "campus." Their relatively high cost limits their accessibility, however, to those with substantial assets and upper-middle incomes.

The third step in reframing is to analyze the rest of the "structure" of housing adaptations. Until recently, analysis in the field has tended toward either theory or application. Design theorists, architects, occupational therapists, gerontologists, older people, and others concerned with the topic do not necessarily speak the same language, even though they make many of the same points. To find and make explicit the common threads in these analyses, and to bridge the gap between theory and application, Pynoos and Regnier suggest twelve principles of housing adaptation in Chapter 3. They derive these principles from accumulated design knowledge, people's behaviors, and social-psychological needs such as privacy, social interaction, choice, and autonomy.

A different but complementary way to tie together theory and application in modifications is to analyze how people behave in the different spaces in a home, as Grayson does in Chapter 4. Grayson also describes in more detail some of the products referred to in other chapters and why so many of them originate in countries other than the United States.

Fourth, reframing a field also benefits from a look at what might make the field obsolete. Most housing adaptations would be unnecessary if all residential settings were completely accessible. Thus, this section introduces the concept of "universal" housing: housing that accommodates people who are older or have disabilities as easily as young families. Every architect has the American Institute of Architects reference booklet than gives average measurements, such as forward and side arm reach from sitting and standing positions, for the average adult male and female. The unspoken implication is that an environment built for this hypothetical "average" person will work for the majority of those who use it. The reality is that it doesn't work well for increasing numbers of adults—older people, people with disabilities, and even short or tall people. It also works poorly for children, who find much of the physical environment too large and unwieldy: shelves are too high, doors too heavy to push open, faucets and knobs unreachable or difficult to manipulate. As our society changes, our images of the "typical user" of the physical environment must change as well. All of us will benefit.

USERS' PERSPECTIVES IN HOME
ADAPTATION

While Section I looks at the physical environment and the field of housing modifications, Section II puts consumers—that's all of us—on center stage. What do consumers want and need? How do we make our decisions about home adaptation? How can we better respect the creative accommodations many of us are already making? How can we advocate for ourselves concerning modifications and help others to advocate for themselves? What advice and financial assistance do we need to make adaptations? What are the income barriers to adaptations? How do we maximize our choices concerning adaptations?

Throughout this book the authors emphasize informed consumer choice in making modifications, both out of respect for the consumer and to increase the likelihood that the consumer will accept and use the adaptation. Older people and people with disabilities show great creativity in modifying their own environments [58]. Consumers are often assumed, however, to be "resistant" to or incapable of making decisions about modifications when their wishes do not match those of professionals.

Few guarantees exist for consumer choice and control in adaptations or services. Governments, insurance companies, and other payers want to minimize spending; public funders, moreover, want to ensure that publicly subsidized services are obtained only by the "truly needy." Such goals limit consumer choice. The personal care assistance model for people with disabilities offers a middle ground: while a public agency assesses consumers' needs to determine eligibility, and sets a maximum allowable rate for the services, consumers hire their own helpers and are reimbursed, usually with Medicaid funds. Some argue that elder services should be similarly organized [59].

Mrs. R may again offer some illumination:

> I finally found a place that they said could help me with fixing up some things around the house. They sent out a man who looked at the whole place over and talked to me for quite a long while. He finally said that my highest priority was bars in the bathroom, so they could pay for that. The funny thing was, he asked lots of questions, but never "What do you want?" Grab bars are all right, but I don't mind my sponge baths nearly as much as I mind—several times every day—those steps.

In Chapter 5, Ohta and Ohta address such paternalistic approaches by housing professionals, researchers, and others. They present a Consumer Decision Model that explains apparent consumer resistance to home adaptations as more rational and understandable than is usually perceived. According to the model, the consumer most likely to make an adaptation is one who believes, for example, that her porch stairs are likely to cause her to injure herself seriously, and that a ramp will solve this problem yet won't cost too much. This exciting conceptualization lays the groundwork for a more practical and effective approach to consumer outreach, marketing, assessment, and decision making.

Building on the Consumer Decision Model, Silverstein and Hyde report in Chapter 6 on how an increasingly important group of consumers—people with cognitive disabilities and their families—make adaptation decisions, and how adaptation considerations for this group differ from others. The chapter reports the findings of a study of caregivers' implementation of home adaptations recommended by professionals, and offers concrete and practical suggestions for both professionals and consumers.

It is increasingly clear that "standardized" or activity-based modifications may not help some people at all, and that individualized modification plans are required to meet individual, complex, nonstandardized needs. Connell and Sanford's task-oriented categorization, presented in Chapter 7, clarifies why. The chapter presents a methodology to maximize the effectiveness of adaptations by taking into account the user's potential to change behavior. After offering a framework linking problems in performing routine activities with aspects of design, two detailed case studies show how the framework is applied. In this innovative treatment of the differences in individual abilities and needs, the authors take a new look at the many complex yet routine tasks of independent living—not only the usual activities and instrumental activities of daily living, but other crucial tasks such as regulating temperature, lighting, and ventilation; home maintenance; and communication.

Finally, a key element in consumer decision-making is the affordability of modifications. Whatever their reaction to modifications of their specific needs, people who can't—or think they can't—afford modifications are unlikely to attempt them. Mutschler, in Chapter 8, explores the incidence of selected building modifications in owner-occupied homes and looks at the effect of income on decision making about adaptations. Not surprisingly, the findings suggest that, while the presence of modifications is associated with disability in all income groups, low incomes and low housing values appear to keep many elderly homeowners with disabilities from making such modifications. Documenting this effect strengthens arguments for better financing.

IMPLEMENTING HOUSING ADAPTATION PROGRAMS

Many different organizations and individuals are delivering the "product" of home modification. Even home health agencies and other providers without formal programs are responding to consumers' concerns about their environments—for example, visiting nurses and home care workers increasingly incorporate such considerations into their client assessments. As with any new field, however, there is much we still need to know about best practices in manufacturing, marketing, and delivering this product. Section III evaluates and offers examples of programs and initiatives for both home modification and home repair services, for both renters and homeowners. It analyzes the findings of a nationwide survey about such programs and discusses issues in establishing them; presents strategies for agencies offering home adaptation services; and looks at housing modifications in the context of subsidized senior housing.

Until recently, little information was available about home modification and repair programs. The findings from a national survey of home modification and repair programs (Chapter 9) go a long way toward overcoming this deficiency. Pynoos, Liebig, Overton, and Calvert find that, although programs are widespread and numerous, most are small add-ons to existing agencies rather than substantial stand-alone organizations; moreover, most experience fragmentation due to multiple sources of funding. In short, the programs are too close to marginal, and many improvements are needed to make them more comprehensive. Assessments and referrals are not standardized, nor do they consistently incorporate both housing and service concerns. Importantly, "in only a few cases are clients asked to demonstrate how they carried out a particular task, a procedure more likely to provide an accurate sense of both personal capabilities and interaction with the environment" (see Chapter 7 for an example of such a procedure). Generally programs focus on developing a *process* for working with other providers, rather than on facilitating changes in the *structure* of service delivery (i.e., on closing the gap between the housing and in-home service delivery systems).

It is not entirely surprising that health or social services agencies face a number of challenges in offering home maintenance, repair, and modification services. Learning from the experiences of other programs may help them to succeed. For example, in making staffing decisions, it would be useful to know that the "more mature and comprehensive" programs tend to integrate staff, subcontractors, and volunteers. Such integration minimizes the problems associated with using only on-staff crew (i.e., recruiting and retaining skilled members and needing to keep an inventory of supplies and tools), using only subcontractors (i.e., quality control and the reluctance of subcontractors to take on small jobs), or using only volunteers (i.e., reliability, recruitment, retention, and liability).

Hereford, in Chapter 10, offers other advice for such agencies based on the experience of the grantees in the Supportive Services Program for Older Persons (SSPOP). This national Robert Wood Johnson Foundation initiative tested the capacity of home health agencies to offer consumer-driven and consumer-financed nontraditional health and health-related services. From early market survey results through program operations, consumers—even those with annual incomes under $10,000—showed strong demand for home repair and maintenance services. The chapter unequivocally recommends that these agencies change their traditional provider-driven way of doing business.

Elderly homeowners, of course, are not the only ones that may benefit from environmental modifications. In Chapter 11, Lanspery reports on how ten state housing finance agencies took the lead in developing services in low-income senior housing through the Robert Wood Johnson Foundation Supportive Services Program in Senior Housing. These findings provide useful guidance to housing sponsors, housing managers, service coordinators, community service providers, and others working with clusters of people. In particular, their experience shows the importance of the linkage and interactions among the physical, organizational, and social environments.

HOUSING ADAPTATION POLICY

Most of the chapters in this book draw conclusions and make recommendations for promoting the availability and accessibility of home modifications and, directly or indirectly, for establishing sound housing adaptation policy. Section IV discusses current laws, policies, and programs related to housing adaptations and links some of the more important findings to policy formulation.

Policies and programs to encourage housing modifications are few and recent. As Talbert, Hyde, and Grayson describe in Chapter 12, consumers and providers have tapped some key sources, such as Older Americans Act programs and local community action agencies, to assist with financing modifications. Consumers, providers, and advocates for older people and people with disabilities are encouraged by the Fair Housing Amendments Act of 1988 (FHAA), analyzed in detail by Newman and Mezrich in Chapter 13, and the landmark 1990 Americans with Disabilities Act (ADA), described in Chapter 12. As important as they are, however, in establishing precedents and raising consciousness, neither the FHAA nor the ADA establishes a comprehensive housing modification policy, especially with respect to the single-family homes in which most older people live.

Lack of research impedes the spread of housing modifications and effective policymaking. It is still unclear which people benefit most from making modifications, which modifications are most cost-effective, how long modifications may forestall a move to a more sheltered setting, and to what extent modifications may substitute for personal assistance. More research is needed on consumer perspectives, effective marketing techniques, and the private sector's experience with home modification.

Section IV addresses these conclusions and recommendations by examining systemic issues in housing adaptation, financing options, implementation policy, and legislation. By placing home modification in the context of important recent legislation—the Americans with Disabilities and the Fair Housing Acts—the section discusses progress to date, remaining gaps, and the likely evolution of current trends, such as efforts to change the focus of long-term care from institutions to homes and communities.

For adaptations to become more widespread and effective, attitudes, policies, and practices must change. The well-recognized policy gap between housing and supportive services needs to be closed, because neither housing modifications nor supportive services alone can succeed in promoting independent living. In fact, providing one without the other risks failure. Assistance in deciding which modifications to make, making the modifications (including financing and the actual work), and obtaining supportive services must all be linked.

With a few recent exceptions [3, 30, 46, 49, 60-62], information on housing adaptation is scarce and hard to find. Consumers need access to information on the modification options available, financing sources, and building contractors who will undertake appropriate, affordable, and timely adaptations. Homeowners also need to learn the value of modifications and the independence, safety, and convenience risks in homes without modifications. Public attitudes of fear and denial hamper the efforts of organizations offering such education. Practitioners and providers also need access to information and to assistance in developing effective programs.

Individual practitioners can promote modifications by educating consumers and recommending specific options. For example, physicians and other health care workers should advise those whose diagnoses or medications make them more prone to falling about removing scatter rugs and installing hand rails, and refer them to agencies that can help. If case managers and others conducting client assessments were trained to identify and solve environmental problems, and assessments explicitly incorporated environmental considerations, recommendations for home modifications could be as common as those for homemaker service.

If practitioners' attitudes are paternalistic, consumers may be less willing to consider changes. Practitioners must learn to respect and work with the many creative ways that people have solved their own problems. A chair or sofa in the midst of bookcases and tables holding lamps, telephone, radio, remote controls, reading materials, games, handwork projects, microwave oven, and small refrigerator might look cluttered and hazardous, but this is one way for a person with mobility impairments to minimize walking.

Opportunities to change attitudes, behavior, and policy with respect to home modifications are many [6]. Concerned individuals and organizations can demand home modification and repair goals in local, state, and national housing and long-term care plans, and can demand accessibility, safety, and low maintenance standards in new construction. They can also create training programs to sensitize remodelers and builders to person-environment fit; de-stigmatize modifications (e.g., by creating resource centers with displays of attractive home adaptations, and by educating realtors to place grab bars, ramps, and lever door handles in the same amenity category as fireplaces and parking spots); promote the testing and developing of new program models with public and private funds; support the growth of providers specializing in modification, repairs, and weatherization; and coordinate home modification funding sources, eligibility requirements, and implementation so that neither providers nor consumers fall through the cracks.

Finally, policymakers must be willing to remove policy and financial obstacles to adaptations. People with low incomes and few liquid assets may find it difficult to make even relatively inexpensive but necessary modifications; major modifications, such as roll-in showers, movable height cabinets, new first-floor bathrooms or bedrooms, elevators, or chair lifts may be beyond the means of all but the wealthiest people. New financial arrangements and incentives have the potential to help. Among the possibilities are: allow "medically necessary" modifications as a tax deductible medical expense; allow other modifications as a tax deduction or credit, similar to those for energy conservation; encourage insurance companies to include housing modifications as a long-term care insurance benefit; expand the types of assistive devices, adaptations, and occupational therapy visits funded by Medicare and Medicaid; promote and expand opportunities to use home equity to finance modifications, such as home equity conversions, reverse mortgages, second mortgages, and home equity loans, by educating consumers as well as banks, finance agencies, and community agencies; and provide incentives for the private sector to play a bigger role in modifying homes.

These suggestions are not beyond the nation's capacity. Confronted by the energy crisis of the 1970s, both public and private entities designed, funded, and implemented energy conservation programs. The housing problems of people with disabilities are no less a crisis and demand no less a response. The energy conservation programs provide a feasible model for housing modification initiatives. These programs usually combined assessments, recommendations for improvements (such as insulation, vents, and replacement windows), and, importantly, financial assistance. Surveys were conducted by utility company or community service agencies and many low-income, elderly homeowners benefited. Housing modification programs could use a similar strategy of outreach, community assessment teams, surveys, expert assistance, and subsidies and loans for lower- and middle-income people [63].

FINAL THOUGHTS

The impetus for this book came from Elaine Ostroff, executive director of Adaptive Environments, a nonprofit Boston group founded in 1979. Elaine and her organization have moved the national agenda forward, and helped to lay the foundation for the Americans with Disabilities Act and the Fair Housing Act, discussed in Chapters 12 and 13. We offer here their strategy to increase the availability and use of home adaptation services:

1. *Document need.* Adaptive Environments [2, 10] found that:

- 53,000 households in Massachusetts needed home modifications
- 52 percent of all people who needed home modifications were over sixty-five
- the greatest need was in the area of small modifications like grab bars and handrails
- the condition most often associated with the need for modifications was arthritis, followed by respiratory and cardiac conditions.

2. *Document existing services, programs, and financing.* Adaptive Environments found that most Massachusetts resources targeted to housing modifications funded new construction, and that the agency most involved was the Massachusetts Industrial Finance Agency. They also found inequities; for example, resources for adaptations for people with visual impairments were much greater than for those with mobility impairments. Finally, this research corroborated earlier findings that modifications averaged under $2,000.

In pursuing research on financing, Adaptive Environments found that Medicaid community-based waivers were, in several states and under certain situations, financing home adaptations. Under these waivers, Medicaid pays for noninstitutional care if it is shown to be cheaper than institutional care. However, the calculations of potential savings, and thus the Medicaid caps on home adaptation coverage, varied. This analysis became an advocacy tool as other states defined their Medicaid plans.

3. *Convene interagency committees for advocacy and networking.* Information in hand, Adaptive Environments invited key staff from all private and public

agencies concerned with disability to participate in a series of meetings on home adaptation. These meetings forged a new awareness about housing and adaptations and generated a common understanding that laid the groundwork for future reforms.

4. *Support policies to create funding sources for home adaptation.* Once a critical mass of aware and committed groups and individuals existed, policy changes were possible. For example, at the time of the interagency meeting, a statewide Massachusetts Housing Finance Agency (MHFA) loan program was the most important source of low-interest financing for home adaptations, but was in danger of termination. Thanks to interagency effort, pressure on the state government, and MHFA support, the program continued to make loans and grants to low-income homeowners for home repairs and adaptations.

5. *Initiate policy actions that support or mandate adaptations.* The data documenting the need for housing modifications were part of the rationale for including housing modification policy in the Massachusetts Housing Bill of Rights, which both parallels and goes beyond the federal Fair Housing Amendments Act.

6. *Educate consumers.* Adaptive Environments hypothesized that a peer-led workshop, giving information about attractive adaptations that also support independence, could change elders' attitudes and empower them to adapt their homes.

In collaboration with the University of Massachusetts at Boston's Gerontology Institute, Adaptive Environments trained older consumers as workshop leaders who, in turn, trained their peers. The goal was for older consumers to become more knowledgeable, plan competently for adaptations, and convey information to friends, rather than have a health professional "prescribe" home adaptations in a crisis, with the older consumer in the role of a passive "patient."

The one-hour workshop, presented in social or educational settings, consists of slides of nonstigmatizing, attractive modifications; self-assessment training, using a worksheet that the group can fill out and discuss together; and information about resources and funding. This workshop was piloted at eight Massachusetts sites to approximately 125 older consumers. The Gerontology Institute polled forty of the attendees nearly one year later to determine the workshop's effects. Thirty-seven were overwhelmingly positive about the value of the information. Seven had made modifications and sixteen intended to. Twenty-four had conveyed information to family and friends, and all felt that this workshop should be offered widely. (Most respondents were healthy. Seventy-five percent had incomes under $25,000. Approximately half lived alone, most of those widowed women.)

7. *Educate providers.* Finally, with public and private funding, Adaptive Environments designed and offered five sets of workshops for different professional audiences such as home care case managers, architects, and developers. The half-day sessions stressed normalization—universal design as well as noninstitutional materials and design—and covered the changing physical capacity of older people, assessment, types of adaptations, the mechanics of adaptation, resources, funding, and new regulations.

The essential message of this strategy, and of *Staying Put*, is one of hope. Better design of new construction, better adaptation of existing construction, and better understanding of how to combine adaptations and services will enable more older people and people with disabilities to live at home safely and autonomously. The rising level of education in the population could also help to increase the demand for and use of home modifications and assistive devices [1, p. 176]. To these ends, we hope that this book will be a resource for faculty, researchers, students, policymakers, and practitioners in several fields (aging, health and human services, social welfare and social policy, housing, urban planning, and disabilities); for builders and remodelers; for housing managers and real estate developers; and for consumers and consumer groups.

Even as the number of U.S. residents who are older or have disabilities is growing, we continue to live in aging dwellings that were not designed to accommodate disability. Although new construction may be desirable, it is safe to say that sufficient numbers of new accessible homes will not be built. Thus, existing homes must be modified. Our challenge is to conduct research and implement programs that lead to new standards for safe and independent living for all. The timing is right to try to meet the challenges.

REFERENCES

1. K. Manton, L. Corder, and E. Stallard, Changes in the Use of Personal Assistance and Special Equipment from 1982 to 1989: Results from the 1982 and 1989 NLTCS, *The Gerontologist, 33*:2, pp. 168-176, 1993.
2. P. Dunn, *An Analysis of the Housing Adaptations Programs in Massachusetts*, Adaptive Environments Center, Boston, 1985.
3. E. E. Malizia, R. C. Duncan, and J. D. Reagan, *Financing Home Accessibility Modifications*, Center for Accessible Housing, North Carolina State University, Raleigh, North Carolina, 1993.
4. Fannie Mae Customer Education Group, *Money from Home: A Consumer's Guide to Home Equity Conversion Mortgages*, #CT066L06/92, Washington, D.C., 1992.
5. P. Porter, Facilitating Aging in Place through Home Repairs, *Long Term Care Advances: Topics in Research, Training, Service & Policy, 6*:2, 1994.
6. J. Pynoos, Toward a National Policy on Home Modifications, *Technology and Disability, 2*:4, pp. 1-8, Fall 1993.
7. U.S. Department of Health and Human Services, *Aging America: Trends and Projections, 1991 Edition*, DHHS Publication No. (FCoA) 91-28001, Washington, D.C., 1991.
8. U.S. Bureau of the Census, *American Housing Survey for the United States in 1987*, U.S. Bureau of the Census, Washington, D.C., 1989.
9. J. Foreman, Balm for Burden of Growing Old, *Boston Globe*, pp. 1 and 8, April 23, 1993.
10. P. Dunn, *An Annotated Bibliography on the Needs, Costs, and Social Impacts of Housing Adaptations*, Adaptive Environments Center, Boston, 1985.

11. G. Robinette, *Access to the Environment*, American Society of Landscape Architects for the U.S. Department of Housing and Urban Development, Washington, D.C., 1978.
12. Batelle Memorial Institute, *Study and Evaluation of Integrating the Handicapped in HUD Housing*, U.S. Department of Housing and Urban Development, Washington, D.C., 1977.
13. U.S. General Accounting Office, *Persons with Disabilities: Report on Costs of Accommodations*, GAO/HRD-90-44BR, U.S. General Accounting Office, Human Resources Division, Washington, D.C., 1990.
14. A. D. Ratzka, *The Costs of Disabling Environments—A Cost-Revenue Analysis of Installing Elevators in Old Houses*, Swedish Council on Building Research, Stockholm, 1984.
15. R. J. Struyk, Current and Emerging Issues in Housing Environments for the Elderly, in *The Social and Built Environment in an Older Society*, pp. 134-168, Institute of Medicine and National Research Council, Committee on an Aging Society, National Academy Press, Washington, D.C., 1988.
16. S. Newman, J. Zais, and R. Struyk, Housing Older America, in *Elderly People and the Environment*, I. Altman, M. P. Lawton, and J. Wohlwill (eds.), Plenum Press, New York, 1984.
17. R. Struyk, M. Turner, and M. Ueno, *Future U.S. Housing Policy: Meeting the Demographic Challenge*, Urban Institute Report 88-2, Urban Institute Press, Washington, D.C., 1988.
18. H. J. Aaron, *Shelter and Subsidies: Who Benefits from Federal Housing Policies?* Brookings Institution, Washington, D.C., 1972.
19. C. Hartman, *Housing and Social Policy*, Prentice-Hall, Englewood Cliffs, New Jersey, 1975.
20. J. Pynoos, R. Schafer, and C. W. Hartman, *Housing Urban America* (2nd Edition), Aldine, New York, 1980.
21. J. Kemeny, *The Myth of Homeownership*, Routledge & Kegan Paul, London, 1981.
22. C. Dolbeare, How the Income Tax System Subsidizes Housing for the Affluent, in *Critical Perspectives on Housing*, R. G. Bratt, C. Hartman, and A. Meyerson (eds.), Temple University Press, Philadelphia, Pennsylvania, pp. 264-271, 1986.
23. C. Perin, *Everything in Its Place*, Princeton University Press, Princeton, New Jersey, 1977.
24. R. G. Bratt, C. Hartman, and A. Meyerson (eds.), *Critical Perspectives on Housing*, Temple University Press, Philadelphia, 1986.
25. J. W. Hughes and G. Sternlieb, *The Dynamics of America's Housing*, Center for Urban Policy Research, New Brunswick, New Jersey, 1987.
26. American Association of Retired Persons, *Understanding Senior Housing for the 1990s: Survey of Consumer Preferences, Concerns, and Needs*, PF4522 (593) D 13899, AARP, Washington, D.C., 1993.
27. M. Faletti, Human Factors Research and Functional Environments for the Aged, in *Elderly People and the Environment*, I. Altman, M. P. Lawton, and J. Wohlwill (eds.), Plenum Press, New York, pp. 195-239, 1984.
28. N. Sheehan, *Successful Administration of Senior Housing: Working with Elderly Residents*, Sage Publications, Newbury Park, California, 1992.

29. S. J. Newman, Housing and Long-Term Care: The Suitability of the Elderly's Housing to the Provision of In-Home Services, *The Gerontologist, 25*:1, pp. 35-40, 1985.
30. R. V. Olsen, E. Ehrenkrantz, and B. Hutchings, *Alzheimer's and Related Dementias: Homes that Help*, New Jersey Institute of Technology, Newark, New Jersey, 1993.
31. R. V. Olsen, E. Ehrenkrantz, and B. Hutchings, Creating Supportive Environments for People with Dementia and Their Caregivers through Home Modifications, *Technology and Disability, 2*:4, pp. 47-57, Fall 1993.
32. J. Pynoos, Public Policy and Aging in Place: Identifying the Problems and Potential Solutions, in *Aging in Place*, D. Tilson (ed.), Scott, Foresman, Glenview, Illinois, pp. 167-208, 1990.
33. V. Regnier and J. Pynoos (eds.), *Housing the Aged: Design Directives and Policy Considerations*, Elsevier, New York, 1987.
34. E. Steinfeld and S. Shea, Enabling Home Environments: Identifying Barriers to Independence, *Technology and Disability, 2*:4, pp. 69-79, Fall 1993.
35. A. Schwartz, Planning Micro-Environments for the Aged, in *Aging: Scientific Perspectives and Social Issues*, D. Woodruff and J. Birren (eds.), Van Nostrand Reinhold, New York, pp. 279-294, 1975.
36. J. P. Dean and S. Breines, *The Book of Houses*, Crown Publishers, New York, 1946.
37. R. W. Kleemeier, Behavior and Organization of the Bodily and External Environment, in *Handbook of Aging and the Individual: Psychological and Biological Aspects*, J. E. Birren (ed.), University of Chicago Press, Chicago, pp. 400-541, 1959.
38. M. P. Lawton, Ecology and Aging, in *Spatial Behavior of Older People*, L. A. Pastalan and D. H. Carson (eds.), University of Michigan Press, Ann Arbor, pp. 40-67, 1970.
39. M. P. Lawton and L. Nahemow, Ecology and the Aging Process, in *The Psychology of Adult Development and Aging*, C. Eisdorfer and M. P. Lawton (eds.), American Psychological Association, Washington, D.C., pp. 619-674, 1973.
40. J. Leon and T. Lair, *Functional Status of the Noninstitutionalized Elderly: Estimates of ADL and IADL Difficulties*, DHHS Publication No. (PHS) 90-3462, National Medical Expenditure Survey Research Findings 4, Agency for Health Care Policy and Research, U.S. Public Health Service, Rockville, Maryland, 1990.
41. A. Campbell, P. E. Converse, and W. L. Rogers (eds.), *Quality of American Life*, Russell Sage Foundation, New York, 1976.
42. W. Donahue, *Housing the Aging*, University of Michigan Press, Ann Arbor, 1954.
43. J. D. Reschovsky, Residential Immobility of the Elderly: An Empirical Investigation, *AREUEA Journal, 18*:2, pp. 160-183, 1990.
44. J. Pynoos, Strategies for Home Modification and Repair, *Generations, 16*:2, pp. 21-25, 1992.
45. Remodeling the Future, *Interiors, 145*, p. 147, August 1985.
46. J. Pynoos, P. Liebig, J. Hultman, and T. Searle, *Home Modifications Resource Guide*, Long Term Care National Resource Center at UCLA/USC, Los Angeles, 1989.
47. B. Hynes-Grace, The Hartford House: Home Modifications in Action, *Generations, 16*:2, pp. 33-34, 1992.
48. M. Rayl, The Friendly Home, Open at Last! *Seniors' Housing News*, pp. 7-8, Spring 1992.
49. J. Overton, Resources for Home-Modification/Repair Programs, *Technology and Disability, 2*:4, pp. 80-88, Fall 1993.

50. R. J. Newcomer, M. P. Lawton, and T. O. Byerts, *Housing an Aging Society: Issues, Alternatives and Policy*, Van Nostrand Reinhold, New York, 1986.

51. P. Kemper, R. Applebaum, and M. Harrigan, Community Care Demonstrations: What Have We Learned? *Health Care Finance Review, 8*:4, pp. 87-100, 1987.

52. R. Lifchez and B. Winslow, *Design for Independent Living: The Environment and Physically Disabled People*, Whitney Library of Design, New York, 1979.

53. F. G. Abdellah and S. R. Moore (eds.), *Surgeon General's Workshop on Health Promotion and Aging*, U.S. Department of Health and Human Services, Washington, D.C., 1987.

54. L. Berg and J. S. Cassells (eds.), *The Second Fifty Years: Promoting Health and Preventing Disability*, National Academy Press, Washington, D.C., 1990.

55. N. M. Silverstein, J. Hyde, and R. Ohta, Home Adaptation for Alzheimer's Households: Factors Related to Implementation and Outcomes of Recommendations, *Technology and Disability, 2*:4, pp. 58-68, Fall 1993.

56. D. L. Breo, At Large: AARP's Call to Arms: Reform Health Care—Now! *Journal of the American Medical Association, 168*, pp. 2706-2707, 1992.

57. S. Pendleton, J. Capitman, W. Leutz, and R. Omata, *State Infrastructure for Long-Term Care: A National Study of State Systems*, Working Paper No. 4, Bigel Institute, Florence Heller Graduate School, Brandeis University, Waltham, Massachusetts, 1990.

58. R. J. Struyk and H. M. Katsura, *Aging at Home: How the Elderly Adjust their Housing without Moving*, Haworth Press, New York, 1988.

59. L. Simon-Rusinowitz and B. Hofland, Adopting a Disability Approach to Home Care Services for Older Adults, *The Gerontologist, 33*:2, pp. 159-167, 1993.

60. L. M. Rickman, C. E. Soble, and J. M. Prescop, *A Comprehensive Approach to Retrofitting Homes for a Lifetime*, NAHB Research Center, Upper Marlboro, Maryland, 1991.

61. *The Directory of Accessible Building Products*, NAHB Research Center, Upper Marlboro, Maryland, 1991.

62. J. Pynoos and E. Cohen, *The Perfect Fit: Creative Ideas for a Safe and Livable Home*, American Association of Retired Persons, #PF 4912 (992) D14823, Washington, D.C., 1992.

63. G. D. Ferguson, M. J. Holin, and W. G. Moss, *An Evaluation of the Seven City Home Maintenance Demonstration for the Elderly: Final Report*, Urban Systems Research and Engineering, Washington, D.C., n.d.

PART I

REFRAMING
HOUSING ADAPTATIONS

Introduction

In this first section of *Staying Put,* we move toward a new vision in the field of housing modifications. Despite a decades-old theoretical framework that supports an integrated notion of person and place, we are still struggling to apply it. Historically, U.S. policy has tried to change the people instead of the places— relocating them, trying to make them adjust to their situation or to one or more programs' requirements, or offering service but ignoring their physical environment. In recent years, we have begun to pay more attention to the physical environment, but often at the expense of addressing service or other needs.

Each of the three chapters in this section tackles a different aspect of developing a new vision in the field:

- Viewing housing adaptations in the context of an increasing number of older and younger people with disabilities, Zola eloquently links aging, disability, housing adaptations, and personal assistance. He presents a needed philosophical analysis that challenges the "disabling" nature of the physical environment and most existing service systems in the United States.
- Regnier and Pynoos link theory and practice through twelve principles that are echoed elsewhere in this book. These principles are part of a multidimensional analysis that includes physical, social, personal, and community elements in a holistic framework.
- Grayson explains why housing adaptation technology is an underdeveloped resource in the United States and presents useful and illustrative examples of

adaptation solutions in a framework of how people use the spaces in their homes.

- All three chapters promote the principle of universal design as the definitive way to change the disabling nature of the physical environment.

Once again we call on Mrs. R to illustrate how a new vision might work in practice:

> The difference between the old program and this new one was like night and day. This time the woman they sent out asked what I wanted, watched how I did things, and helped me think about changes that might not occur to me—like asking whether the glare from the morning light affects my cooking or reading, with my eyes the way they are.
>
> She laid out different things I could do, and gave me an idea of how much each would cost. Some things were pretty cheap, and some I didn't care about, but other things that I'd like to do would add up. Then she said they could help figure out whether one of these reverse mortgages would be worth my while, or if I could take out a loan from the state. Now, I'd already looked into some kind of fix-up loan a while back, after my children said they cared more about me being able to stay on here than inheriting the house. But the bank said my income was too low for any of their loans.
>
> Then she told me that they even have volunteers who can take care of that bad corner of the fence and give my yard a good spring cleaning.
>
> Now this is a program that gives an old lady the idea that she might have a future to look forward to.

CHAPTER
2

Living at Home:
The Convergence of Aging
and Disability

Irving Kenneth Zola

People who are aging and people who have disabilities have traditionally been split into two opposing camps by providers of service and often by themselves [1, 2]. Social as well as therapeutic advances, however, have resulted in the two becoming increasingly intertwined, with important implications for health policy. This chapter traces some aspects of this intertwining, and how it plays itself out in regard to housing adaptations and at-home care.

We have seen dramatic increases in survival rates for infants, younger people, and older people with disabilities—increases that are expected to grow even more dramatically in the coming years. People with a whole range of chronic diseases and disabilities are reaching old age, and more adults remain alive sufficiently long to experience age-associated chronic illness and disability. These changing demographics have led to the need for increased housing adaptations and personal services, and for policies that incorporate a recognition of the need for options and flexibility in meeting these challenges.

For years infant mortality has steadily decreased, in large part because of improvements in standards of living, prenatal care, and medical therapeutics. Though the numbers are as yet small, it is clear that there are increasing numbers of low-birth-weight and other infants surviving into childhood and beyond with manifest chronic impairments. Many children who would have died from causes such as leukemia, spina bifida, or cystic fibrosis now survive into adulthood or longer. Diagnostic advances, as well as some life-extending technologies, allow survival rates of people with spinal cord injuries. As recently as the 1950s, death was likely in the very early stages or soon after because of respiratory and other complications. Thus in World War I only 400 men with wounds that paralyzed them from the waist down survived *at all*, and 90 percent of them died before they reached home. By World War II, 2,000 men with paraplegia lived and 1,700— over 85 percent of them—were still alive in the late 1960s [3]. Each decade since has seen a rapid decline in the death rate and thus an increase in long-term survival—first of those with paraplegia, then with quadriplegia, and now, in the 1980s and '90s, with head injuries [4].

This is only the most dramatic example. Many chronic diseases once thought inevitably to cut short the life span (e.g., diabetes) are now, with diet and therapeutics, having almost negligible effects. Life-extending interventions are available for many other diseases, from cancer to heart disease to multiple sclerosis, muscular dystrophy, and even AIDS.

The aging population itself will be even more at risk for what were once thought to be "natural" occurrences such as decreases in mobility, visual acuity, and hearing, and for other musculoskeletal, cardiovascular, and cerebrovascular changes whose implications are only beginning to be appreciated. Moreover, they will very likely have more than one chronic condition [5] and this co-morbidity is almost certain to exacerbate disease in nonlinear ways [6]. In absolute numbers, all census data affirm that the fastest-growing segment of the U.S. population is made up of those over the age of sixty-five. In 1880 their number was less than two million (3%) of the total population, but by 1990 it had reached nearly thirty-two million (at least 12%). Put another way, throughout most of history only one in ten people lived past sixty-five; now nearly eight out of ten do. The most phenomenal growth (under-predicted in the 1960s and '70s) will be in the even older age groups, those over eighty-five. This age group, while constituting 1 percent of the total population in 1980, is projected at over 5 percent in 2050, or nearly a quarter of all elderly people [7].

This aging of the population has important service implications. While only 5 percent of those sixty-five to seventy-four require assistance in basic activities of daily living, about one-third do so by age eighty-five [8-10]. Moreover, even these estimates of disability and service needs may be conservative according to a detailed compilation of future trends [11]. For not only is the over-eighty-five age group likely to get even older, but under current medical policy, people are receiving progressively more "care" (however defined) in the last year of life.

Thus, no matter how one defines or measures it, the number of people in the United States with conditions that interfere with their full participation in society is steadily and dramatically increasing.

Still another unappreciated aspect of most chronic conditions, including those most common among older people, is that although permanent, they are not necessarily static. While we do, of course, recognize at least in terminology that some diseases are "progressive," we are less inclined to see that there is no

Still another unappreciated aspect of most chronic conditions, including those most common among older people, is that although permanent, they are not necessarily static. While we do, of course, recognize at least in terminology that some diseases are "progressive," we are less inclined to see that there is no one-time, overall adaptation/adjustment to the condition. Even for a recognized progressive or episodic disorder, such as multiple sclerosis, attention only recently has been given to the continuing nature of adaptations [12]. The same is also true for those with end-stage renal disease [13]. With the survival into adulthood of people with diseases that once were fatal come new changes and complications. Problems of circulation and vision for people with diabetes, for example, may be due to the disease itself, the aging process, or even the original life-sustaining treatment [14].

We are also finding an emergence of secondary disabilities even for supposedly more stable conditions like spinal cord injuries [15], cerebral palsy [16], and spina bifida [17]. Perhaps the most well-known example of a new manifestation of an old disease is the so-called post-polio syndrome [18]. Polio has been considered a stable chronic illness. Following its acute onset and a period of rehabilitation, most people had reached a plateau and expected to stay there. For the majority, this may still be true, but for at least a quarter, it is not. Large numbers of people are experiencing new problems some twenty to forty years after the original onset. The most common are fatigue, weakness in muscles previously affected and unaffected, muscle and joint pain, breathing difficulties, and intolerance to cold. Whether these new problems are the mere concomitant of aging, the reemergence of a still lingering virus, a long-term effect of the early damage or even of the early rehabilitation programs, or something else, is still at issue [19]. Whatever the etiology of this phenomenon, there will likely be many more manifestations of old diseases and disabilities as people survive decades beyond the acute onset of their original diseases or disabilities [20]. The dichotomy between people with a "progressive" condition versus those with a "static" one may well be, generally speaking, less distinct—and, indeed, more of a continuum—than once thought.

While these concepts, observations, and numbers make an empirical point about the prevalence and changing face of disability, this is not to claim that the conditions themselves "cause" or even "increase" disability. On the contrary, as the Independent Living Movement has long pointed out [21], disability is a social construction, the result of an interplay between particular conditions with existing resources and the social, political, economic, and physical environments. From this perspective, physical obstacles or barriers to access to support services, rather than the person's condition, cause the disability [22]. In any case, the culminating point of this essay is that having a serious disability and growing old no longer represent disparate populations. The two groups increasingly share issues. Two particularly important issues are where they will live and with what assistance.

LIVING AT HOME:
CHALLENGES AND POLICY SOLUTIONS

The changing nature of disability, the increasing number of younger and older people with disabilities, and three other factors are hastening the convergence of aging and disability. First, recognition has grown that chronic illness and disability among all age groups are the major health problems of the late twentieth century. Consequently, the treatments themselves, while becoming more palliative (aspirin for arthritis) and adaptive (insulin for diabetes), are at the same time life-long and administered regularly by "patients," their families, and their networks, and in their own homes. Second, this period has also seen a series of critiques of almost every form of long-term institutional care—whether in mental hospitals, chronic-disease hospitals, or nursing homes—by all age groups and people with all types of disabilities and their advocates. Third, groups representing both older and younger people with disabilities have made efforts to strengthen their case by forming coalitions and alliances.

These trends must be viewed against the historical background of a longstanding schism between younger people with disabilities and older people, and their respective advocates. Many younger people with disabilities who value independence and control feel little incentive to ally themselves with older people, "because of traditional stereotypes of older people as frail, chronically ill, declining, and 'marginal' to society" [23, p. 86]. Similarly, older people have stereotypes about younger people—for example, problems have arisen where older and younger people with disabilities live together in subsidized housing. Some have argued, especially since about the mid-1980s, that the two groups have more in common than not, and that they should increase their influence by joining forces; but "to date, the joint allegiance of advocates for disabled persons and elderly persons to general principles has not been easily translated into a politics of unified action" [23, p. 83]. Convergence is impeded by the fact that health and supportive service systems for older people and for younger people with disabilities have developed quite differently and have remained largely separate. Those established for older people are generally provider-based, rely on a medical model, and assume that frailty prevents older clients from controlling their daily lives: "Homecare programs for the elderly have been reluctant to embrace a philosophy of client control with real bite" [24, p. 55]. Systems serving younger people, by contrast, tend to be consumer-based and reflect the independent living movement's emphasis on consumer control and autonomy [25, p. 90].

Increasingly, however, older people and their advocates talk about autonomy, choice, and control. The Social Security Disability Insurance Program, which became law in 1956, assumes that "a disability prevents an individual from being autonomous" [26, p. 80], and thus emphasizes dependence; while the 1990 Americans with Disabilities Act "assumes that people with disabilities are able and want to make decisions about their lives" [26, p. 80]. The so-called "aging network" is serving more and more people under sixty-five. Many health care reform proposals reflect an age-neutral approach. More and more states have integrated at least some independent living options into their long-term care policies [25, p. 92]. Thus, over time, the similarities rather than the differences between the two groups are emerging. The refrain "There's no place like home" has thus become a popular theme for all ages for the delivery and receipt of long-term care.

Adapting the Home

It will, however, not be entirely the same home from which the shift to the hospital originally took place. Technology has made the home a friendlier environment for procedures previously thought possible only in the hospital under close medical supervision. Examples include improved ability to maintain sanitary and sterile conditions, electrical power for motors to run a variety of machines and fail-safe measures (back-up generators) when power fails, easy access to public and private transportation and to information and professional advice, and surveillance and telemonitoring systems for peoples' conditions and regimens [27]. Although some health care may place certain individuals at greater risk, it is in the eyes of many a risk worth taking. Studies of end-stage renal disease suggest that those in control of their services not only do better in the long run but, in the face of such an unpredictable disease and technology, also feel more in control of their lives and better about themselves [28].

Mobility and access problems are also of great relevance both to people with disabilities and older people but their solution will have more universal applicability. One of the most intensive and detailed studies on the housing needs of low-income people who are elderly and have disabilities [29] found that one out of every ten Houston residents require special architectural modifications in their homes. One-third of the older residents and over one-half of the people with disabilities require grab bars, and at least one-fifth need ramps. This need for ramps and railings nearly doubles from the sixty to sixty-five age group to the seventy-five-and-older category. For those with a "severe" as opposed to "moderate" disability, two-fifths need ramps and one-third need railings. Given the numbers, it is not surprising to find that 25 percent of those who are over sixty-five and have disabilities would like to move from their current home in the next year.

Such problems, however, are largely correctable, and usually at low cost. If accessibility is incorporated into the design prior to construction, the costs of accessible units are only slightly more than conventional ones [30, 31]. According to the Batelle Memorial Institute [32], the cost of barrier-free design can range from .25 to 4.2 percent of the fixed costs, depending upon the type of units to be made accessible and whether it is new construction or renovation. The average cost of making 10 percent of newly constructed units of an apartment building accessible is less than 1 percent of construction costs. Estimates made by the

Society of Landscape Architects indicates that the exterior environment, such as steps, handrails, parking, and site lighting, can be made accessible along with the interiors for slightly more than 1 percent of construction costs when incorporated in the initial plans [33]. Estimates provided by the United States General Accounting Office [34], in the wake of the Americans with Disabilities Act, have not been markedly different.

Inflation may, of course, raise these estimates. They will also vary, depending on expanded and developing standards of accessibility and how much any specific adaptation will "necessarily" lead to other changes (e.g., increase in apartment size). Thus a *New York Times* article claims that compliance with Local Law 58, "a law that requires nearly every new or substantially renovated apartment to be designed for the disabled," would add "5 to 8% to costs" [35]. On the other hand, as such design installation and equipment features become more commonplace, the actual cost (because of government and insurance company support as well as business interest) is likely to go down and the property value is likely to increase. The latter is not idle speculation. To get a full federal tax deduction I had to prove that a newly constructed outside ramp and a wheelchair accessible bathroom did *not* increase the value of my house.

Such accessibility is not high-tech [36, 37]. Dramatic improvements can result from doors 32 inches wide, small ramps, and grab bars in bathrooms. (In the Durham Emergency Repair Program, these types of modifications averaged only $82 per project [38].) Even in retrofitting, the options are more viable than ordinarily realized. Dunn evaluated Project Open House, a New York City area program which adapts the homes of a wide spectrum of people with disabilities [39]. For its clients, physical access in and out of the homes and aids relating to toileting, bathing, and grooming (all usually in bathrooms) were the two most important housing adaptations. The latter had a most direct effect on one of the most "troublesome" aspects of the care of both older people and people with disabilities—their independence in matters of personal hygiene. The former adaptation had a direct effect on people's spending more time in community activities and, in conjunction with other factors, on their employment. Striking was also the effect on household members, reducing many physical, emotional, and energy strains on them. In general, the older the individuals, the more important such adaptations were, because older people were more likely to be relying on other people's assistance (e.g., spouses, aging parents). For the vast majority of people with disabilities, these adaptations improved their feelings of safety and security and helped ensure their continued residence in familiar surroundings among friends, family, and community. An important caveat, however—in line with the earlier point in this chapter about the changing nature of disability—was that within a couple of years, the needs of 40 percent of the clients had changed. It is not clear how much of this was due to new needs created by new possibilities or new needs created by changing health conditions [40]. On the other hand, all of these adaptations were achieved at an average sum of $1,507, an amount which in several cases was equivalent to a year's cost for ambulance service and stretcher bearers for those in inaccessible housing who required frequent medical attention [39].

Ratzka has extended the implications of such work in terms of much more costly adaptations like the installation of elevators [41]. He finds such renovations in Sweden are 40 percent less costly than the institutional care they replace and estimates that as many as 40 percent of the moves of people with disabilities into nursing homes could have been avoided by housing modifications. He also examines the issue of long-term costs. In the 1930s, fifty years before this report, there was apparently a debate on whether to include elevators in the housing project area in which he concentrated his analysis. If included, the resulting increase in break-even rents would have been 3 percent. A comparison of these additional costs with costs of *NOT* making housing accessible showed that each year Swedish society is losing the equivalent of forty million U.S. dollars, for a total of nearly one and a half billion U.S. dollars lost by the 1980s. All in all, it costs thousands of times more than the original investment would have been. Similarly, Chollet estimates that renovating housing in the United States yields benefits from thirteen to twenty-two times their costs in reduced support services [42]. Lewis documented similar benefits vis-a-vis children [43]. Kiewel makes a comparable argument for all age groups based on the experiences of a Minnesota program [22].

Striving for accessible homes may have an effect not only on such specific issues as the ability of people to "age in place" and of younger people with disabilities to enhance their autonomy, but also on the very "production" of disability. Injuries are generally regarded as one of the most preventable causes of disability. While public attention often focuses on traffic accidents, the home, except for teenagers and young adults, is the major location for injuries. This increases directly with age. In both Sweden [41] and the United States [44], persons age sixty-five or older account for more than 75 percent of deaths due to falls, even though they compose less than 15 percent of the population. The over-sixty-five population experiences more injuries in the home *than in all other places combined* [45]. And this tendency increases precipitously as the older population ages [46]. As many as one-third of older persons residing in the community report a fall or a tendency to fall [47]. But these figures may be an *underestimate!* Not only may less serious falls be under-reported but the elderly themselves may purposefully hesitate to report a fall for fear of restriction of activities or placement in a nursing home [48]. Such a fear is not unrealistic for, after all, in both the United Kingdom and France (and probably the United States also), falls *without* fracture are among the most common causes of admission of the elderly to geriatric hospitals, residential facilities, and nursing homes [47]. A study in Toulouse, France noted that 39 percent of 295 persons aged seventy and over who had fallen but suffered no serious physical injury were institutionalized upon their family's request [49].

As for the specific location (or fear) of such falls, the vast majority occur on staircases and slips on wet surfaces [45]. Not surprisingly, bathrooms are the highest-risk area in relation to the amount of time people spend using them. Falls there, because of confined spaces with wet slippery surfaces, plenty of hard projecting contact edges, and hot water, generally lead to the most serious injuries [50].

Getting people to adapt their homes, however, is no easy matter [40, 51-53]. It will likely require a multifaceted approach. One important change must come in policies and practice. This presents many challenges, especially since adaptations of single-family homes are not part of the Americans with Disabilities Act [54]. One possibility is to upgrade the safety standards of all entrance and toilet facilities in hotels and other public accommodations (e.g., requiring non-slip surfaces and grab bars near toilets and in baths and showers) and to encourage such adaptations in the private sphere. For the latter, a tax incentive program is worth considering [55]. A simple example can be found in the way the United States responded to the energy crisis of several years ago. The government instituted an allowable income tax deduction for installing insulation or performing certain other energy-saving activities. Surely, as I have argued, an "accessible society" is also in the national interest. Why not allow a similar deduction for installing nonslip surfaces, grab bars, and ramps? Tax deductions are not the only way such a policy might be formalized. How about reductions in house insurance premiums? If we make a case for the safety effect of smoke alarms, surely we can do so for accessibility.

Another change needed to accomplish the goal must be in attitudes: people in the United States must learn to think of individuals' needs and abilities as constantly changing, and of the built environment as flexible and adaptable. At Het Dorp, for example, such expectations were part of the design [56]. This village in The Netherlands had a general crew of workers whose major task was to be available to adapt the built environment, inside and out, to the changing needs of the residents. The convergence of aging and disability may help to promote such attitudes in the United States.

Personal Assistance

Whatever the condition of the built environment, an important issue of control in living at home is "dependence" on others for assistance. Although the vast majority of older people and of people with disabilities are by no means isolated, and only a very small percentage are in long-term care institutions [57], Jones and Veter [58] conclude that caring does not seem to involve a large network of informal or formal caregivers. Whether in Europe [59], New Zealand [60], or the United States [61], the primary caregiver in more than 70 percent of all instances is a woman working largely alone. Moreover, she may not be a blood relative of the person she is caring for, and more than 40 percent of these caregivers are themselves over the age of sixty-five. Interestingly, when the caregiving is shared with others it is not likely to be done equitably nor is it likely to be the most personal services, such as washing and dressing, which are shared. And when males are the primary caregiver, the amount of personal services shrinks even further, perhaps even to the detriment of the recipient [62].

It is ironic that at a time of an ever-growing number of younger and older people in need, most of whom want to stay home, the very group most involved in providing informal care is under personal, financial, and societal pressure to enter and stay in the job market. They are accurately described as "women in the middle," juggling responsibilities for young children or spouses or older children with disabilities with caring for aged parents (not necessarily their own) and paid employment [63, 64].

That women retain the overwhelming responsibility for such care will be good neither for them nor for society. Future demographics make the continuation of such a pattern unlikely. With the post-World War II baby boom past, American families continue to shrink. They tend to live farther and farther apart. With greater pressure for women to contribute more to family income, jobs with flexible hours and working conditions—so essential to these caregivers—will necessarily become less desirable; even now, they usually offer lower wages, with little vertical mobility. And, finally, the fact that one of every two marriages ends in divorce will necessarily attenuate women's ties to their in-laws. Though "burnout" may not be imminent for those currently giving care, it is easy to see that there will be a future social burnout—a diminishing supply of female caregivers.

For many reasons, then, an increasing shift to out-of-hospital and out-of-institution care is a good, necessary, and even inevitable phenomenon. It must, however, be acknowledged that for some the shift will come too late. Some families will already be so depleted of energy and resources that they simply will not be ready to try again. For some, the attendant risk and responsibility will be too great, while for others, there will simply be no available family. The shift of assistance to the home is thus more complex than a mere physical shift in the location of services.

Initiatives which enhance the possibilities of "living at home" for all of us include family leave legislation, as well as programs to facilitate home sharing. These, however, are but stop-gap measures. To allow the majority of us to live and age in place, we will need to seek support outside the family. Limited amounts of "respite care" are available in some situations but this service too often kicks in only when the family is at the end of its rope. We need forms of assistance integrated into our way of life so that family relationships can be sustained, not replaced. A provocative form has sprung from the Independent Living Movement and its model of personal assistance services [65]. Such services are not embedded in a home health care model designed to meet a person's episodic acute-care needs during post-hospital convalescence, but are more self-directed and intended to meet a person's continuous chronic care needs. Service users are regarded as consumers and they and their families as capable of supervising their own care [66].

One plan to deal with these necessities, drafted by the World Institute on Disability, is called the Personal Assistance for Independent Living Act. While the proposed law is national, it would result in the creation of state and local agencies to connect people requiring personal assistance with individuals and organizations desiring to provide such services. The proposed law is built on the four basic principles articulated in *Toward Independence*:

- making services available to fill a broad range of needs at any time, anywhere, for any purpose
- not limiting eligibility by age, disability type, or income
- allowing for all degrees of consumer control of the services and their administration
- providing reasonable wages and benefits for personal assistance [67].

Under such a bill any person with a chronic illness or disability who requires assistance in daily living activities in order to continue living in a community or familial setting would be eligible to receive personal assistance services [68]. They might include:

- personal services, such as personal hygiene, dressing, transferring, feeding, giving medications, operating and maintaining assistive devices.
- household services, including meal preparation, cleaning, and laundry.
- child and infant care assistance to parents who have disabilities and require assistance in child-rearing.
- cognitive services, such as assistance with money management, planning, and decision making.
- communication services, such as assisting the individual who has a disability with reading and letter writing.
- security-enhancing services, such as monitoring alarms and periodic contact with the individual to ensure that she or he is safe.
- mobility services, including escorting and driving the individual to his or her destination.

Such a program of services—aimed at continued integration and providing family support as well as personal assistance—would be beneficial to all age groups and all disabilities.

CONCLUSION

A physical environment more flexible in orientation (i.e., not designed exclusively for able-bodied users) and in design (e.g., more adjustability in height and placement and reflecting a range of cognitive and sensory needs) requires as much a change in perception as a change in architecture. If society perceives that the needs and abilities of people are constantly changing, it might alter its attitudes toward the built environment from stressing "permanence" and "maintenance" to valuing "flexibility" and "adaptation." Designing equally flexible personal assistance services to be delivered within this adaptive environment would enable most people with disabilities to live independently and actively in noninstitutional settings. This is true whether their disabilities are age-related, injury-induced, or associated with childhood illness, and whether they are short-term or long-term.

And so we return to where we began—with the notion that aging and disability are intertwined, not special and separate concerns, and that dealing constructively with these concerns is in the interests of the entire society. The Swedish Secretariat for Future Studies called such a vision *A Caring Society* [69]. This report, while recognizing each person's uniqueness, also acknowledged our interdependence and promulgated a concept of "special needs" and policies which were based not on breaking the rules of order for the few, but on designing a flexible world for the many [70,71]. In short, what is done in the name of aging and disability today will have meaning for all of society's tomorrows.

REFERENCES

1. M. A. Nosek, Political Responses to Long-Term Disability, in *Aging with Spinal Cord Injury*, G. G. Whiteneck et al. (eds.), Demos, New York, pp. 263-274, 1992.
2. J. A. Racino and J. Heumann, Independent Living and Community Life: Building Coalitions among Elders, People with Disabilities, and Our Allies, *Aging and Disabilities*, pp. 43-47, Winter 1992.
3. President's Committee on Employment of the Handicapped, *Designs for All Americans*, Washington, D.C., 1967.
4. M. J. DeVivo, R. D. Rutt, K. J. Black, B. K. Go, and S. L. Stover, Trends in Spinal Cord Injury Demographics and Treatment Outcomes between 1973 and 1986, *Archives of Physical Medicine and Rehabilitation, 73*, pp. 424-430, 1992.
5. L. M. Verbrugge, The Iceberg of Disability, in *The Legacy of Longevity*, S. M. Stahl (ed.), Sage, Newbury Park, California, pp. 55-75, 1990.
6. L. M. Verbrugge, J. M. Lepkowski, and Y. Imanaka, Co-Morbidity and Its Impact on Disability, *Milbank Quarterly/Health and Society, 67*, pp. 450-484, 1989.
7. D. M. Gilford (ed.), *The Aging Population in the Twenty-First Century: Statistics for Health Policy*, National Academy Press, Washington, D.C., 1988.
8. P. H. Feinstein, M. Gornick, and J. N. Greenberg, The Need for New Approaches in Long-Term Care, in *Long-Term Care Financing and Delivery Systems: Exploring Some Alternatives*, P. H. Feinstein, M. Gornick, and J. N. Greenberg (eds.), U.S. Health Care Financing Administration, Washington, D.C., Pub. No. 03174, pp. 7-12, 1984.
9. National Center for Health Statistics, *Americans Needing Help to Function at Home*, Public Health Service Advance Data No. 92, U.S. Department of Health and Human Services, Washington, D.C., Pub. No. 83-1250, 1983.

10. J. P. Fulton, S. Katz, S. S. Jack, and G. E. Hendershot, Physical Functioning in the Aged: United States, 1984, *Vital and Health Statistics*, 10 (167 DHHS Publication No. PHS 89-1595), National Center for Health Statistics, Hyattsville, Maryland, 1989.

11. M. N. Haan, D. P. Rice, W. A. Satariano, and J. V. Selby, Guest Editors, Living Longer and Doing Worse? Present and Future Trends in the Health of the Elderly, special issue of *Journal of Aging and Health, 3*, pp. 133-307, May 1991.

12. N. Brooks and R. Matson, Managing Multiple Sclerosis, in *The Experience and Management of Chronic Illness*, J. Roth and P. Conrad (eds.), JAI Press, Greenwich, Connecticut, pp. 73-106, 1987.

13. U. Gerhardt and M. Brieskorn-Zinke, The Normalization of Hemodialysis at Home, in *The Adoption and Social Consequences of Medical Technologies*, J. Roth and S. B. Ruzek (eds.), JAI Press, Greenwich, Connecticut, pp. 271-317, 1986.

14. D. C. Turk and M. A. Speers, Diabetes Mellitus: A Cognitive-Functional Analysis of Stress, in *Coping with Chronic Disease*, T. G. Burish and L. A. Bradley (eds.), Academic Press, New York, pp. 191-217, 1983.

15. R. B. Trieschman, *Spinal Cord Injuries—Psychological, Social, and Vocational Rehabilitation*, Demos, New York, 1988.

16. H. Sato, Secondary Disabilities of Adults with Cerebral Palsy in Japan, *Disabilities Studies Quarterly, 9*, p. 14, 1989.

17. K. B. Funne, N. Gingher, and L. M. Olsen, *A Survey of the Medical and Functional Status of Members of the Adult Network of the Spina Bifida Association of America*, Spina Bifida Association of America, Rockville, Maryland, 1984.

18. G. Laurie and J. Raymond (eds.), *Proceedings of Rehabilitation Gazette's 2nd International Post-Polio Conference and Symposium on Living Independently with Severe Disability*, Gazette International Networking Institute, St. Louis, 1984.

19. L. S. Halstead and D. Wiechers, *Late Effects of Poliomyelitis*, Symposia Foundation, New York, 1985.

20. R. B. Trieschman, *Aging with Disability*, Demos, New York, 1987.

21. N. Crewe and I. K. Zola (eds.), *Independent Living for Physically Disabled People*, Jossey-Bass, San Francisco, 1983.

22. H. D. Kiewel, Serving Community Needs for Home-Accessibility Modifications, *Technology and Disability, 2*:4, pp. 40-46, Fall 1993.

23. R. Binstock, Aging, Disability, and Long-Term Care: The Politics of Common Ground, *Generations, 16*:1, pp. 83-88, 1992.

24. C. Sabatino and S. Litvak, Consumer-Directed Homecare: What Makes it Possible? *Generations, 16*:1, pp. 53-58, 1992.

25. G. DeJong, A. Batavia, and L. McKnew, The Independent Living Model of Personal Assistance in National Long-Term Care Policy, *Generations, 16*:1, pp. 89-95, 1992.

26. L. Beedon, Autonomy as a Policy Goal for Disability & Aging, *Generations, 16*:1, pp. 79-81, 1992.

27. K. Dawson and A. Feinberg, Hospitals in the Home, *Venture*, pp. 38-43, August 1984.

28. N. Kutner and D. Brogan, Disability Labelling vs. Rehabilitation Rhetoric for the Chronically Ill: A Case Study in Policy Contradictions, *Journal of Applied Behavior, 21*, pp. 169-183, 1985.

29. J. Gilderbloom, M. Rosentraub, and D. Bullard, *Designing, Locating and Financing Housing and Transportation Services for Low Income, Elderly, and Disabled Persons*, University of Houston Center for Public Policy, Houston, 1987.
30. P. A. Dunn, *An Analysis of the Housing Adaptation Programs in Massachusetts*, Adaptive Environments Center, Boston, 1985.
31. P. A. Dunn, *An Annotated Bibliography on the Needs, Costs, and Social Impacts of Housing Adaptation*, Adaptive Environments Center, Boston, 1985.
32. Batelle Memorial Institute, *Study and Evaluation of Integrating the Handicapped in HUD Housing*, U.S. Department of Housing and Urban Development, Washington, D.C., 1977.
33. G. O. Robinette, *Access to the Environment*, U.S. Department of Housing and Urban Development, Washington, D.C., 1978.
34. U.S. General Accounting Office, *Persons with Disabilities. Reports on Costs of Accommodations*, GAO/HRD-90-44BR, U.S. General Accounting Office, Human Resources Division, Washington, D.C., 1990.
35. J. Richman, A New York Law that Disables Builders, *New York Times*, p. A23, November 23, 1988.
36. R. Tideiksaar, Home Safe Home—Practical Tips for Fall-Proofing, *Geriatric Nursing*, pp. 280-284, November/December 1989.
37. R. Tideiksaar, Environmental Adaptations to Preserve Balance and Prevent Falls, *Topics in Geriatric Rehabilitation, 5*:2, pp. 78-84, 1990.
38. P. Porter, Facilitating Aging in Place through Home Repairs, *Long Term Care Advances: Topics in Research, Training, Service & Policy, 6*:2, 1994.
39. P. A. Dunn, *The Impact of Housing Upon the Independent Living Outcomes of Individuals with Disabilities*, doctoral dissertation, Florence Heller Graduate School for Advanced Studies in Social Welfare, Brandeis University, Waltham, Massachusetts, 1987.
40. R. J. Struyk and H. M. Katsura, *Aging at Home: How the Elderly Adjust Their Housing Without Moving*, Haworth Press, New York, 1987.
41. A. D. Ratzka, *The Costs of Disabling Environments—A Cost-Revenue Analysis of Installing Elevators in Old Houses*, Swedish Council of Building Research, Stockholm, 1984.
42. D. J. Chollet, *Cost-Benefit Analysis of Accessibility*, U.S. Department of Housing and Urban Development, Washington, D.C., 1979.
43. B. E. Lewis, *Inventors, Explorers and Experimenters: How Parents Adapt Homes for Children with Mobility Problems*, doctoral dissertation, Massachusetts Institute of Technology, Cambridge, Massachusetts, 1985.
44. National Safety Council, *National Safety Council Accident Facts, 1980 Edition*, National Safety Council, Chicago, 1980.
45. J. G. Collins, Persons Injured: Disability Days Due to Injuries, U.S., 1980-81, *Vital and Health Status Series 10*, U.S. Public Health Service Pub. No. PHS85-1577, Washington, D.C., 1985.
46. S. R. Cummings, J. Kelsey, M. Nevitt, and K. Dowd, Epidemiology of Osteoporosis and Osteoporotic Fractures, *Epidemiological Reviews, 7*, pp. 178-208, 1985.
47. Kellogg International Work Group on the Prevention of Falls by the Elderly, The Prevention of Falls in Later Life, *Danish Medical Bulletin, 34*(Special Supplement Series)4 (Gerontology), pp. 1-24, April 1987.

48. R. Tideiksaar, *Falling In Old Age: Its Prevention and Treatment*, Springer, New York, 1990.
49. J. L. Albarede and B. Vellas, *Restriction d'Activités Après la Chute de la Personne Agée*, Rapport à O.M.S. Centre International de Gerontologie Sociale, March 1, 1985.
50. W. Wrightson, New Zealand: Linking Design with Health, *Action on Accessibility: Proceedings of the International Accessibility Mini-Summit, September 1990*, Center for Accessible Housing, North Carolina State University, Raleigh, pp. 25-32, 1991.
51. J. E. Kincade Norburn, S. Bernard, T. Konrad, A. Woomert, G. H. DeFriese, W. D. Kalsbeek, G. G. Koch, and M. G. Ory, Self-Care and Assistance from Others in Coping with Functional Limitations among a National Sample of Older Adults, *Journal of Gerontology: Social Sciences, 48B*:2, pp. S101-S109, 1995.
52. J. Pynoos, Toward a National Policy on Home Modification, *Technology and Disability, 2*:4, pp. 1-8, Fall 1993.
53. E. Steinfeld and S. Shea, Enabling Home Environments: Identifying Barriers to Independence, *Technology and Disability, 2*:4, pp. 69-79, Fall 1993.
54. J. West (ed.), *The Americans With Disabilities Act: From Policy to Practice*, Milbank Memorial Fund, New York, 1991.
55. D. C. Schaffer, Tax Incentives, in *The Americans With Disabilities Act: From Policy to Practice*, J. West (ed.), Milbank Memorial Fund, New York, pp. 293-312, 1991.
56. I. K. Zola, *Missing Pieces: A Chronicle of Living with a Disability*, Temple University Press, Philadelphia, 1982.
57. M. H. Cantor, The Family: A Basic Source of Long-Term Care for the Elderly, in *Long-Term Care Financing and Delivery Systems: Exploring Some Alternatives*, P. H. Feinstein, M. Gornick, and J. N. Greenberg (eds.), U.S. Health Care Financing Administration, Washington, D.C., pp. 107-112, 1984.
58. D. A. Jones and N. J. Vetter, A Survey of Those Who Care for the Elderly at Home: Their Problems and Their Needs, *Social Science and Medicine, 19*, pp. 511-514, 1984.
59. L. Reif and B. Trager (eds.), *International Perspectives on Long-Term Care*, Pantheon, New York, 1985.
60. A. Jack, *Who Cares for the Dependent Disabled?* presented to the New Zealand Public Health Association Conference, 1985.
61. S. A. Stephens and J. B. Christianson, *Informal Care of the Elderly*, Lexington Books, Lexington, Massachusetts, 1986.
62. S. M. Allen, *Dehospitalization and Spousal Caregiving: Are Wives at Risk?* doctoral dissertation, Brown University, Providence, Rhode Island, 1992.
63. J. Aronson, Women's Sense of Responsibility for the Care of Old People: "But Who Else Is Going To Do It?" *Gender & Society, 6*:1, pp. 8-29, 1992.
64. E. Brody, Women in the Middle and Family Help to Older People, *Gerontology, 21*, pp. 471-480, 1981.
65. S. Litvak, H. Zukas, and J. E. Heumann, *Attending to America: Personal Assistance for Independent Living*, World Institute on Disability, Berkeley, California, 1987.
66. G. DeJong and T. Wenker, Attendant Care, in *Independent Living for Physically Disabled People*, N. Crewe and I. K. Zola (eds.), pp. 157-170, Jossey-Bass, San Francisco, 1983.

67. National Council on the Handicapped, *Toward Independence—An Assessment of Federal Laws and Programs Affecting Persons with Disabilities—With Legislative Recommendations*, Superintendent of Documents, Washington, D.C., 1986.

68. E. Abberbock, The Personal Assistance for Independent Living Act, *Independent Living*, pp. 43-44, November/December 1989.

69. Secretariat for Future Studies, *Care and Welfare at the Crossroads*, FRN, Stockholm, 1982.

70. R. Lifchez, *Rethinking Architecture: Design Students and Physically Disabled People*, University of California Press, Berkeley, 1987.

71. M. Orleans and P. Orleans, High and Low Technology—Sustaining Life at Home, Advanced Technology and Health Care in the Home, *International Journal of Technology Assessment in Health Care, 1*, pp. 353-363, 1985.

CHAPTER
3

Design Directives in Home Adaptation

Jon Pynoos and Victor Regnier

Housing for the elderly is one of the most unappreciated of the important issues confronting our society. Housing for all age groups bears significantly on the quality of life, affecting physical health, status, friendship formation, and access to neighborhood services. Older persons place special importance on housing because they are likely to spend more time in it, have more difficulty taking care of it, and have stronger psychological attachments to it (having more often lived in the same place for many years) than their younger counterparts. If there is a poor fit between the capabilities of older persons who have become frail and their environments, they may give up activities unnecessarily or carry them out in a dangerous manner, either of which can contribute to accidents, isolation, and premature or unnecessary institutionalization.

Environment-behavior researchers typically approach the problem of understanding the relationship between the physical environment and the behavior of older persons by developing and testing theories. Designers and planners, however, are often faced with the need to make decisions and judgments with scanty data that rarely resemble testable research hypotheses. Intuition and the ability to problem solve often take precedence over rigorous application of empirically based research findings or an elaborate theoretical framework. Consequently, there is a wide gap between environment-behavior theory and everyday necessary decisions that must be made to manage or design the physical environment.

This chapter attempts to bridge the gap between the theoretical framework researchers use to understand the environment and the practice or application of decisions by designers and planners. After discussing why this gap exists, twelve principles for environments for frail older persons will be presented. Each principle is accompanied by a series of interventions or strategies intended to provide researchers, designers, and planners with ways to implement them. A final section discusses the impact of policies and regulations on achieving the principles and suggests how the principles may enhance applied research on environmental interventions.

Lawton suggests that research in environment-behavior has four principal orientations: 1) an orientation to place, which involves a focus on specific places or settings; 2) an orientation to design, which focuses on the creation and shaping of the setting and the objects used by people; 3) an orientation to social-psychological processes, which recognizes the primary interest of behavioral and social science researchers (i.e., in psychological processes as they relate to the environment); and 4) an orientation to policy, which recognizes the relationship between the environment and the national/regional/local plans and strategies that have been established to respond to social and environmental problems [1].

This chapter addresses the orientations to design and policy. We emphasize implications for the existing home environment because of the strong preference of the great majority of older persons to age in place and the increasing emphasis on home care services for the frail elderly.

GUIDELINE ORGANIZATION SCHEMES

Over the course of the relatively brief history of environment-behavior (E-B) research a number of organizational schemes have been utilized. One approach is to organize information by "scale level," ranging from features within the unit (small, private spaces) to community-level considerations (large, public spaces) [2-4]. A second approach methodically considers each of the typical spaces (bedroom, kitchen, etc.) and the behavioral characteristics of each.

A third approach organizes information around the process of implementation [5, 6]. In this approach, guidelines are organized to match the sequence that normally accompanies the development of a project. The information is general in nature at the beginning of the process, when decisions are conceptual; later, more specific choices are made with detailed data about application.

A fourth approach, often found to be most useful, organizes guidelines so as to correspond with behaviors in relation to specific spaces or design elements [7-9]. This is appealing to architects because design often begins with the process of "programming" the building through assigning and specifying special requirements for specific rooms. For example, Howell's work on the relationship between circulation and sociability directly communicates the positive social outcomes associated with common spaces tethered to main circulation spaces [10]. In another example, doors are the locus of various behaviors which mediate what is identified here as the principle of "privacy." The twelve principles outlined in this chapter provide a systematic approach to the behavioral issues that are relevant to housing for older people and should be considered in any discussion of home adaptations.

TWELVE ENCOMPASSING PRINCIPLES

We believe that residential settings for older persons could be improved by bridging broad theory and application by utilizing consistent environment-behavior categories or principles. Toward this end, we identify twelve specific principles that have surfaced in the design and policy application literature. We offer these principles in an effort to create a research framework that is sensitive to program and environmental design concerns, rather than being led by theory building at the expense of application. Because this framework is informed by the range and types of decisions and considerations made by designers and policymakers, it represents a conduit through which social science-based research can more tangibly influence the management, program, policy, and design arenas.

The twelve principles are based on common themes in the literature [1, 11-18]. They were selected because they have a universal or timeless quality about them. While they have particular relevance for older persons, these principles are also applicable to other segments of the population. Although some are present and identified in the work of Cohen et al. [11], as they relate to nursing homes, and others are recognizable from the theory sections of textbooks that deal with environmental effects, we know of no comprehensive list of those principles that address the needs of those living in their own homes.

Each of the twelve principles is accompanied by a discussion explaining in broad terms why it is important and examples of how it can be applied. These interventions are intended to be illustrative and do not represent an exhaustive list. Many of the principles are interdependent, and some are conflicting. Others represent ends of a continuum. For example, "privacy" and "social interaction" address two opposite aspects of the environment. "Safety" and "challenge" have a similar conflicting quality. These interrelationships are referred to in cautionary notes that follow the presentation of the principles involved and their related interventions. The final section of the chapter discusses the importance of broader macropolicy for implementation of the principles.

Application of these twelve principles will vary depending on the type of dwelling unit and the extent of modifications. Table 1 rates each of the twelve variables with regard to planned and existing environments. For example, privacy, which is an important and critical concern in planned group living arrangements, is a major attribute of an existing home environment. Thus, although all principles are important, Table 1 reveals a number of issues that may be less important to address within an existing home environment.

Table 1. Relevance of Twelve Principles within
Planned and Existing Environments

	Environmental Context	
Environment Behavior Principles	Planned Environment	Retrofitted Existing
1. Privacy	X	O
2. Social interaction	X	X
3. Control/choice/autonomy	X	X
4. Aesthetics/appearance	X	X
5. Personalization	X	O
6. Orientation/way finding	X	O
7. Safety/security	X	X
8. Accessibility and functioning	X	X
9. Stimulation/challenge	X	X
10. Sensory aspects	X	X
11. Adaptability	X	X
12. Familiarity	X	O

Note: X = high relevance, O = low relevance.

Privacy

Provide opportunities for a place of seclusion from company or observation where one can be free from unauthorized intrusion. Privacy affords a sense of self and separateness from others. Privacy is usually provided by having one's own dwelling unit within which there is a bedroom or study. Sometimes privacy is achieved by methods such as: 1) informing others not to interrupt when one is working on a project, 2) putting a "do not disturb" notice on a door, 3) taking the phone off the hook, and 4) using an answering machine to screen calls even when the person being called is present. Altman defines privacy as "the selective control of access to the self" [19]. When asked what privacy means, individuals often respond: "being alone" or "no one bothering, distracting, or disrupting me." It becomes difficult to maintain or enforce these boundaries as an older person becomes more frail and dependent on others for help in such tasks as bathing or toileting. The ultimate loss of privacy occurs, however, when an older person has to move in with children, share a house with someone else, or share a room with one or more unrelated individuals whom he or she has not known previously.

According to Archea, "No matter how we conceptualize privacy, we cannot escape the fact that the behavior required to attain or maintain it occurs in an environment for which the physical properties can be specified" [20]. The physical environment can be used to channel and obstruct the visual and auditory information upon which the regulation of privacy depends. For example, features such as walls, doors, mirrors, and windows can either facilitate or inhibit the flow of information an older person can acquire. These physical properties can also affect what others can learn about an older person by controlling the probability that his or her behavior can be monitored. An auditory monitor is a potential home adaptation that enhances privacy by allowing a dependent person to close the bedroom door, yet to call or ask for help.

Social Interaction

Provide opportunities for social exchange and interaction. Creative social relationships between individuals can facilitate problem solving and emotional development, as well as motivate individuals to engage in more stimulating and lively experiences [21]. Older people without peer associations can experience isolation, which may lead to depression. Social interaction can reduce isolation and increase life satisfaction by allowing the older person to share problems, life experiences, ideas, and everyday events with someone who also benefits from the exchange. The attractiveness of this aspect of the environment is clearly demonstrated in the appeal of retirement communities, representing a life style that involves both organized and informal social interaction. One can create a neighborhood connection by adding features such as porches, bay windows to look in and out, flower boxes, mail boxes, personalized front doors, and play equipment for grandchildren or neighborhood children. Such features function as symbols of life, individuality, and openness. A simple home adaptation that promotes socialization is a telephone with larger, more readable buttons and an auto-dial feature that allows a person with visual or memory impairments to call friends more easily.

Control/Choice/Autonomy

Promote opportunities for residents to make choices and control events that influence their lives. Controlling aspects of one's social and physical environment has been embraced by social psychologists as a fundamental basis for positive social adjustment. Independence, which is frequently the single most cherished aspect of life for the frail, has its basis in choice, control, and autonomy. Older persons are more alienated, less satisfied, and more task-dependent in settings that are highly restrictive and regimented or promote dependency. Having control, or a sense of mastery, or feeling that one is in control enhances quality of life and morale [22]. A number of design interventions for choice and control are possible. They range from the simple—e.g., improving lighting to enhance both safety and productive activities—to the more complex—e.g., adding a roll-in shower with accessible controls to allow a person using a wheelchair to take his or her own shower. In one instance, renovations enhancing autonomy for a ten-year-old boy with a disability included easy access to the kitchen and a laundry chute so that he could do his share of household chores [23].

Choice can be enhanced by assessing and discussing the usefulness of environmental modifications prior to arranging services; providing alternative solutions, including products, designs, and devices; and analyzing the risks and benefits of the proposed changes and the status quo. On a cautionary note, choice/control must be congruent with competence.

Aesthetics/Appearance

Design environments that appear attractive and provoking. The overall appearance of the environment sends important messages to older persons and their family and friends about that person's physical, mental, and spiritual state of well-being [23, 24]. Thus, appliances and aids such as grab bars, handrails, and fixtures should be designed so as to appear attractive and "normal" rather than symbolic of institutional and hospital-like settings. For example, they may be made of wood instead of metal; and modifications may be designed to match or enhance the existing structure.

Personalization

Despite adaptive changes, the environment should remain as personal or individual as possible. Self-expression or personalization reinforces an older person's sense of identity, as well as expressing this identity to others. It is also a way of demonstrating to others that the space is occupied by a single, unique individual. Personalization is a compelling intrinsic feature of living in one's own home. Claire Cooper has written, for example:

> The furniture we install, the way we arrange it, the picture we hang, the plants we buy and tend, are all expressions of our images of ourselves, all are messages about ourselves that we want to convey back to ourselves and to the few intimates that we invite into this, our house [25].

Moreover, practitioners and researchers increasingly recognize that personalizing is critical to successful adaptive changes (see Chapters 5, 6, and 7). The need for personalization must, then, be balanced with the professionals' tendency to reduce "clutter" when modifying homes to increase safety.

Orientation/Way Finding

While this is rarely an issue when a person remains at home, orientation can arise as an adaptation issue when a frail older person experiences cognitive problems or moves to another home, such as the home of an adult child or other relative, or a foster home. In these situations, it becomes important to promote a sense of orientation within the environment, reduce confusion, and facilitate way finding. Older people with cognitive problems are particularly prone to have difficulty in orienting themselves, even in their own homes. Interventions which can provide landmarks for orientation include signs, graphics, and architectural differentiation in the form of wall treatments and objects. Other sensory cues such as aromas from cooking may reinforce these landmarks. Features that allow people to orient themselves with regard to the surrounding context, such as windows that open to a unique feature of the external environment (e.g., a garden or view), can also be helpful.

Safety/Security

Provide an environment that ensures each user will sustain no harm, injury, or undue risk. Older people experience not only a high rate of home accidents but also more than twice the number of resulting deaths compared with other age groups [26]. Falls and burns cause the most serious accident-related problems. Research suggests proper design can help prevent many accidents and lessen the severity of injury. Design interventions which contribute to safety and security include the following:

- Safety features such as grab bars, handrails, nonslip flooring, and ramps can be added to home environments in an unobtrusive and nonstigmatizing manner. For example, as already noted, grab bars or handrails made of wood or colored materials may be more acceptable than those made of metal.
- The environment can be made more resilient and less dangerous for older persons who are likely to fall—for example, replace existing items with round edges on furniture and fixtures and carpet hard floor surfaces to absorb impact.
- The environment should compensate for sensory losses. For example, compensate for greater susceptibility to glare, which could contribute to a fall, with features such as overhangs, north-facing skylights, and window shades.
- Modifying unsafe furniture, finishes, and fixtures may allow older persons to keep items of sentimental value and thereby reduce resistance to making the home safer. For example, rather than removing slippery throw rugs, firmly secure them.
- Safety and security throughout the home can be enhanced through the installation of items such as smoke detectors, security alarm systems, door peepholes, outdoor lights, and locking devices on doors and windows.
- Provide bathtub and shower temperature controls that regulate unpredictable water temperature swings. These can protect the older person from accidental burns and scalds.

- Reduce dangerous clutter by eliminating unnecessary items and improving storage capacity.
- Install supportive railings, nonslip floor surfaces, and lighting on stairs and in bathrooms because accidents are likely to occur in these places.

As a cautionary note, efforts to improve safety and security can conflict with efforts to stimulate, challenge, personalize, or meet the need for control, choice, and autonomy.

Accessibility and Functioning

Consider manipulation and accessibility as the basic requirement for satisfying concerns about functionality. Older people often experience problems manipulating the environment (windows, doors, HVAC equipment, appliances) due in part to chronic diseases such as arthritis. Reach-capacity and muscle-strength impairments can affect stopping, bending, sitting, and standing. Ambulation can become a problem, making it harder to get from one place to another without frequent rest stops. These limitations can make it difficult to navigate and fully utilize an environment [27]. Adaptations to the environment can make it easier to manipulate, as can the specification of fixtures, equipment, and devices that are designed to be manipulated by individuals with limited grip capacity or twisting ability. Making the environment convenient and easy to access for both individuals and caregivers will often alleviate ambulation limitations. Some design interventions which address accessibility and functioning include the following:

- Adequate handrails positioned in strategic places can compensate for changes in floor levels, often a major problem in the home environment.
- Changes in grade often occur between the front door and the street, where surfaces can be wet and slippery. Falling on pavement can be especially traumatic. Handrails located at the appropriate level and designed for good grasp control are important.
- Older people will often create a "control center" near a couch or favorite chair that centralizes access to light switches, television remote devices, telephone instruments, and reading materials. Securing or reorganizing electrical cords, throw rugs, and living room furniture can enhance safety without reducing access.
- Strategically placed night lights can help make reaching the bathroom in the middle of the night a safer trip.
- Many of the most severe safety problems exist or occur in kitchens. Changes that make it easier to access food, cutlery, dinnerware, and pots and pans can help reduce risks associated with climbing a step stool or injuries resulting from retrieving a heavy pot from a deep drawer under the counter.

- Redesigning closets, storage areas, and shelves for ease of access can compensate for reduced reach capacity, a common problem, especially among older, shorter women.
- Controls for HVAC systems, water valves, doors, windows, and lights often require handle adaptations or replacement fixtures that are accessible as well as easy to turn, twist, or pull.
- Unlike repairs to a leaky roof or to a malfunctioning heating system, safety-oriented home modifications do not always seem "necessary" to the older person. Improving attitudes toward safety can facilitate adjustments before an avoidable accident occurs. Involving the older person and the family in environmental assessment or negotiating safety features can also facilitate implementation.
- Making improvements in the home often requires capital and coordination with semiskilled and skilled workers. Programs for making home modifications should be structured to overcome the problems many older people face in coordinating the delivery of services and paying for environmental improvements.

Stimulation/Challenge

Provide a stimulating environment that is safe but challenging. Stimulation keeps the older person active, alert, and aware. A lack of stimulation can lead to inactivity and depression. One difficulty in increasing safety is that challenge is often reduced. An appropriate degree of challenge is highly desirable. Institutional environments are often faulted for their lack of variety or for their sensory monotony. A stimulating environment is especially important to combat boredom, a common problem of persons with mobility impairments. For example, color, smells, surface textures, and sounds give environments a richness of character that often reinforces their individuality and complexity. Spatial variety and hierarchy can make an environment more interesting to experience. The challenge of fitting other people, plants, and animals into a stimulating physical setting is the essence of making an environment a memorable place. One could dramatize time changes such as daylight, seasons, and daily weather by adding such features as window boxes, skylights, corner windows, and French doors; or features such as greenhouses, aquariums, aviaries, vegetable gardens, and bird baths that may promote productivity, alertness, and activity.

Sensory Aspects

Changes in visual, auditory, and olfactory senses should be accounted for in environments. Many older people experience problems with vision and hearing that can place them at a disadvantage in the environment [28]. Environments with high levels of sound and low lighting levels can inhibit socialization and manipulation of the environment.

The amount and source of light can affect basic visual acuity and glare. Color distortions brought about by the aging of the eye muddle color distinctions and mute color differences. The use of natural light in combination with indirect artificial lighting can have pleasing and effective results. The design interventions or adaptations that follow from this principle include:

- Control the glare from light from exposed windows through the use of exterior overhangs or window treatments (e.g., louver-type shades, shading tints).
- Replace difficult-to-read instructions or numbers on appliance controls such as on stoves, thermostats, telephones, and washing machines with larger, easy-to-read graphics.
- Increase the level of illumination, when needed, with special attention to task-related activities (e.g., cooking, reading, sewing). This may require additional outlets as well as fixtures.
- Illuminate light switches to make them easier to locate.
- Insulate or replace windows to dampen noise.

Adaptability

An adaptable or flexible environment can be easily modified to fit a specific new use or situation. As older persons age, their abilities are likely to change, and often the setting within which they live no longer fits their capabilities [29]. Consequently, some older persons carry out activities in unsafe environments, give up some tasks, or move to another setting in spite of their strong preference to stay in the same place. For a setting to meet the diminished capabilities of frail older persons, it must either include supportive features (e.g., ramps, grab bars, handrails) or be able to be retrofitted. Unfortunately, many housing units cannot easily be adapted to the changing needs of older persons because of stairs, bathrooms being located on only one floor, and other problems associated with accessibility. Such problems are particularly difficult for people who use wheelchairs. In addition, the availability of modifications is limited by inadequate reimbursement policies and the lack of an adequate delivery system for home modifications.

Interventions for adaptability include:

- Improve the system for financing and carrying out home modifications.
- Ease the reluctance of some older persons to make changes by making available products that are attractive and "normal looking" rather than constructed out of institutional materials and appearing to be made for hospital and nursing home settings.

- Provide educational programs to the general public concerning hazards and problems in the home and what can be done to remedy them.
- Improve environmental assessment procedures for the home, and train professionals in their use.
- Provide zoning options or condition-use permits that allow accessory apartments to be placed in single-family residential areas. This can encourage other persons who need housing to live with frail older persons and provide services or assistance.
- Promote universal design in single-family housing, with features such as nonslip flooring, grab bars, accessible bathrooms, adjustable kitchen counters and shelving, and the flexibility to live on a lower-level floor should that be necessary.
- Make sure that adaptations do not defeat efforts to maintain a homelike, personalized environment.

Familiarity

Adaptations should be accomplished in a manner that maintains the sense of the familiar. For some older people, changing the setting can be disorienting [30]. The environment should also constitute a familiar frame of reference in which rooms have a vernacular reference point. When making home modifications:

- Maintain familiar objects and their arrangement to the greatest extent possible, including maintaining habitual traffic patterns and well-known views.
- Avoid institutional materials.
- Incorporate changes into the existing decorating scheme, for example, make a ramp look like part of the existing porch.

DISCUSSION

Our ability to implement these environment-behavior principles and their accompanying interventions is significantly affected by government policy. Reimbursement policies, regulations, land-use zoning, and building codes all influence what is built and how it is managed, as well as the availability of programs. In many instances, these policies have been moving in directions that make it harder rather than easier to create environments that will improve the quality of life for frail older persons [31-33].

On the other hand, codes can be important in improving safety and accessibility. For example, the Fair Housing Amendments Act of 1988 will increase accessibility in multi-unit housing, especially for those using wheelchairs, allowing more disabled and elderly persons to age in place. However, codes have often ignored features that could improve safety for older and younger persons alike.

For example, while local codes pertaining to single-family homes often require handrails on stairs, there is a great deal of variation in their placement. Moreover, virtually no local codes require single-family housing to have such features as grab bars in showers or bathtubs, even though they would improve safety for all age groups.

The environment is an important component of the quality of life, especially for frail older persons who are more dependent on it than their healthier counterparts. This chapter has stressed the importance of linking clear principles to interventions that designers, planners, older persons, and policymakers can use. Many of these principles will interact and some may conflict with each other. The interventions and strategies to implement the principles will therefore require that architects, planners, managers, and older persons themselves be not simply technicians but problem solvers.

Attempts to improve the quality of life for frail older persons must be viewed in the context of government policies that place constraints on how home adaptation is provided, for example, by affecting the amount of money available. Policy affecting environments for frail older persons could be improved if the principles and their accompanying interventions could be proven to save costs and improve the quality of life. In order for this to occur, much more systematic research needs to be conducted on the impact of environmental interventions on the quality of older persons' lives. Following the method proposed by Zeisel [34], these principles and interventions could be useful in carrying out such applied research, which would affect both theory building and design innovation.

REFERENCES

1. M. P. Lawton, *Environment and Aging*, Center for the Study of Aging, Albany, New York, 1986.
2. I. Green, B. Fedewa, C. Johnston, W. Jackson, and H. Deardorff, *Housing for the Elderly: The Development and Design Process*, Van Nostrand Reinhold, New York, 1975.
3. J. Zeisel, G. Epp, and S. Demos, *Low-Rise Housing for Older People: Behavioral Criteria for Design*, HUD-483, U.S. Government Printing Office, Washington, D.C., 1977.
4. J. Zeisel, P. Welch, G. Epp, and S. Demos, *Mid-Rise Elevator Housing for Older People*, Building Diagnostics, Boston, 1983.
5. B. Chambliss, *Creating Assisted Living Housing*, Colorado Association of Homes and Services for the Aging, Denver, 1989.
6. P. Welch, V. Parker, and J. Zeisel, *Independence through Interdependence*, Department of Elder Affairs, Commonwealth of Massachusetts, Boston, 1984.
7. AIA Foundation, *Design for Aging: An Architect's Guide*, AIA Press, Washington, D.C., 1985.
8. L. Aranyi and L. Goldman, *Design of Long Term Care Facilities*, Van Nostrand Reinhold, New York, 1980.

9. M. Calkins, *Design for Dementia: Planning Environments for the Elderly and Confused*, National Health Publishing, Owings Mill, Maryland, 1988.
10. S. C. Howell, *Designing for the Aging: Patterns of Use*, MIT Press, Cambridge, Massachusetts, 1980.
11. U. Cohen, J. Weisman, K. Ray, V. Steiner, J. Rand, R. Toyne, and S. Sasaki, *Environments for People with Dementia: Design Guide*, Health Facilities Research Program, Washington, D.C., 1988.
12. M. P. Lawton, *Planning and Managing Housing for the Elderly*, Wiley, New York, 1975.
13. V. Regnier and J. Pynoos (eds.), *Housing the Aged: Design Directives and Policy Considerations*, Elsevier, New York, 1987.
14. L. M. Rickman, C. E. Soble, and J. M. Prescop, *A Comprehensive Approach to Retrofitting Homes for a Lifetime*, NAHB Research Center, Upper Marlboro, Maryland, 1991.
15. H. D. Kiewel, Serving Community Needs for Home-Accessibility Modifications, *Technology and Disability, 2*:4, pp. 40-46, Fall 1993.
16. R. V. Olsen, E. Ehrenkrantz, and B. Hutchings, Creating Supportive Environments for People with Dementia and Their Caregivers through Home Modifications, *Technology and Disability, 2*:4, pp. 47-57, Fall 1993.
17. B. R. Connell, J. A. Sanford, R. G. Long, C. K. Archea, and C. S. Turner, Home Modifications and Performance of Routine Household Activities by Individuals with Varying Levels of Mobility Impairments, *Technology and Disability, 2*:4, pp. 9-18, Fall 1993.
18. J. E. Kincade Norburn, S. Bernard, T. Konrad, A. Woomert, G. H. DeFriese, W. D. Kalsbeek, G. G. Koch, and M. G. Ory, Self-Care and Assistance from Others in Coping with Functional Limitations among a National Sample of Older Adults, *Journal of Gerontology: Social Sciences, 50B*:2, pp. 5101-5109, 1995.
19. I. Altman, Privacy Regulation: Culturally Universal or Culturally Specific? *Journal of Social Issues, 33*, pp. 66-87, 1977.
20. J. Archea, The Place of Architectural Factors in Behavioral Theories of Privacy, *Journal of Social Issues, 33*, pp. 116-137, 1977.
21. I. Rosow, *Social Integration of Aged*, Free Press, New York, 1967.
22. E. Langer and J. Rodin, The Effects of Choice and Enhanced Personal Responsibility for the Aged, *Journal of Personality and Social Psychology, 34*, pp. 191-198, 1976.
23. R. D. Lynch, Karl's House, *Technology and Disability, 2*:4, pp. 30-39, Fall 1993.
24. C. Hartman, J. Horowitz, and R. Herman, Involving Older Persons in Designing Housing for the Elderly, in *Housing the Aged: Design Directives and Policy Considerations*, V. Regnier and J. Pynoos (eds.), Elsevier, New York, pp. 153-176, 1987.
25. C. Cooper, The House as Symbol of Self, in *Architecture and Human Behavior*, Part II, No. 4, J. Lang et al. (eds.), Dowden, Hutchinson and Ross, Stroudsburg, Pennsylvania, pp. 130-146, 1974.
26. J. Pynoos, E. Cohen, L. J. Davis, and S. Bernhardt, Home Modifications: Improvements that Extend Independence, in *Housing the Aged: Design Directives and Policy Considerations*, V. Regnier and J. Pynoos (eds.), Elsevier, New York, pp. 277-304, 1987.
27. L. Noelker, *Environmental Barriers to Family Caregiving*, paper presented at the annual meeting of the Gerontological Society of America, Boston, 1982.

28. L. G. Hiatt, Designing for the Vision and Hearing Impairments of the Elderly, in *Housing the Aged: Design Directives and Policy Considerations*, V. Regnier and J. Pynoos (eds.), Elsevier, New York, pp. 341-372, 1987.

29. E. Steinfeld, Adapting Housing for Older Disabled People, in *Housing the Aged: Design Directives and Policy Considerations*, V. Regnier and J. Pynoos (eds.), Elsevier, New York, pp. 307-340, 1987.

30. M. E. Hunt and L. A. Pastalan, Easing Relocation: An Environmental Learning Process, in *Housing the Aged: Design Directives and Policy Considerations*, V. Regnier and J. Pynoos (eds.), Elsevier, New York, pp. 421-440, 1987.

31. J. Pynoos, Public Policy and Aging in Place: Identifying the Problems and Potential Solutions, in *Aging in Place: Supporting the Frail Elderly in Residential Environments*, D. Tilson (ed.), Scott, Foresman, Glenview, Illinois, pp. 167-208, 1990.

32. J. Pynoos, Toward a National Policy on Home Modification, *Technology and Disability, 2*:4, pp. 1-8, Fall 1993.

33. E. Steinfeld and S. Shea, Enabling Home Environments: Identifying Barriers to Independence, *Technology and Disability, 2*:4, pp. 69-79, Fall 1993.

34. J. Zeisel, *Inquiry by Design*, Brooks Cole Publishing, Monterey, California, 1981.

CHAPTER
4

Technology
and Home Adaptations

Paul John Grayson

It is almost self-evident that people arrange their living space in ways that suit their needs. As people age and their physical and sensory capabilities decline, they tend to rearrange or modify their home setting to accommodate their current abilities. Some home adaptations are simply changes in the arrangement of existing furniture or accessories. Others introduce a new appliance or a mechanical or electrical system encompassing new technologies.

Applying technology to improve the quality of life is not new. From the earliest of times, humankind has tried to find ways to make life easier and to improve security, privacy, personal control, and comfort within the built and natural environments. Technology is so woven into contemporary life that we are at times unaware of the profound and pervasive ways it assists us to manage and perform daily activities. Without technology, civilization could not have progressed. In everyday life, we routinely use such technological achievements as a telephone, a microwave oven, an automobile, or an airplane without considering their magnificence. We give little thought to the intricacies and the technological engineering feats involved in such commonplace appliances as a door lock or door hinge, a refrigerator, a stove, or electric lights. Even devices as simple as a comb, a tooth brush, or a pair of scissors are applications of technology. Without such tools our quality of life would not even be considered minimal by contemporary standards.

Webster's Seventh New Collegiate Dictionary's definition of "technology" includes: "the totality of the means employed to provide objects necessary for human sustenance and comfort." For our application, the term "technology" is further expanded to include those objects, elements, or spaces that enable users to perform tasks that they want or need to, but cannot easily perform because of physical, sensory, or cognitive impairment. Thus, "technology" as used herein refers to the totality of the means to enable a person to remain as independent as possible despite disabilities.

Generally, as the level of technology sophistication rises, so do costs. However, even sophisticated home adaptation technologies can prove cost-effective—for example, when they permit independent aging in place at a lower total cost than a nursing home placement or when they eliminate or reduce the need for a caregiver. Another benefit may be a sense of pride and a measure of control over one's daily activities.

The application of technology, whether low-tech or high-tech, can enhance independent living, encourage self-help, reduce stress and strain on caregivers, and improve the quality of life, not only for older people but for all. In this chapter, we consider the home adaptation market and industry, explore areas of the home to illustrate these points, review innovative products that are currently available or are being developed, and discuss the concept of universal life span design.

MARKET OUTLOOK AND
THE HOME ADAPTATION INDUSTRY

United States manufacturers have been reluctant to make major changes to existing designs or to develop new products that assist people with disabilities to remain independent. One reason is that, in the United States, our litigious nature causes some manufacturers deep concern about the exposure to liability related to new products. Another reason is their uncertainty about the market potential. Some manufacturers perceive older people as uniformly sick, and in need of medically oriented products and environments; others perceive them as uniformly healthy. Some manufacturers think older people are "easy marks," while others believe they are unwilling to purchase new products. All too often, products and appliances used by older persons with limited strength, or with impaired vision, hearing, speech, or mobility, have been designed with little sensitivity to such contingencies. Many manufacturers focus more on the convenience and cost of the manufacturing process than on lasting quality and functional convenience for the consumer. As a result, design and marketing strategies emphasize the standard of a youthful consumer of average height, weight, and physical and mental abilities. But who is average? The reality is that we are all different.

Overseas, manufacturers have long had a different outlook that results from public policies supporting independent living for people who are older or have disabilities. These policies include extensive community-based home care, health services, and financial assistance to encourage home modifications. Thus, in Europe and Japan numerous innovative and supportive products for older persons are available. Many of the products and designs referred to in this chapter are not yet available in the United States or are only gradually becoming available through dealer import arrangements.

Due to this lack of a strong manufacturer commitment in the United States, it has fallen to frail older people, younger people with disabilities, or their caregivers to adapt products to suit individual needs. For example, individuals with low vision may modify an illegible thermostat or stove control dial with a contrasting marking, such as a brightly colored self-adhesive transfer dot. They may devise coding systems, such as using one wide rubber band around a can to identify the contents as corn and two to indicate cream-style corn, or wrapping contrasting color tapes around pot handles to make the handles more visible and reduce spills and burn hazards. The prevalence of such adaptations suggests both the need and the opportunity to provide more efficient and safer products.

The elderly are a rapidly growing market with increasing need for new and innovative products. However, as a group, they are not prone to make impulsive buying decisions. They want to be fully aware of a product's benefit and value, and are interested in proven results [1]. In addition, some older people are slow to accept new products that may enhance their independence, either because of cost or because they wish to keep using familiar objects, even if such objects are disabling. However, as more enabling products come to the marketplace, and as older people become more informed about their advantages, these products will become more readily acceptable. Reducing the stigma associated with adaptive devices, whether high- or low-tech, will also increase the market for and ultimately the availability of such products. We are only at the beginning of a trend toward using assistive technology to make it easier for older people and people with disabilities to function independently in their homes.

Caregivers offer another market for both low- and high-tech devices: technology can help to reduce caregiver stress and strain. For instance, in response to caregiver difficulties getting frail older people in and out of bed, Japanese manufacturers have developed a series of adjustable and adaptable beds, including:

- a bed that splits at the foot, allowing a section of the mattress to drop down on each side so that the bedridden person's feet come down to the floor. Simultaneously, the head of the bed rises, and the middle tilts, so that the bed gradually rotates the person from a lying to a standing position; the caregiver needs only to guide, rather than lift or carry.
- a bed that converts into a chair while the person is in it—the caregiver can roll the chair-bed into activity spaces.
- an adjustable-height remote-controlled rehabilitation bed with a wheeled floor-mounted overhead beam rig that can raise a patient horizontally or seated in a sling to permit a caregiver to make the bed. The overhead rig permits a caregiver to lower a patient into a portable bathtub unit (stored under the bed) or to roll-up a portable wash/dry flush commode or a portable

sink (with standard faucet controls and a flexible hose for hair washing). The caregiver can transfer a patient into a wheelchair using the overhead rig or lower overhead rails to create a set of parallel training bars for patient mobility rehabilitation with or without use of an overhead rolling support harness.

Completing a home adaptation project requires the ability to search out options, arrange for purchase, contract for services, and make payment. If frail or disabled residents cannot manage these activities independently, family members or outside sources such as friends and service providers need to assist. Information and decision-making assistance may also be needed for older people or people with disabilities who are not aware of the need for home adaptation, the options available, and the potential benefits to autonomy and quality of life. These factors, addressed more fully in other chapters, are particularly true of high-tech adaptations.

It is important to note that, although some elders in the United States have the resources to purchase innovative products, many do not. How can they acquire products that encourage independence, if they do not have the means to buy them? *Coping with Daily Life* [2] offers many examples of uncomplicated, low-tech assistive devices that can be made easily, with a minimum amount of time and at low cost. Additional sources of information for home modification solutions may be found in the References section of this chapter [1, 3-7]. However, for more costly high-tech devices, new financing mechanisms are needed.

Still, perhaps the most important aspect of introducing technology is the need for the user to select assistive technology by means of informed choice. Too many times family members, service providers, or designers, with all good intentions, impose technology on a frail elder without reviewing options adequately or offering a "hands-on" introduction to the proposed adaptation. Technology adopted through individual choice (see Chapters 2, 5, 6, and 8) will more likely be used and appreciated. A user who is not involved in the selection process is much less likely to accept and use the adaptation.

USE OF TECHNOLOGY AND LEVELS
OF ADAPTATION

Home adaptation technology options vary from low-tech to high-tech. For example, many frail elderly have difficulty getting into and out of bed. Installing a vertical pole from floor to ceiling, near the head of the bed and a few inches away from the edge, would provide stability when grasped, thus minimizing the potential for falls resulting from a lack of balance or from dizziness caused by a sudden change of position. This form of technology could be represented herein as a low-tech tool. If the tool were fitted with a sensor device that is programmed to turn on the night lights when touched, the pole would then represent a medium-tech element. If the pole had a bracket arm that rotated and could move from a mattress height level to a standing level, serving as a "helping hand" guiding the elder person from a horizontal to a standing position on voice command, it would qualify as a high-tech component.

Whole systems can be high-tech, such as "Smart House" or "Intelligent House" technology. These systems can perform multiple functions, including:

- checking whether the stove was left on without a pot on a burner, and if so, turning it off
- locking exterior doors and windows at night
- ensuring that the bathtub water does not overflow
- serving as a voice reminder—for example, "Time to take your medicine."

Some adaptations are simple and require little effort, while others require careful planning and contracting of services. In thinking about modifications it is useful to divide them into three "levels."

Level I

Use of various types of aids (such as reaching and grabbing aids, bathing and personal hygiene aids, eating and cooking aids, and communication aids), including any new product or replacement product or service that does not require physical, mechanical, or electrical changes to the existing space. Requires ability to determine need, locate source, review options, obtain, purchase, arrange delivery, unpack, set up, plug in (if necessary), and use it.

Examples: a large-numeral clock, a microwave, a large button telephone, increased lamp wattage, a tactile-marked meat thermometer or bread cutting board, "easy grip" utensils.

Level II

Retrofitting the home by replacing a fixed or built-in element, or installing a new element. The retrofit may involve minor carpentry, painting, plumbing, mechanical, electrical, or other contractor service. Requires ability to determine need and to plan the retrofit; arrange, contract for, and review the installation; and, if acceptable, pay for services.

Examples: widening a doorway, removing a threshold, installing a security or emergency response system, or installing electrical outlets at more appropriate locations and heights. Providing rocker three-way switches, motion detector room lights, night lights, or recessed step lights to reduce the risk of falling. Installing grab bars, a hand-held shower hose in a bathtub, or a transfer bench at a roll-in shower alcove. Providing an automatic faucet and thermostatic water temperature control in the kitchen or bathroom to prevent scalds and eliminate the problem of a user forgetting to turn off the faucet. Replacing an ordinary stove with a heat-resistant glass induction cooking surface and a counter height oven to reduce pot spills, burns, and strains from bending. Installing a home automation system that can be programmed to lock up doors at night, permit monitored guest entry, turn off appliances or water faucets, or send an emergency message to a local health center. Replacing an existing toilet seat and cover with a wash/dry unit and an automatic flush valve that operates when the user gets off the seat. (Many of these assistive devices are in use at transportation facilities, hotels, and office buildings.)

Level III

Making major alterations to the home. Such modifications frequently disrupt the use of space for a period of time. Requires ability to plan, design, budget, schedule the work, bid, contract and oversee the work, make accommodation while work is proceeding, and pay for the services when satisfactorily completed.

Examples: removing and replacing built-in equipment, doors, and electrical or heating systems, walls, windows, closets, floor materials, and bathroom or kitchen plumbing fixtures. Installing adjustable height counters and accessible cabinets. Eliminating steps. Installing ramps, a residential elevator, a lift, an automatic door opener, a roll-in shower, a walk-in bath-tub, and an adjustable height toilet.

Each user has different needs for home adaptation solutions drawn from one or more of these levels and varying from low- to high-tech. The following sections of this chapter describe several areas in the home to illustrate potential uses of home modifications and technology to create an enabling environment for older persons.

USE OF TECHNOLOGY AND HOME ADAPTATION
APPROACHES FOR DIFFERENT TYPES OF SPACES

In this section design criteria are described, for each area of the home, that will help a resident to compensate for many types of disabilities. These features may either be designed into the original construction or added as an adaptation later on.[1] Readers will note many examples of the use of technology in these descriptions. While in many cases the same goals can be accomplished with less innovative technology, in other cases, application of such technology can make a significant difference in the frail or disabled person's functional independence.

---

[1] For a useful and interesting description of an accessibility renovation, see [8].

Included in this section are illustrations of specific areas in a hypothetical residence that could serve the needs of an elderly couple aging in place, as well as a younger family. The goal is to provide as flexible and adaptable an environment as possible. Although using all the features described would require considerable resources, the examples attempt to identify a range of options.

Site

The exterior of a home that is easy for anyone to use and meets the needs of people with disabilities may include: a pathway that is firm underfoot, is non-slippery in wet or icy weather, and provides tactile edges; covered or enclosed parking convenient to a level entrance that is wheelchair-accessible; curb cuts that provide a smooth path of travel from roadway to sidewalk; paths with gentle slopes; area lighting activated by timers, photoelectric cells, motion or smart card proximity detectors; and radiant heating coils embedded in the pathways in northern climates to melt snow and ice.

Entrance

A safe and convenient entrance might provide: a covered area for protection from the weather, with an illuminated space at the entrance door and a package shelf; a lighting system activated by a motion detector; a secure entrance door providing a keyed or magnetic card reader lock system and a lever handle that is easy to use; a pull bar to permit ease in closing the door from a wheelchair; peepholes at standing and seated heights; a closed-circuit TV camera with monitors for use from any room to identify the caller and remotely release the lock for entry.

Vestibule

Practical features for a vestibule include: space to maneuver a wheelchair; a transfer bench that can serve as a seat for changing shoes; a place for mail and packages and for removing and storing outer garments, shoes, and boots; a coat closet with a pull-down counter-weighted clothes pole that is accessible to a person in a wheelchair, and with an alcove or recess for storing a wheelchair, walker, stroller, or baby carriage; sliding doors between the vestibule and living spaces to permit more comfortable passage and to serve as space savers in lieu of hinged doors; mechanical door openers activated by switches or infra-red controls and provided with fusible link devices for door release in case of fire or other emergency; and a radiant heating system built into the first floor if on-grade.

Concept for an Accessible Entrance Vestibule (see Plan A)

This "universal" arrangement serves all people, not just those who are older or have disabilities. Over the entranceway is a covered area with a light fixture that is activated by a motion detector. Adjacent to the door are an intercom and door buzzer with a closed-circuit TV camera connected to a communications center inside. A bedridden person or other resident can identify visitors remotely from a monitor and then, if desired, activate a remote control to release the entrance door lock. A flush threshold is protected from water intrusion by means of a continuous flush drain across the entrance door. It provides a level, smooth path of travel for a person using a wheelchair, and also reduces tripping hazards, especially useful for people with visual or mobility impairments. The entrance door has lever handle hardware and a pull bar across the exterior to permit a person using a wheelchair to open or close the door easily. A package shelf, with boot and shoe storage below, along with a transfer seat, is provided. Two closet sections with sliding doors offer space to store a wheelchair or stroller and coats. The second of these is outfitted with an adjustable-height clothes pole accessible to a person using a wheelchair, eliminating the need to stretch overhead to hang up one's garments.

Passageways and Stairs

Interior circulation is especially important to a person who wishes to remain at home despite a disability. Such circulation space should provide: sufficient passageway width (48″) for a wheelchair and an ambulatory person; provision of a handrail for balance; nonslip flooring (if carpeted, low-pile and securely fastened material); three-way light switches, preferably rocker type, at entrances from other spaces; sufficient illumination to minimize potential for falls; lighting that can be adjusted with the use of dimmers both for energy efficiency and for individualization by the user; stairs with handrails on both sides; contrasting color at the stair nosing and the tread; step lights; and a bench at the top or bottom of a stair to serve as a resting place.

Common Spaces

Key design features for living, dining, and family rooms and dens could include: nonslip floor material, either fixed rugs or wall-to-wall carpet with tightly woven low-height pile; twelve-inch-high baseboard of carpet or cork as a kick-plate and doors with Plexiglass® skirts or a plastic laminate finish to reduce wheelchair leg damage; windows conveniently located with accessible hardware that is easy to grasp, turn, and lock; window shades, blinds, and draperies that can be opened or closed with a remote control device; furniture without sharp corners and with sturdy base supports; chairs with firm support legs and arms that extend

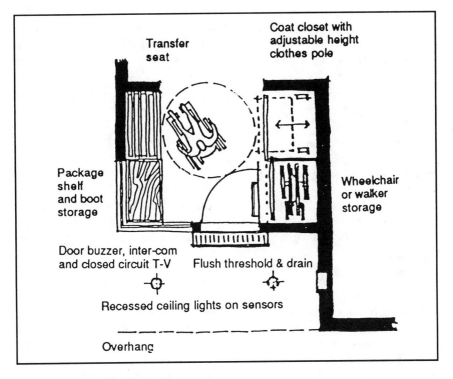

Plan A — Concept for an accessible entrance vestibule.
Source: Environments for Living, Winchester, Massachusetts.

far enough forward to maximize the ability to move from a seated to a standing position.

The control center and TV monitor for a home automation and security system can be located in any room (but preferably in a room where the resident spends the most time, such as a bedroom, living room, or kitchen) and could:

- Provide closed-circuit TV monitoring and intercom to front door and other security areas permitting automatic visual contact when the doorbell is sounded, two-way communication, and the remote unlocking or locking of any exterior door or window without getting up from chair or bed.
- Program or change heating and cooling temperatures; turn any lights in the home or yard on or off at any time or at programmed times; monitor all mechanical, electrical, and other systems for malfunction, fire, smoke, water overflow in a sink or bathtub, a stove left on, or a window or exterior door left open; and, if needed, sound an alarm and send a signal to the appropriate municipal service.

- Provide an emergency response system that can be voice-activated from any space in the home to provide a direct link to local medical support, and to send a personal signal to family members or a friend at an office or at another home.

- Provide a telephone/intercom link with all rooms, external communication, and message center.

- Raise or open any exterior window shutter or interior blind, curtain, or drapery, to help control heating, cooling, and light (an emergency spring will open shutters in case of fire).

- Control assistive devices such as an adjustable bed.

Throughout the dwelling unit all convenience outlets, self-illuminated light switches, thermostats with tactile markings, and power panels should be located in positions accessible to people who use wheelchairs or have low vision.

Kitchen

Kitchen features that promote independence include: a counter, sink, or stove that can be adjusted to a comfortable height for any standing person or a person using a wheelchair. Cabinets and storage areas positioned for accessibility. Flexible hose on sink. Refrigerator, freezer, and oven units located at counter height to eliminate bending. Locating the kitchen/dining table at the end of the counter to permit leveling of the counter with the table, thus eliminating the need to pick up heavy dishes or pots. Cork or vinyl floor finishes for convenient maintenance and resiliency. Walls painted, papered, or finished with plastic laminates or other easy to clean material to provide convenient maintenance. Control system that permits both general room lighting and task lighting adjustment to higher or lower intensities. Contrasting colors on work surfaces for people with low vision to ease meal preparation (e.g., a cutting board with a dark surface on one side provides contrast for light colored meat, such as chicken). Large-sized knobs with tactile indicators on stove and refrigerator controls, measuring cups, and weighing scale.

Concept for an Accessible Kitchen (see Plan B)

At the heart of this state-of-the-art kitchen is a communications center containing a desk and a home automation system control unit with a telephone, intercom, closed-circuit TV monitor to the front door and other parts of the house with a remote lock release system for exterior doors, an emergency response system, location annunciator for fire and smoke detectors, status and programmed timers for all mechanical and electrical systems, and a control device for remote opening and closing of windows and shutters.

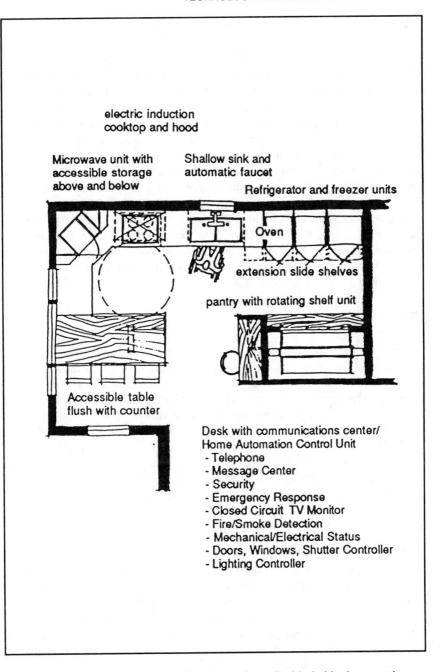

electric induction cooktop and hood

Microwave unit with accessible storage above and below

Shallow sink and automatic faucet

Refrigerator and freezer units

Oven

extension slide shelves

pantry with rotating shelf unit

Accessible table flush with counter

Desk with communications center/
Home Automation Control Unit
- Telephone
- Message Center
- Security
- Emergency Response
- Closed Circuit TV Monitor
- Fire/Smoke Detection
- Mechanical/Electrical Status
- Doors, Windows, Shutter Controller
- Lighting Controller

Plan B — Concept for an accessible kitchen for a disabled older homemaker.
Source: Sekisui's "Life Care–Model Home," Mitaka, Japan.

A unique pantry design provides for a shelf system that moves up and down. When the called for shelf arrives at the transfer counter, the slide-down glass door automatically opens. The assembly is, therefore, usable by a person using a wheelchair or a person standing. This illustration also shows an above-counter mounted oven, refrigerator, and freezer that provide convenient access to these appliances. Further, extension slides are provided under each appliance to permit the placement of supplies or food. The shallow depth sink provides clearance to permit a person using a wheelchair to work at the sink. The flush top electric induction cooking surface helps to reduce accidental spills, and minimizes burns and other hazards. Controls are mounted on the front panel for ease of use by older persons, while providing below-counter access for a person using a wheelchair. Relocatable under-counter storage carts with a variety of configurations for pots, dishes, or supplies are also provided. The microwave oven located in the corner is mounted six inches above the counter to facilitate the placement of cooking containers when the door opens. The accessible dining table is flush with the counter extension, to enable a person to slide the dishware onto the dining table without lifting.

Bedroom

Those who need assistance with activities of daily living, especially people with severe chronic illnesses who spend much of their day in bed, may require various types of assistive technology such as: A ceiling-mounted transfer system running from bed to bathroom, which can be operated by a hand held remote controller; an adjustable bed with a remote controller which can be raised from residential height to hospital level for convenient use for health care services. Night light activated automatically or by remote controller. A TV monitor linked to a home automation system (as described in the section on common spaces). A closet with a pull-down counter-weighted pole. All room door hardware with lever handles, all drawer and closet door hardware with large pull bars.

A Concept for an Adaptable Life Span Bedroom

This concept was designed to anticipate and address changing needs as residents age in place; it illustrates how a designer can apply universal design principles to solve specific problems. For example, assume an elderly couple with a husband who is mobile but experiences balance problems when getting in and out of bed, standing at the lavatory, getting onto and off of the toilet, and getting into and out of a chair. Simple modifications that would help him remain independent are floor-to-ceiling modular support poles at the table, bed, and lavatory, and a commode lift at the water closet (see Plan C).

Assume, however, that the husband eventually develops a severe mobility problem and requires caregiver assistance with bathing and toileting. This

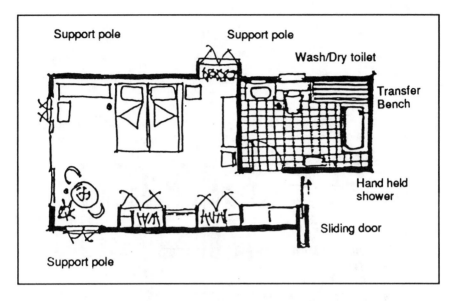

Plan C — Concept for an adaptable life span bedroom.
Source: Environments for Living, Winchester, Massachusetts.

adaptable design provides for future installation of a ceiling-mounted transfer lift, with a track running between bed and bathroom, to help reduce the stress and strain on a caregiver transferring the husband from bed to bath to toilet. One of the most common compensation claims filed by health care workers in the United States is for back injuries. A pre-established framed opening in the wall between the bathrooms and bedroom has been provided in this design, as have removable wall panels for future modification if required (see Plan D).

Bathroom

The most important and generally neglected planning area in the home is the bathroom. Its location is very crucial and in some cases a second-floor location is an obstacle to remaining at home. Access and equipment considerations may include: Sliding door with automatic open/close mechanism instead of a hinged swinging door. Floor area adequate for maneuvering a wheelchair. Adjustable-height counter top with lavatory and knee space for person using a wheelchair. Infra-red automatic control lavatory faucet with pre-set water temperature. Under-counter wheeled storage cart for supplies. An adjustable height wash/dry toilet with heated seat and infra-red controlled automatic flush valve. Fold-away grab bars to permit transfer from a wheelchair from either side of toilet. Wet area shower and bathing alcove with transfer bench for use at shower and tub, and with

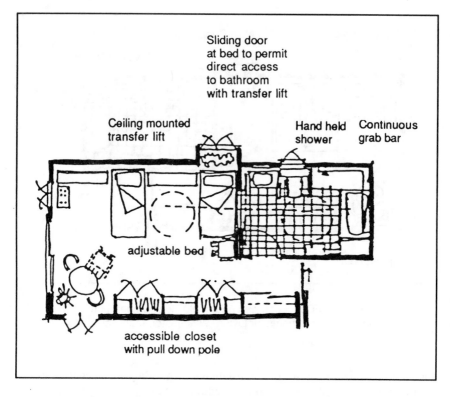

Sliding door
at bed to permit
direct access
to bathroom
with transfer lift

Ceiling mounted
transfer lift

Hand held
shower

Continuous
grab bar

adjustable bed

accessible closet
with pull down pole

Plan D — Concept for an adaptable life span bedroom.
Source: Environments for Living, Winchester, Massachusetts.

continuous grab bar across bench for convenient transfer. Clothes hooks and drying lines mounted at convenient seated and standing height. Pre-set water temperature controls to prevent scalding. Heated towel rack with wall mounted hair/body dryer. Nonslip floor material with continuous drain across flush threshold at sliding door to wet area shower. Lighting intensity controlled with dimmers. A ceiling-mounted transfer lift.

Concept for a Bathroom of Universal Design
(see Plan E)

This compartmentalized bathroom provides a wet area shower with hand-held shower, a transfer bench, and standard bathtub that permits safe access from the transfer bench. A continuous floor drain and pitched floor keep water away from the adjoining space. An accessible lavatory has an automatic faucet and water temperature control. The fold-up, adjustable-height arm supports at the wash/dry

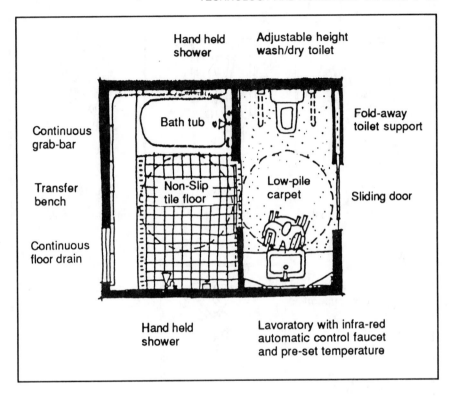

Plan E — Concept for a bathroom of universal design.
Source: Environments for Living, Winchester, Massachusetts.

toilet will permit right or left transfer from a wheelchair, or will aid a person with stability difficulties. A continuous grab bar along the transfer seat and bathtub doubles as a hanger for a soap dish, a shampoo bottle rack, washcloths, and towels.

Utility and Laundry Area

A person who wishes to remain independent in instrumental activities of daily living may need an accessible utility area. Some suggestions for this area are: Adjustable height counter with soaking sink. Raised washer/dryer. Adjustable-height ironing board with room to maneuver a wheelchair. Accessible cabinets and drying lines. Wheeled carts for supplies. Adjustable-height sewing/folding/ sorting table. Lighting intensity controlled with dimmers. Power panel, convenience outlets, and room light switches mounted at accessible heights.

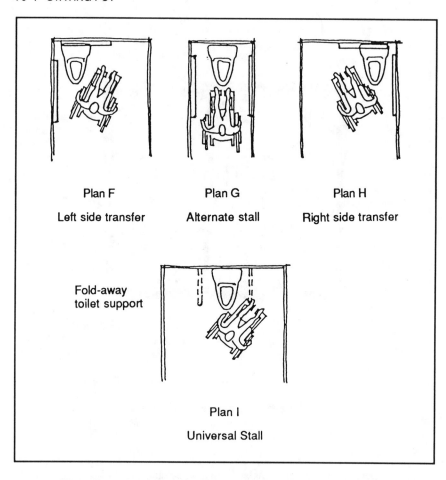

Plans F-I — Options for customizing toilet layouts (conceptual).
Source: Environments for Living, Winchester, Massachusetts.

UNIVERSAL DESIGN

No discussion of technology and home adaptation would be complete without a description of universal design. Universal design is the principle by which environments and products are designed to meet the needs of as broad a range of users as possible. Such environments accommodate people with disabilities as comfortably as able-bodied people. Universal Life Span design is accessible, adaptable, barrier-free, and safe. It strives for an environment that improves the quality of life for a frail older person, for a wheelchair user of any age, or for a young child. For example, a universal bathroom design might include a wet area shower with a transfer bench, a hand-held shower, a nonslip floor surface, and adequate space in which to maneuver a wheelchair. This design would enable a person with a disability to shower independently; it would also allow a young child to wash safely and independently without adult concern about "getting the floor wet." Another example of universal design is the provision of step lights on a flight of stairs, which improve safety for any user.

Universal design, in seeking to accommodate the broadest range of people, minimizes the need for major modifications if the able-bodied occupant becomes disabled. Its features help to reduce the need for costly modification. To accommodate differently abled people in neither a medical model nor a "Peter Pan," never-grow-old model of the built environment, universal design emphasizes function rather than style. For example, it focuses on user needs and enhances safety and security. Universal design permits us to think in terms of the life span. Since aging is associated with some impairments that may limit our independence, we need to think in terms of an environment that can easily adapt as needs change. In Japan, housing manufacturers are experimenting with a form of design known as Life Span housing. Life Span housing functions for both able-bodied and disabled persons.

CONCLUSION

The current and expanding interest in the application of technology has dynamic implications for home adaptation. Particularly beneficial is its potential in encouraging independent aging in place for the elderly and for persons with disabilities, and in reducing stress and strain on caregivers.

In modifying an existing residence or in planning a new home, thought should be given to the residents' ongoing and potential needs as well as the needs of others who may use the space in the future. Whenever possible, our goal should be to achieve a universally accessible environment that will not require costly or major modifications as needs change. When modifications are required, however, the user should participate in the decision-making process, so that the results will more effectively serve that particular individual's needs.

First of all, assistive devices for the elderly or for persons with disabilities can make the difference between independence and dependency, or between remaining a part of the community and being institutionalized. For example, in many industrialized nations, home automation systems for people who are elderly or have disabilities provide the eyes, ears, memory, and communication links to community-based supporting services and to friends or relatives.

Second, technology can be applied to make appliances and equipment more universally functional and more easily adapted to changing needs. For example, mechanically adjustable kitchen or workroom countertops or cabinet heights are more convenient for all people to use.

Barriers to the widespread use in the United States of technology in home adaptations include: higher than necessary initial costs to consumers, due to the inadequacy of current third-party reimbursement systems; the uncertainty of manufacturers about the perceived size of the market, which results in decreased interest in research and development; and the lack of resource centers that could adequately and impartially disseminate product data to permit informed consumer choice. Other factors include the lack of flexible zoning regulations that would permit accessory apartments in suburban residential areas, and resistance by developers and builders to the idea that accessible, adaptable features in new construction represent an "all-win" approach that can enhance their competitive edge.

If we, as building professionals and service providers, become innovators and leaders of change, we will open up a whole new market by reinventing environmental design using principles of universal design. Even more important, this evolution can have a tremendous impact, especially in the context of the Americans with Disabilities and Fair Housing Acts (see Chapter 12). Universal design is inclusive. Its flexibility and adaptability mean that we don't have to add things to the environment to improve the quality of life for those with special needs. The building environment thus is not reactive, but proactive.

The challenge for building professionals and service providers, then, is to research needs, with user involvement, and to become innovators. The use of technology can become a vehicle for change in the way we define our environment, and in reinventing the built environment we can enhance the quality of life for all.

REFERENCES

1. L. M. Rickman, C. E. Soble, and J. M. Prescop, *A Comprehensive Approach to Retrofitting Homes for a Lifetime*, NAHB Research Center, Upper Marlboro, Maryland, 1991.
2. *Coping with Daily Life: Handbook of Technical Aids*, Les Editions Papyrus, Quebec, PQ, 1988.
3. *The Directory of Accessible Building Products*, NAHB Research Center, Upper Marlboro, Maryland, 1991.
4. R. V. Olsen, E. Ehrenkrantz, and B. Hutchings, *Alzheimer's and Related Dementias: Homes that Help*, New Jersey Institute of Technology, Newark, New Jersey, 1993.
5. J. Pynoos and E. Cohen, *The Perfect Fit: Creative Ideas for a Safe and Livable Home*, American Association of Retired Persons, #PF 4912 (992) D14823, Washington, D.C., 1992.
6. E. E. Malizia, R. C. Duncan, and J. D. Reagan, *Financing Home Accessibility Modifications*, Center for Accessible Housing, North Carolina State University, Raleigh, North Carolina, 1993.
7. Fannie Mae Customer Education Group, *Money from Home: A Consumer's Guide to Home Equity Conversion Mortgages*, #CT066L06/92, Washington, D.C., 1992.
8. R. D. Lynch, Karl's House, *Technology and Disability*, 2:4, pp. 30-39, Fall 1993.

BIBLIOGRAPHY

Action for Accessibility: Proceedings of the International Accessibility Mini-Summit, September 1990, Center for Accessible Housing, North Carolina State University, Raleigh, 1991.

Aging Design Research Program, *Design for Aging: Strategies for Collaboration between Architects and Occupational Therapists,* AIA/ACSA Council on Architectural Research, ISBN 0-935502-07-6, Washington, D.C., 1993.

Arlen, G. *Senior Net Services: Toward a New Electronic Environment for Seniors,* Aspen Institute Communications and Society Program, Project on Enhancing the Social Benefits of New Electronic Technologies, Queenstown, Maryland, 1991.

Chellis, R. D. and P. J. Grayson, *Life Care: A Long-Term Solution?* D. C. Heath, Lexington Books Division, Lexington, Massachusetts, 1990.

Cocharane, G. M. and E. R. Wilshire (eds.), *Home Management: Equipment for the Disabled* (6th Edition), Headington, Oxford, United Kingdom, 1987.

Connell, B. R., J. A. Sanford, R. G. Long, C. K. Archea, and C. S. Turner, Home Modifications and Performance of Routine Household Activities by Individuals with Varying Levels of Mobility Impairments, *Technology and Disability,* 2:4, pp. 9-18, Fall 1993.

DeJong, G., *Independent Living & Disability Policy in the Netherlands: Three Models of Residential Care & Independent Living,* World Rehabilitation Fund, International Exchange of Information in Rehabilitation, New York, 1984.

Design for Aging: 1992 Review, American Institute for Architects in Cooperation with the American Association of Homes for the Aging, Washington, D.C., 1992.

Dickman, I. R., *Making Life More Livable: Simple Adaptations for the Home for Blind and Visually Impaired Older People,* American Foundation for the Blind, New York, 1983.

Enders, A. and M. Hall (eds.), *Assistive Technology Sourcebook,* ResnaPress, Washington, D.C., 1990.

Goldman, N. (ed.), *Achieving Physical and Communication Accessibilities,* National Center for Access Unlimited, Washington, D.C., 1991.

Kelly, C., and K. Snell, *The Source Book: Architectural Guidelines for Barrier-Free Design,* Barrier-Free Design Centre, Toronto, Ontario, 1992.

Kiewel, H. D., Serving Community Needs for Home-Accessibility Modifications, *Technology and Disability,* 2:4, pp. 40-46, Fall 1993.

Mullick, A., Bathing for Older People with Disabilities, *Technology and Disability,* 2:4, pp. 19-29, Fall 1993.

Olsen, R. V., E. Ehrenkrantz, and B. Hutchings. Creating Supportive Environments for People with Dementia and Their Caregivers through Home Modifications, *Technology and Disability,* 2:4, pp. 47-57, Fall 1993.

Overton, J., Resources for Home-Modification/Repair Programs, *Technology and Disability,* 2:4, pp. 80-88, Fall 1993.

Porter, P., Facilitating Aging in Place through Home Repairs, *Long Term Care Advances: Topics in Research, Training, Service & Policy,* 6:2, 1994.

Preiser, F. E., J. C. Vischer, and E. T. White (eds.), *Design Intervention: Toward a More Humane Architecture,* Van Nostrand Reinhold, New York, 1991.

Salmen, J. P., illus. by H. Mandel, *The Do-Able Renewable Home: Making Your Home Fit Your Needs*, American Association of Retired Persons, Consumer Affairs Program Department, Washington, D.C., 1985.

The Study of Emergency Response Systems for the Elderly, MacLaren Plansearch for the Research Division of Canada Mortgage and Housing Corporation under Part V of the National Housing Act, Ottawa, 1988.

Silverstein, N. M., J. Hyde, and R. Ohta, Home Adaptation for Alzheimer's Households: Factors Related to Implementation and Outcomes of Recommendations, *Technology and Disability*, 2:4, pp. 58-68, Fall 1993.

Steinfeld, E. and S. Shea, Enabling Home Environments: Identifying Barriers to Independence, *Technology and Disability*, 2:4, pp. 69-79, Fall 1993.

Tilson, D. (ed.), *Aging in Place: Supporting the Frail Elderly in Residential Environments*, Professional Books on Aging, Scott, Foresman, Glenview, Illinois, 1990.

Wilshire, E. R., *Equipment for the Disabled: Hoists and Lifts*, Mary Marlborough Lodge, Eynsham, Oxford, United Kingdom, 1985.

Wrightson, W. and C. Pope, *From Barrier-Free to Safe Environments: The New Zealand Experience*, World Rehabilitation Fund, International Exchange of Information in Rehabilitation, New York, 1989.

Zacharias, C. (ed.), *Independent Living Environments for Seniors and Persons with Disabilities: Proceedings of Directions '91*, Canadian Aging & Rehabilitation Product Development Corporation, Winnipeg, Manitoba, 1991.

PART II

USERS' PERSPECTIVES IN HOME ADAPTATION

Introduction

Home adaptation is the process of creating a better fit between the user and the physical environment. In considering adaptation, the focus is often on the physical environment. This section looks at the human—in particular, the consumer—side of the equation.

Those of us working in the field of home adaptation are often convinced of the usefulness of adaptations to support older people's independent functioning. But how do potential users view the situation? Mrs. R pretty well sums up some of the factors:

> Another thing about that old agency—they checked over my house and said I should put a handrail down my front stairs. I could get up and down just fine if I wanted to, but I never use my front stairs—they're just for company. And even if I could afford it, a railing would make my house look like that housing project for the elderly downtown.

This section explores these and other factors that are part of the user's perspective.

First, a ground-breaking effort by Ohta and Ohta presents a credible hypothesis regarding the process older people may use in making decisions about home adaptation. Drawing from the literature on compliance with medical recommendations as well as their own experience in home adaptation research, the authors posit that seniors use four criteria in deciding whether to make recommended adaptations: susceptibility to the target problem; severity of the problems if the adaptation is not accomplished; likely effectiveness of the adaptation; and cost (both financial and behavioral) of the proposed adaptation.

The next chapter explores the unique adaptation needs of people with Alzheimer's disease. In the first half of the chapter Silverstein and Hyde compare home adaptation needs of the cognitively impaired to those of the frail elderly. In the second half of the chapter the authors use the Ohta and Ohta model to report on new research which seeks to understand how this group of consumers, the dementia caregivers, view home adaptation. While adaptation needs for people with Alzheimer's differ in many ways from adaptation needs for other disabilities, the findings point to issues that family members of elders with many types of disabilities may face.

In Chapter 7, Connell and Sanford present the results of the first study using a new and important methodology that looks at how people with disabilities use their physical environment to complete tasks. Using this methodology, the authors look closely and individually at the fit between the abilities of a person with an impairment and the aspect of their environment that must be changed to allow completion of a task. When one ability is compromised, individuals may change behavior patterns, rather than the physical environment, to compensate. Connell and Sanford's two case studies supplement the more theoretical portions of the text and help us understand how we can break out of the stereotyped prescription of grab bars and lever handles to help consumers who are older or have disabilities to find adaptations and products that meet their individual needs.

In Chapter 9, Mutschler analyzes National Long Term Care Survey data to determine which people are making changes to their homes and explore the effects of income on their behavior. As would be expected, homeowners are more likely than renters to make adaptations. Those with more impairments in their ability to perform activities of daily living are more likely to have adaptations in their homes than those with fewer ADL impairments. (Renters, however, are almost equally likely to have adaptations regardless of their disability level, due to the existence of standard features such as grab bars in many senior housing units.) Not surprisingly, income has a major effect on the likelihood that an older person with a disability will be living in a home that is adapted to his or her needs.

Taken together, these four chapters support the view that older people are often creative and independent in the face of disabilities. While an adaptation may make life easier, it is only one means to an end, and not necessarily the one that the older person finds most empowering. Frail elders may devise behavioral strategies to cope with their limitations, such as asking a relative for help or rearranging the methods and timing for completing tasks. Or they may simply use more time and effort to get something done despite their disability, and may relish the sense of accomplishment that comes from doing the task themselves the way they always have despite, or even because of, this added effort. Respecting the decision-making process and creativity of potential adaptation users in one sense adds some complications, but in another sense it makes the field more stimulating and interesting than even its proponents had previously thought.

The section has policy implications as well. For while adaptation is slowly becoming a recognized part of the long-term care service continuum, and there is some hope that third party payers will absorb some of the financial costs of adaptations, this section makes it clear that a standardized approach to adaptation will not meet the needs of many older people and people with disabilities. Any system that recommends and funds adaptations will need to conform to the diverse perspectives and felt needs of the physically dependent, but often fiercely independent, users.

CHAPTER
5

The Elderly Consumer's Decision to Accept or Reject Home Adaptations: Issues and Perspectives

Russell J. Ohta and Brenda M. Ohta

Modern technology has made available to elderly individuals a wide variety of adaptations for the home capable of facilitating functional independence and minimizing the occurrence of injury. The actual acceptance and use of these adaptations by the elderly, however, is clearly dependent upon a host of factors. It appears that the housing literature has focused primarily on the development of adaptations to meet the physical needs of the elderly, and the affordability of these adaptations to those for whom they are designed. When psychological factors are mentioned in the literature, however, they are usually assigned a secondary or auxiliary role to the development and affordability issues. They have generally been regarded as a backdrop rather than as a major player on the stage where human behavior occurs. Correspondingly, their treatment in the housing literature has not been highly systematic, comprehensive, or cohesive. Thus, in the area of housing adaptations for the elderly, the impact of psychological factors has not gained conceptual or research prominence. This chapter seeks to bring psychological factors out of the backdrop and onto the stage as a major player. To achieve this, the chapter presents an organized, model-based exploration of salient issues in elderly consumers' acceptance and use of home adaptations, describes alternative approaches to viewing consumer resistance, and considers implications for research and intervention.

PREVALENCE AND PREFERENCE FOR
HOME ADAPTATIONS

Mrs. Campbell is an eighty-seven-year-old widow who resides alone in her home of thirty-five years. For the past eight months her health has been on the decline due to congestive heart failure, arthritis which limits her mobility, and diminished vision due to cataracts and glaucoma. It takes Mrs. Campbell considerable effort to maneuver around her home environment, which is strewn with stacks of magazines and newspapers along pathways, and with numerous throw rugs. In addition, she holds on to the shower curtain when getting in and out of her combination bathtub/shower and utilizes the toilet paper holder to support herself in getting on and off of the toilet. A recent professional assessment of her home environment and functional abilities indicated that: 1) the clutter along pathways should be removed and throw rugs should be secured or, preferably, removed; 2) a grab bar and tub transfer seat should be installed; and 3) a raised toilet seat with nearby grab bar should be installed. Mrs. Campbell flatly refused all professional recommendations, stating that she is managing adequately with her home as is.

The case is quite typical. The solutions are rather standard. The outcome is not uncommon.

Despite what may appear to be the "logical" advantages of home adaptations, housing professionals are faced with making sense of some challenging data. First, the actual prevalence of home adaptations is very low. Only about 10 percent of frail elderly households have been found to have any modifications in their home [1, 2]. Furthermore, attempts to estimate the extent of unmet need by asking frail elderly to specify adaptations which "would be helpful" or "would make things easier or more comfortable" have resulted in modest figures at best [1, 3-5]. Finally, it has been found that elderly individuals are less likely than housing experts to rate prosthetic aids (defined as the provision of a barrier-free environment and aids to physical independence and mobility) as very important or essential housing features [6]. What could account for these prevalence/preference data?

A MODEL FOR UNDERSTANDING THE ACCEPTANCE
AND USE OF HOME ADAPTATIONS
BY THE ELDERLY

A Consumer Decision Model has been developed to examine salient issues in elderly consumers' acceptance and use of home adaptations. Before describing this model, however, it is necessary to understand the historical significance of the Health Belief Model from which the current model is derived.

Historical Origins

The Health Belief Model [7, 8] grew out of a set of applied research problems facing a group of investigators in the Public Health Service between 1950 and 1960. The development of the model therefore grew simultaneously with the solution of practical problems.

The problems being faced centered around the widespread failure of people to accept disease preventives or screening tests for the early detection of asymptomatic disease (including prevention or tests for TB, cervical cancer, dental disease, rheumatic fever, polio, and influenza). The failure to accept these measures existed despite the fact that they were usually provided free of charge, or at very low cost.

What was therefore needed was a model which would be not only useful in addressing a particular program problem, but also adaptable to other problems, and capable of explaining the resistance/reluctance of people to engage in health-related actions even when they were being charged little or nothing to do so.

Over the succeeding years, the Health Belief Model which emerged was extensively researched and applied to a wide variety of health contexts. By 1984, a critical review of forty-six investigations found very substantial empirical evidence that Health Belief Model dimensions are important contributors in explaining and predicting individuals' acceptance of health and medical care recommendations [9].

To date, there has been no application of the Health Belief Model to the area of home adaptations. However, the extensive history and success of the model in other health-related areas provide sound reason to believe that it would be useful here as well, and could provide an important foundation for understanding elderly consumers' acceptance and use of home adaptations.

The Consumer Decision Model

The Consumer Decision Model presented here represents an application of concepts derived from the Health Belief Model to the area of home adaptations for the elderly. According to this Consumer Decision Model, the likelihood that elderly consumers will seek, adopt, and utilize home adaptations will depend upon 1) their perceptions of the threat posed by the target concerns identified by housing professionals, and 2) their perceptions of the specific adaptations available for dealing with the target concerns. Specific components of this model are discussed in the sections that follow.

Perceptions of Threat

Perceived threat of the target concern is comprised of two types of beliefs: those related to *susceptibility* and those related to *severity*.

Perceived Susceptibility

At issue here is how likely the elderly individual feels he/she is to experience the target concern. Individuals vary widely in their feelings of personal vulnerability or their assessment of subjective risk. At one extreme might be the individual who denies any possibility of experiencing a given target concern. In a more moderate position is the person who may admit to the statistical possibility of experiencing a target concern, but views this possibility as not likely to occur. Finally, a person may express a feeling that he/she is in real danger of experiencing a target concern. The consumer might ask the following questions. How likely am I to encounter a problem with this? Is this likely to happen to me? Am I personally vulnerable, at risk? Am I luckier than most?

Perceived Severity

At issue here is how serious the elderly individual feels the consequences would be if the target concern occurs. Feelings concerning the seriousness of a target concern also vary from person to person. This dimension includes evaluations of both medical/clinical consequences (e.g., death, disability, and pain) and possible social consequences (e.g., effects on performance of activities, family life, and social relations). The consumer might ask the following questions. If I did encounter this problem, how important would the consequences be? Would the outcome be disastrous, insignificant, or somewhere in between? Would the results be life-threatening, debilitating, or merely inconvenient?

Perceptions of Specific Adaptations

Perceptions of specific adaptations include two types of beliefs: those related to *efficacy* and those related to *costs*.

Perceived Efficacy of Adaptation

At issue here is how effective the elderly individual feels the specific adaptation would be in dealing with the target concern. The person's *beliefs* about the effectiveness of an adaptation, not the objective facts about its effectiveness, are the issue here. The consumer might ask the following questions. If I adopt and utilize this adaptation, would it make a difference? Would it do what the experts tell me it will do? Do I know from either personal experience or the experience of others that this adaptation will not work? Does the adaptation make me more dependent by forcing me to avoid risk and not utilize remaining abilities? Does it take all the challenge out of my environment?

Perceived Costs of Adaptation

At issue here is how costly the elderly individual feels the specific adaptation to be. The potential negative aspects believed to be associated with an adaptation can be viewed in terms of three types of costs: financial, behavioral, and social. With regard to *financial costs*, the consumer might ask the following questions. Is this an expensive adaptation for me? Can I afford it? With regard to *behavioral costs*, the consumer might ask the following questions. Does the adaptation disrupt my lifestyle? Is the adaptation inconvenient to use? Is it emotionally upsetting or unpleasant? Does it affect my self-esteem? With regard to *social costs*, the consumer might ask the following questions. Do I find the adaptation to be unsightly in my home? Would I be embarrassed to have my friends see the adaptation in my home?

CONDITIONS FAVORABLE TO CONSUMER RECEPTIVITY

According to the Consumer Decision Model presented previously, an individual's perception of his/her susceptibility to a target concern, and of the severity of its consequences, combine to provide the impetus to act. In addition, the individual's perception of the efficacy of the adaptation in reducing susceptibility to (or the severity of) the target concern, and of the costs associated with the adaptation, determine the desired course of action. The conditions most favorable to consumer receptivity to home adaptations are depicted in Figure 1. As can be seen, the elderly consumer can be expected to be most receptive to home adaptations when all of the following conditions are met.

- Perceived susceptibility to the target concern is high.
- Perceived severity of the target concern is high.
- Perceived efficacy of the specific home adaptations is high.
- Perceived costs of the specific home adaptations are low.

There are, however, numerous ways in which consumer receptivity to home adaptations can be jeopardized. First, if the elderly person does not feel personally susceptible to the target concern, he/she can be expected to feel little need for any adaptation to deal with target concern. Second, if the elderly person feels personally susceptible, but the consequences of the target concern are deemed minor, he/she can still be expected to feel little need for any adaptation to deal with the target concern.

Even if the elderly consumer were "sufficiently threatened," however, his/her particular course of action would not yet be defined. Perceived threat can be best thought of as a necessary, but not sufficient, condition to accept home adaptations. The actual course of action taken is still subject to the consumer's perceptions of the home adaptations available. For example, if the elderly person views the

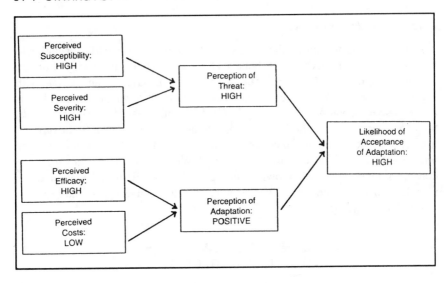

Figure 1. The conditions most favorable to consumer
receptivity to home adaptations.

efficacy of specific home adaptations as questionable, he/she will probably see
little reason to accept the adaptations. Or, if the specific home adaptations are
viewed as efficacious, but the costs associated with them are seen as high, he/she
will probably still hesitate to accept the adaptations.

Given these many conditions which could serve to dampen consumer receptivity, consumer resistance to home adaptations should not surprise us.

APPROACHES TO
VIEWING CONSUMER "RESISTANCE"

The Consumer-as-Noncompliant

The traditional approach of housing professionals may be akin to the medical
model's treatment of the noncompliant patient. In the medical model of health
care, the patient is viewed as the dependent, uninformed recipient of medical care
and advice from a knowledgeable and beneficent physician. The patient either
accepts the care and advice of the physician or fails to accept it (i.e., is noncompliant). It is to the patient's benefit, and every attempt should be made to
encourage the patient's compliance with the physician's orders.

Similarly, when the elderly consumer is receptive to home adaptations, the
interests of the housing professional and those of the elderly individual are likely

to be highly compatible. Dealing with the elderly under these circumstances should pose few problems, and should in fact be very reinforcing for housing professionals. On the other hand, when the elderly consumer is not receptive to home adaptations, the interests of the housing professional and those of the elderly individual may conflict. It is here that housing professionals are likely to be most challenged (and frustrated) in their dealings with the elderly, who may be viewed as noncompliant.

Hints that housing professionals may subscribe to the "consumer-as-noncompliant" approach to viewing consumer resistance come from the language they use to describe such situations. For example, the summary of the Institute of Medicine's report comments that only a small percent of the frail elderly (the 10% figure presented earlier) carried out any modification of their dwelling "despite the rationality of a strategy of housing modification" [10, p. 13].

This approach is even more strongly suggested by the comments of professionals which were reported by Pynoos et al.:

> Focus group members reported that it was difficult to convince some older persons that they needed to make a change. . . . Some older persons would not give up their independence or their lifestyle, including clutter and throw rugs, until they accepted the fact that something had to change or they would have to leave their home [11, p. 293].

Language such as this makes it difficult to avoid the impression that housing professionals may view the elderly consumer who resists home adaptations as being unexplainably irrational and/or seriously uninformed (or misinformed) with regard to imminent threats and appropriate solutions. If this is the case, then the assumption would be that the standard of what constitutes logic and knowledge is determined solely by the housing professional. Conversely, it would imply that the resistant consumer's decision, and the reasons for that decision, could not possibly be justifiable. At this point, the housing professional's role would appear to closely parallel that of the physician in the medical model.

The Consumer-as-Self-Advocate

An alternative approach to viewing the elderly consumer's refusal to make home adaptations rejects the notion that housing professionals alone should determine what constitutes logic and knowledge. Instead it simply, yet profoundly, allows for the possibility that the consumer's rejection of home adaptations may be a justifiable, rational decision based upon acceptable information. In short, this approach acknowledges that the consumer may be right.

The implications of adopting the consumer-as-self-advocate approach are twofold. First, it forces an examination of the assumptions and data customarily used by housing professionals to promote home adaptations. Second, it gives considerable credit to consumers and recognizes their many years of accumulated experience in making consumption decisions (both general and health-specific). This approach thus empowers consumers and legitimizes their experiences and beliefs.

Consider the various ways in which consumer receptivity to home adaptations may be less than enthusiastic (see the Consumer Decision Model presented earlier). To begin with, the consumer may not feel personally susceptible, either currently or in the future, to the target concern identified by housing professionals. Although housing professionals may use the actual or likely presence of any difficulty in performing an activity as the marker which identifies target concerns or problem areas, the consumer may feel otherwise. The mere presence of difficulty in performing an activity may not be equated with the existence of a problem, and thus the elderly consumer may not necessarily feel that he/she is highly susceptible to a target concern. Furthermore, the consumer may have utilized personal and family health histories to conclude that he/she will not be highly susceptible to the target concern in the future.

Next, the consumer may not feel that the consequences of the target concern are very severe. Housing professionals may be concerned about the negative effect of an individual struggling to perform, or being unable to perform, an activity. However, the consumer may feel that an added expenditure of time or effort, or even a complete inability to perform a given activity, are no more than inconveniences which can be tolerated and to which adjustments can readily be made. The consumer may use information from personal experiences, and those of family and acquaintances, to decide that the consequences of a target concern are not particularly severe. That the situations of even frail elderly may not be serious enough to warrant adaptations to the home has been raised by Macken [3].

Furthermore, the consumer may question the efficacy of home adaptations. It may be easy to assume that home adaptations have a positive impact on the elderly's ability to function independently. Housing professionals themselves, however, recognize that sound empirical data documenting this impact (as opposed to anecdotal reports) still do not exist [12-14]. The consumer, on the other hand, may challenge the purported efficacy of home adaptations based upon direct, personal experience of what works or does not work, or the vicarious but trusted experience of friends and relatives. Furthermore, the consumer may be concerned about iatrogenic problems (i.e., problems arising as a result of using the home adaptations). That iatrogenic problems, such as insufficient challenge and stimulation, can arise from "risk aversion" and an overly supportive environment has been addressed by Kane et al. [15] and Lawton ([16], see also Chapter 3 of this book).

Finally, the consumer may find the costs associated with home adaptations to be unacceptable. Housing professionals have recognized that home adaptations should not be unsightly, but rather should be unobtrusive and noninstitutional in appearance [11, 17, 18]. The financial expense of home adaptations has also been a concern of housing professionals, although findings have shown that consumer income level is not related to the presence of home adaptations [2, 19, 20]. Whether housing professionals accept it or not, unobtrusive, and affordable home adaptations can still have prohibitive behavioral (and emotional) costs for the elderly consumer. Changes in behavior pattern, even those which may appear minor, may be viewed by elderly consumers as too disruptive and may even mean ascribing to oneself such undesirable labels as "at risk," "dependent," or "feeble." The rejection of home adaptations may therefore take on existential implications, and may represent a Sisyphean battle for personal meaning through the refusal to accept defeat by a dominant adversary (i.e., the aging process).

IMPLICATIONS FOR
RESEARCH AND INTERVENTION

The Consumer Decision Model presented in this chapter provides a framework for considering various psychological factors capable of affecting elderly consumers' acceptance of home adaptations. Consistent with this model is the following agenda for assessing the reaction of elderly consumers to specific adaptations designed to address particular target concerns. First, organize target concerns by major categories (e.g., difficulty in physical activities of daily living vs. instrumental activities of daily living), subcategories (e.g., difficulty in toileting vs. bathing), and tasks (e.g., difficulty getting on/off the toilet vs. flushing the toilet). Second, wherever possible include a range of adaptations for dealing with each target concern (e.g., low-tech to high-tech). Third, develop assessment items which are sensitive to consumer perceptions of the target concerns (i.e., perceived susceptibility and severity) and the possible solutions (i.e., perceived efficacy and costs).

The utility of assessing consumer perceptions in this way can be diverse. Such assessments may certainly be helpful in explaining observed consumer behaviors. In addition, such assessments may be useful in predicting consumers' reactions to home adaptations that are made without their wholehearted endorsement. Perhaps more importantly, such assessments may help to isolate the exact reasons consumers have for rejecting home adaptations. What happens with this knowledge, however, would depend upon the housing professional's approach to viewing consumer "resistance."

If the "consumer-as-noncompliant" approach is adopted, the housing professional may concentrate on "educating" the consumer to the gravity of the threat he/she faces (in terms of susceptibility and severity) and the advisability of the recommended adaptations (in terms of efficacy and costs). In short, the intervention would consist of an attempt to align the consumer's perceptions with those of the housing professional.

If, on the other hand, the "consumer-as-self-advocate" approach is adopted, a multi-level response may occur. It would still be imperative that the consumer be provided with all pertinent information. However, what passes for "data" would be critically evaluated. Implicitly, this would challenge others in the field to supply the missing data if such in fact exist (e.g., demonstrating the efficacy of home adaptations). Furthermore, the housing professional would acknowledge the consumer's own sources of information, and would be willing to accept as legitimate and valid a consumer's decision not to accept home adaptations. The professional would not be viewed as "correct," the refusing consumer as "incorrect," and the resulting situation as "unfortunate" or a "failure." The circumstance would be seen as no more, and no less, than an exercise of self-determination.

REFERENCES

1. J. D. Reschovsky and S. J. Newman, Adaptations for Independent Living by Older Frail Households, *The Gerontologist, 30*:4, pp. 543-552, 1990.
2. R. J. Struyk and J. Zais, *Providing Special Dwelling Features for the Elderly with Health and Mobility Problems*, Urban Institute, Washington, D.C., 1982.
3. C. L. Macken, A Profile of Functionally Impaired Elderly Persons Living in the Community, *Health Care Financing Review, 7*:4, pp. 33-49, 1986.
4. B. J. Soldo and C. F. Longino, Social and Physical Environments for the Vulnerable Aged, in *The Social and Built Environment in an Older Society*, Institute of Medicine (ed.), National Academy Press, Washington, D.C., pp. 103-133, 1988.
5. J. Pynoos, Toward a National Policy on Home Modification, *Technology and Disability, 2*:4, pp. 1-8, Fall 1993.
6. P. L. Brennan, R. H. Moos, and S. Lemke, Preferences of Older Adults and Experts for Physical and Architectural Features of Group Living Facilities, *The Gerontologist, 28*:1, pp. 84-90, 1988.
7. M. H. Becker, The Health Belief Model and Sick Role Behavior, *Health Education Monographs, 2*, pp. 409-419, 1974.
8. I. M. Rosenstock, Historical Origins of the Health Belief Model, *Health Education Monographs, 2*, pp. 328-335, 1974.
9. N. K. Janz and M. H. Becker, The Health Belief Model: A Decade Later, *Health Education Quarterly, 11*, pp. 1-47, 1984.
10. Institute of Medicine (ed.), *The Social and Built Environment in an Older Society*, National Academy Press, Washington, D.C., 1988.
11. J. Pynoos, E. Cohen, L. J. Davis, and S. Bernhardt, Home Modifications: Improvements that Extend Independence, in *Housing the Aged: Design Directives and Policy Considerations*, V. Regnier and J. Pynoos (eds.), Elsevier, New York, pp. 277-303, 1987.
12. V. Regnier, Design Problems in Enhancing Productivity and Independence in Housing for the Elderly, in *The Social and Built Environment in an Older Society*, Institute of Medicine (ed.), National Academy Press, Washington, D.C., pp. 218-249, 1988.
13. R. J. Struyk, Current and Emerging Issues in Housing Environments for the Elderly, in *The Social and Built Environment in an Older Society*, Institute of Medicine (ed.), National Academy Press, Washington, D.C., pp. 134-168, 1988.

14. E. Steinfeld and S. Shea, Enabling Home Environments: Identifying Barriers to Independence, *Technology and Disability,* 2:4, pp. 69-79, Fall 1993.
15. R. L. Kane, R. A. Kane, and S. B. Arnold, Prevention and the Elderly: Risk Factors, *Health Services Research, 19,* pp. 945-1006, 1985.
16. M. P. Lawton, Housing and Living Environments of Older People, in *Handbook of Aging and the Social Sciences* (2nd Edition), R. H. Binstock and E. Shanas (eds.), Van Nostrand Reinhold, New York, pp. 450-478, 1985.
17. E. Steinfeld, Adapting Housing for Older Disabled People, in *Housing the Aged: Design Directives and Policy Considerations,* V. Regnier and J. Pynoos (eds.), Elsevier, New York, pp. 307-339, 1987.
18. R. D. Lynch, Karl's House, *Technology and Disability,* 2:4, pp. 30-39, Fall 1993.
19. R. J. Struyk and H. M. Katsura, *Aging at Home: How the Elderly Adjust Their Housing without Moving,* Haworth Press, New York, 1988.
20. J. E. Kincade Norburn, S. Bernard, T. Konrad, A. Woomert, G. H. DeFriese, W. D. Kalsbeek, G. G. Koch, and M. G. Ory, Self-Care and Assistance from Others in Coping with Functional Limitations among a National Sample of Older Adults, *Journal of Gerontology: Social Sciences, 50B*:2, pp. S101-S109, 1995.

CHAPTER
6

The Importance of a Consumer Perspective in Home Adaptation of Alzheimer's Households

Nina M. Silverstein and Joan Hyde

As many as four million people in the United States have Alzheimer's disease or a related disorder [1], and the National Institute of Aging expects this number to increase to fourteen million by the year 2050 [2]. From the onset of symptoms, the lifespan of a person with Alzheimer's can extend to over twenty years. Thus, while the number of elders with physical disabilities continues to grow, along with related home adaptation needs, a second group of home adaptation users, older persons with cognitive disabilities, is mushrooming alongside them.

Lawton reported that the great majority of people with Alzheimer's disease reside in the community with their spouses or adult children. He observed:

> Almost all published material on designing for the person with Alzheimer's disease assumes that the appropriate environment is the nursing home. . . . Our thinking about environment as a therapeutic agent must take into account [the] diverse residences for older people with some element of dementia. The redesign of these dwelling units may well become a community-based service that will enable demented individuals to remain at home [3, p. 344].

If this large noninstitutionalized population of elders with cognitive impairments is to be appropriately served, then home adaptation programs must respond to their needs. In particular, the perspectives, wants, and needs of family caregivers are central, since the purpose of home adaptation in these cases is to allow

91

the caregivers to gain control of their situation. In keeping with this approach, the next section uses the authors' research findings and the experiences of others in the field to address the following questions:

- How is home adaptation for the cognitively impaired different from other home adaptation?
- What information is currently available about home adaptation for the cognitively impaired and what additional information is needed?
- What are the most common adaptation recommendations currently being made for this population?
- For the purposes of providers, researchers, and policymakers, what kind of framework or system is suitable for this field?

The third section focuses more narrowly on the authors' findings with respect to:

- the issues involved in (and barriers to) the use of adaptations for this user group.
- how adaptations and recommendations can be made more useful for those with dementia and their caregivers.

BACKGROUND

Some Preliminary Answers to These Questions

How is home adaptation for the cognitively impaired different
from other home adaptation?

Home adaptation for those with cognitive impairments is different from other types of home adaptation in several respects. First, providers must demonstrate an awareness of and sensitivity to cognitive as well as physical impairments and the recommendations offered must function prosthetically for both. Second, the caregiver is as much the "user" of the adaptation as the impaired person, and is the decision maker in terms of assessing the usefulness of the adaptation and its likelihood of implementation. Third, while most adaptations for those with physical frailties are targeted to existing problems, many adaptations recommended for individuals with Alzheimer's are designed to prevent potential problems.

What information is currently available about home
adaptation for the cognitively impaired and what
additional information is needed?

Many community support programs for Alzheimer's caregivers do, in fact, provide information and recommendations regarding home adaptation or brief home adaptation "audits," and several guides list possible adaptations as well as a few articles and reports of preliminary research in the field. Most available literature takes the form of descriptions of adaptations that families may find helpful.

The first systematic documentation regarding home adaptation for dementia was undertaken as part of a multi-faceted project under the leadership of Jon Pynoos at the Andrus Gerontology Center. In-house interviews were conducted with twenty-five families enrolled in a home adaptation program, all of whom received recommendations, funding, and other assistance for implementing adaptations. The project produced several articles and a practical report for families and professionals entitled *The Caring Home Booklet: Environmental Coping Strategies for Alzheimer's Caregivers* [4]. This booklet addresses the role of the environment in supporting the needs of those with Alzheimer's disease and caregivers in the home. It covers behavior problems and management strategies; caregiver reluctance to change the environment; help available for making changes; need for alternative settings; and strategies for environmental management of such issues as behavior problems, memory loss, wandering, incontinence and difficulty with toileting, personal hygiene, hallucinations, aggressive behavior, eating, boredom, destructive or dangerous behavior, and safety. Appendices list mail-order retailers of adaptive products and supplies, activity resources, clues for reducing behavior problems, and a caregiver-oriented bibliography.

Another valuable guide for families and professionals, *Home Modifications: Responding to Dementia* [5], was released by the Research Center of the Corinne Dolan Alzheimer's Center. The researchers surveyed by telephone fifty-nine families who were caring for someone with dementia regarding their use of and satisfaction with home adaptations. In the foreword the authors stated:

> When we began this project, we had no way of knowing what our results would indicate. By the time the study was concluded, we had learned that families devise a great number of ingenious solutions to the many difficult problems that arise when caring for a loved one with dementia. Every one of the respondents we interviewed made at least one environmental modification. Of these, 78% indicated that the modifications made the caregiver's life easier, while 68% said that the modifications helped the confused person. This positive response to environmental modifications seems to indicate that more information should be available to caregivers.

A more recent guide, *Homes that Help: Advice from Caregivers for Creating a Supportive Home* [6], is based on interviews with ninety veteran caregivers who had cared for loved ones in all types of home settings. A wide range of behavioral and physical adaptation recommendations are described under three main goals:

First, the home should be calming and reassuring. Second, it should be safe and supportive. Third, [it] should provide activities that engage your loved one, sustain his or her remaining strengths, and encourage independence [6, p. 5].

Although the materials described are a good beginning, both providers and family caregivers require more information on useful adaptations.

What are the most common adaptation recommendations currently being made for this population?

The authors of this chapter, in their preliminary work with three provider agencies, generated a list of the ninety-nine most commonly recommended adaptations for this population (see next section). The list can provide a useful checklist for providers and caregivers considering possible adaptations. Another list of most-often-made adaptations is available in Calkins [5]. The problem with lists such as these is that they give providers and others working in the field little guidance as to which adaptations are appropriate for particular users and circumstances. Thus, a systematic understanding of the issues is crucial. Both the caregiver's perspective and outcomes regarding the functioning of the cognitively impaired person must be considered.

For the purposes of providers, researchers, and policymakers, what kind of framework or system is suitable for this field?

At the Spring 1992 Alzheimer's Association conference, Calkins reported on a systematic framework for discussing home adaptation in this area [7]. As in all environment-behavior (E-B) studies, this framework addresses the physical environment, human behavior in the environment, and the interactions between the two. First, Calkins defines six types of adaptations:

- Structural changes to the home (moving walls, doorways)
- Adaptation modifications (changing existing features of home such as railing or locks)
- Special equipment (such as grab bars)
- Assistive devices (which Calkins points out can be difficult for those with dementia to learn to use)
- Material adjustments (moving furniture to create a wandering path, keeping poisons locked away)
- Behavioral modifications (changes in how activities are carried out such as giving someone a sponge bath)

Calkins then classifies the reasons for (or purposes of) adaptations. The list includes safety-related adaptations, changes made to assist people with age-related physical disabilities, modifications to support independence in recreational and daily living activities, modifications that address orientation and confusion, and adaptations that simplify caregiver tasks or reduce caregiver confusion or frustration.

Hiatt briefly discusses the environment side of the equation, and suggests that adaptations may be an effective way to help meet behavioral goals for cognitively impaired individuals [8]. For examples, adaptations may help to:

- Support attention span
- Support social interchange, sensitivity to personal spaces
- Maximize remaining vision
- Motivate by aroma
- Support hearing
- Encourage motion
- Cue memory

Little work has been done to date to link our understanding of behavior and behavioral goals to our knowledge regarding the adaptations available to assist cognitively impaired individuals. It is likely that family caregivers have considerable insight into this relationship, which focused interviewing techniques may elicit. These relationships could then be further tested.

RESEARCH FINDINGS

Issues and Barriers to the Use of Adaptations for this User Group

The Role of Caregiver

Calkins [7] and others [9, 10] have noted that the few studies that have been done focus more on the physical adaptation and less on the behavior, needs, and subjective experiences of the impaired person or caregiver. The authors of this chapter concur: Researchers to date have neglected to emphasize the transactional aspects of home adaptation, placing their focus on either the person and the disability or on the environment. To the extent that adaptations are recommended, the emphasis has usually been either on assessing physical characteristics of the caregiving household (such as clutter, unsecured exits, stairs, and cooking hazards) or on patient characteristics (including wandering, sleep cycle disturbances, and difficulties with activities of daily living). Little attention has been paid to the third step in good E-B practice: understanding the relationship of the environment to the behavior.

In this case the "behavior" to be considered includes that of the caregivers. Key to implementation but often ignored is the congruence of adaptation recommendations with the strengths, values, and preferences of the caregiver who must implement and live with them. In a situation that allows caregivers few tangible successes, home adaptation may be an area in which concrete steps lead to concrete positive results, as well as a greater feeling of control. More information is needed on how families utilize professional advice with respect to home adaptation.

Family support as an integral component in the care of people with Alzheimer's disease has been well documented [11-13]—indeed, focusing on family caregivers has become an important branch of inquiry within Alzheimer's research (see, e.g., [14-16]). Caregivers across the United States may avail themselves of support groups and educational workshops that provide them with information and coping strategies with respect to erratic behavior and social losses, as well as learning techniques to compensate for the declining competencies of the person for whom they are caring. In many locations, caregivers also receive information and recommendations regarding home adaptation both for behavior management and to improve the safety of the home environment for the person with Alzheimer's disease. This type of information is critical. Hall notes that in the early stages of the disease the client can be taught to structure his or her own schedule and environment to maintain comfort and function; however, "as the disease progresses . . . tighter control is required to maintain normative behavior. . . . In the ambulatory demented phase . . . the caregiver must assume responsibility for monitoring and structuring of the client's environment" [17, p. 37].

Studies by Handler [18] and Pynoos and Ohta [19] suggest that home adaptation is indeed an important factor in managing the person with Alzheimer's disease in the community. Both studies tested the hypothesis that home adaptation will improve patient behaviors and reduce caregiver burden. While the researchers concluded, based on their limited samples, that home adaptation as an intervention may be effective, they also acknowledged that caregivers do not always comply with provider recommendations. Pynoos and Ohta noted that caregivers are often reluctant to change the environment:

> In many instances the caregiver did not make adjustments to the home which the researchers believed would minimize danger/promote functioning of the patient, such as providing alert signals on doors or safety guards on electric outlets [19, p. 2].
>
> Reluctance on the part of the caregiver may come from the negative image of a stigmatized environment, cost of making change, difficulty in identifying resources or uncertainty over whether the modification will be effective. Yet many of the preventative measures that are recommended are non-therapeutic in nature, low cost, and relatively simple to make [19, p. 5].

The Decision-Making Process for Caregivers

The authors' recent study of Alzheimer's caregivers' implementation of home adaptation recommendations builds on the model created by Ohta and Ohta [20]. Described in Chapter 5 of this book, the model hypothesizes that four factors are important to older consumers when they decide whether to implement home adaptation recommendations: 1) the likelihood that the target problem will occur without the adaptation, 2) the severity of the target problem, 3) the potential effectiveness of the adaptation, and 4) the cost of the adaptation. The model used for this research differed from the Ohta model in two respects. First, the decision-making process of caregivers, rather than that of the impaired elders themselves, was examined in this study. Second, the adaptations addressed were intended for those with cognitive impairments, rather than with physical frailty.

The primary objective of this project was to assess the relationship between home adaptation recommendations made by geriatric nurse practitioners to Alzheimer's caregivers and the level of implementation achieved. More specifically, the aims of the study were to:

- Determine the degree to which professional perceptions of barriers to implementation, the caregiver's perceptions of the recommended adaptation, and patient characteristics affect the perceived likelihood of following through with the recommendations
- Determine the degree to which the type of target problem addressed through the recommended adaptation affects the perceived likelihood of following through with the recommendation.

The Difference between Caregivers' and Users' Perceptions

The first phase of the study documented professionals' perceptions of barriers to the implementation of adaptation recommendations. These perception "consensus scores" would later be tested as predictor variables of the caregivers' level of implementation of recommendations. Health care professionals from the Harvard Geriatric Education Center, in addition to professional staff and support group leaders from the Alzheimer's Association of Eastern Massachusetts, were surveyed in Spring 1990 regarding ninety-nine home adaptation recommendations. These adaptations were compiled by a review of environmental assessment forms used by three Boston-area community agencies that provide in-home assessment and counseling for Alzheimer's caregivers.

The professionals were asked whether they perceived any of four barriers to a recommendation: whether the recommendation cost too much, required outside help, required a change in caregiver behavior, or required a change in household appearance. Table 1 illustrates the range of adaptation recommendations reviewed and provides summary scores [21].

Table 1. Professionals' Perceptions of Barriers to Home Adaptation
Recommendations to Family Caregivers of Persons with Alzheimer's
(Percent) (n = 18)

Recommendation	Financial Output	Needs Outside Help	Requires Change in Caregiver Behavior	Requires Change in Household Appearance	Overall
1. Add additional bathroom	100.0	88.9	27.8	72.2	72.2
2. Fence in yard	94.4	88.9	16.7	72.2	68.1
3. Build ramp	88.9	72.2	22.2	72.2	63.9
4. Install stair/elevator chair	83.3	72.2	22.2	77.8	63.9
5. Fence in swimming pool	94.4	77.8	16.7	50.0	59.7
6. Install additional locks on exit doors	72.2	83.3	38.9	38.9	58.3
7. Install movement monitor	94.4	66.7	50.0	11.1	55.6
8. Install handrails in hallway	72.2	72.2	11.1	66.7	55.6
9. Install safety locks on windows	77.8	77.8	16.7	33.3	51.4
10. Install alarm system	100.0	77.8	11.1	11.1	50.0
11. Install grab bars in bathroom	66.7	61.1	11.1	55.6	48.6
12. Render automatic locks on storm/screen doors inoperable	61.1	83.3	38.9	11.1	48.6
13. Install gate on stairway	61.1	55.6	22.2	50.0	47.2
14. Install locks on closet doors	55.6	61.1	38.9	27.8	45.8
15. Install locks on doors to cellar and attic	55.6	66.7	33.3	27.8	45.8
16. Install door buzzer	72.2	77.8	22.2	5.6	44.4
17. Improve poor lighting conditions in stairs, hallways, and bathrooms	72.2	61.1	11.1	33.3	44.4
18. Remedy overloaded electrical sockets	61.1	77.8	16.7	16.7	43.1
19. Install refrigerator lock	55.6	66.7	38.9	11.1	43.1
20. Use hospital bed	66.7	38.9	16.7	44.4	41.7
21. Repair frayed electrical wires	55.6	77.8	11.1	16.7	40.3
22. Install lock on yard fence	61.1	66.7	22.2	11.1	40.3
23. Add non-skid strips to stairs	44.4	33.3	5.6	77.8	40.3
24. Install radiator covers	72.2	38.9	5.6	44.4	40.3
25. Insulate hot water pipes	66.7	66.7	5.6	16.7	38.9
26. Install childproof kitchen cabinet locks	55.6	50.0	33.3	16.7	38.9
27. Repair step carpeting	61.1	55.6	11.1	27.8	38.9
28. Tape or paint stair edges	33.3	38.9	16.7	61.1	37.5
29. Install smoke detectors and insure proper placement	50.0	61.1	11.1	27.8	37.5

Table 1. (Cont'd.)

Recommendation	Financial Output	Needs Outside Help	Requires Change in Caregiver Behavior	Requires Change in Household Appearance	Overall
30. Use hand held shower	50.0	33.3	44.4	11.1	34.7
31. Install bed rails	55.6	44.4	11.1	22.2	33.3
32. Provide clocks in multiple rooms	50.0	5.6	33.3	38.9	31.9
33. Use shower chair or tub seat	61.1	16.7	33.3	11.1	30.6
34. Use reflector tape on floor or walls to guide patients	33.3	22.2	5.6	61.1	30.6
35. Use wheelchair	55.6	27.8	16.7	22.2	30.1
36. Remove auxiliary heating sources	33.3	33.3	38.9	16.7	30.1
37. Store household kitchen appliances under lock and key	22.2	11.1	72.2	11.1	29.2
38. Protect upholstered furniture	22.2	5.6	33.3	66.7	29.2
39. Have commode available	38.9	16.7	16.7	38.9	27.8
40. Create and utilize signs for identification cues	22.2	0	38.9	50.0	27.8
41. Store sharp kitchen tools in locked cabinets	16.7	11.1	72.2	11.1	27.8
42. Store razor blades in locked cabinets	16.7	11.1	72.2	11.1	27.8
43. Change to electric razor	50.0	0	55.6	0	26.4
44. Eliminate shiny, glaring surfaces	33.3	22.2	22.2	27.8	26.4
45. Store medications in locked cabinet	22.2	11.1	66.7	0	25.0
46. Simplify clothing	61.1	0	38.9	0	25.0
47. Immobilize stove, remove dials	5.6	16.7	55.6	22.0	25.0
48. Use vinyl tablecloth	11.1	0	38.9	44.4	23.6
49. Use automatic dial telephone	50.0	0	33.3	11.1	23.6
50. Remove clutter	0	11.1	50.0	33.3	23.6
51. Remove area rugs	0	0	33.3	61.1	23.6
52. Put decals on glass doors	16.7	5.6	22.2	44.4	22.2
53. Store household cleansers and insecticides in locked cabinet	16.7	11.1	61.1	0	22.2
54. Store matches and lighters in locked cabinets	16.7	11.1	61.1	0	22.2

Table 1. (Cont'd.)

Recommendation	Financial Output	Needs Outside Help	Requires Change in Caregiver Behavior	Requires Change in Household Appearance	Overall
55. Rearrange furniture to protect from radiators	5.6	16.7	16.7	44.4	20.8
56. Lower hot water temperature to <120°	27.8	38.9	16.7	0	20.8
57. Use walker	44.4	16.7	16.7	5.6	20.8
58. Install outlet covers	38.9	5.6	16.7	22.2	20.8
59. Store valuable items in locked or inaccessible area	27.8	11.1	50.0	5.6	20.8
60. Store tools under lock and key	11.1	5.6	66.7	0	20.8
61. Regularly replace batteries of smoke detectors	16.7	22.2	38.9	5.6	20.8
62. Remove low furniture, i.e., coffee tables and stools	0	11.1	27.8	38.9	19.4
63. Store firearms under lock and key	11.1	5.6	61.1	0	19.4
64. Post pictures as cues	5.6	5.6	33.3	33.3	19.4
65. Have easy access to fire extinguisher	27.8	16.7	33.3	0	19.4
66. Clear path in center of room	0	0	50.0	27.8	19.4
67. Use sturdy chairs that do not tip	38.9	0	16.7	16.7	18.1
68. Post calendar, cross off days and record appointments and activities	5.6	0	61.1	5.6	18.1
69. Use straw and finger foods	5.6	5.6	55.6	5.6	18.1
70. Limit smoking area to non-carpeted area with non-upholstered chair	0	0	61.1	11.1	18.1
71. Tape electrical cords across walkways	11.1	11.1	16.7	33.3	18.1
72. Remove or pad sharp corners on furniture	16.7	0	11.1	44.4	18.1
73. Post lists of AD family member's and caregiver's responsibilities	0	0	55.6	11.1	16.7
74. Check trash before discarding	0	0	66.7	0	16.7
75. Remove firearms	5.6	0	61.1	0	16.7
76. Post daily schedule	5.6	0	50.0	5.6	15.3
77. Double tape area rugs	16.7	22.2	16.7	5.6	15.3

Table 1. (Cont'd.)

Recommendation	Financial Output	Needs Outside Help	Requires Change in Caregiver Behavior	Requires Change in Household Appearance	Overall
78. Remove fake fruit/look-alike decorations	0	0	22.2	38.9	15.3
79. Keep patient's belongings in one place	0	0	38.9	16.7	13.9
80. Limit rummage areas	0	0	50.0	5.6	13.9
81. Use cane	33.3	11.1	11.1	0	13.9
82. Use sturdy plastic plates	16.7	0	33.3	5.6	13.9
83. Remove car keys from easy access	0	0	55.6	0	13.9
84. Have AD family member wear ID bracelet	33.3	11.1	11.1	0	13.9
85. Remove small magnets from refrigerator	0	0	27.8	22.2	12.5
86. Have copies of a current photo of AD family member	22.2	11.1	16.7	0	12.5
87. Use selfcare devices, i.e., curved hairbrush handles and utensils	33.3	0	16.7	0	12.5
88. Use non-skid tub mat	22.2	0	22.2	5.6	12.5
89. Use nightlights in hallways and bathrooms	11.1	0	22.2	16.7	12.5
90. Remove electrical cords across walkways	0	5.6	16.7	22.2	11.1
91. Notify police and offer photo	0	11.1	33.3	0	11.1
92. Notify neighbors	0	11.1	33.3	0	11.1
93. Remove small ingestible objects from environment	0	0	22.2	22.2	11.1
94. Hide an extra set of keys outside the house	5.6	0	33.3	0	9.7
95. Post emergency numbers near telephone	0	0	33.3	5.6	9.7
96. Provide large deep ashtray for smoker	5.6	0	33.3	0	9.7
97. Use non-skid bathroom mats	22.2	0	16.7	0	9.7
98. Keep furniture arrangement consistent	0	0	33.3	0	8.3
99. Place ID info in AD family member's wallet and clothing pockets with note about being forgetful	5.6	0	22.2	0	6.9

A "simple" recommendation like "removing an area rug" may not be simple at all, as 61 percent of the professionals noted that a barrier existed due to the change required in the household appearance. Further, storing medications in a locked cabinet may require a change in the caregiver's behavior, and 68 percent of the professionals surveyed thought that this might be a barrier to implementation. Caution should be exercised in interpreting these data in that the perceived strength of the barrier was not asked.

Matching Adaptations to Caregiver Perceptions and Needs

The second phase of the study addressed the match between adaptation recommendations and caregiver perceptions. Data were collected in the Boston metropolitan area during Spring 1991. Four geriatric nurse practitioners representing three community agencies conducted assessments in thirty-one Alzheimer's households. The care recipients ranged in age from fifty-seven to ninety while their caregivers ranged in age from thirty-three to eighty-four. Over half (55%) of the caregivers were spouses and over a third (39%) were adult children. The duration of the illness reported by the caregivers averaged 4.33 years and ranged from one to ten years. The nurses' assessment included the Zarit Burden Interview [22], an ADL checklist, and a home environment assessment designed by the authors. Like Calkins, the researchers categorized adaptations by purpose. Nurses were asked to identify the "target problem" the adaptation was intended to address. These areas related to:

• Cognitive and behavioral impairments
• ADL impairments
• Caregiver ease
• Safety

Table 2 lists the recommendations by the target problems addressed, as noted by the geriatric nurse practitioners. An adaptation recommended to address one target problem for one care recipient may have been recommended to address other target problems for other care recipients. For example, installing additional locks on exit doors was recommended to address cognitive and behavioral impairments as well as safety and caregiver ease.

An average of twenty-five and a median of thirty-one recommendations were made, with one family caregiver receiving fifty-three recommendations. This is considerably higher than the fifteen to twenty recommendations per caregiver which the research team had anticipated. One caregiver expressed the feelings of many when, explaining why she had not made all the adaptations recommended, she said, "It was just too much for me to deal with."

Table 3 depicts the adaptations that were most frequently recommended.

Table 2. Recommended Adaptations by Target Problem

	Cognitive or Behavioral Impairment	Safety	Caregiver Ease	Impairment in ADLs
1. Create and utilize signs for identification cues	X	X	X	X
2. Install additional locks on exit doors	X	X	X	
3. Simplify clothing			X	X
4. Install childproof cabinet locks		X	X	
5. Immobilize stove—remove dials	X	X		
6. Double tape or remove area rugs	X	X		
7. Post emergency numbers near telephone	X	X		
8. Use hand-held shower			X	
9. Have patient wear ID bracelet	X			
10. Install hand rails		X		
11. Install grab bars in bathroom		X		
12. Store medications in locked cabinet		X		
13. Add non-skid strips to stairs	X	X		

Three of the top five recommendations dealt with concerns about potential wandering and two related to the potential for poisonous ingestion. Adaptations that promoted care recipient independence were less frequently recommended.

Table 4 provides the specific categories addressed within each target problem and the percent of recommendations made regarding each. Almost half (45%) of the recommendations addressed problems related to cognitive or behavioral impairments, while 31 percent of the recommendations addressed safety concerns, 20 percent addressed caregiver ease, and only 3 percent addressed impairments in activities of daily living. In fact, fewer than 1 percent of the recommendations made were specifically targeted to promote independence for the care recipient.

A social worker called the thirty-one family caregivers approximately one month after the nurse's visit to assess the caregiver's initial response to the home adaptation recommendations. At the time of the telephone interviews, 68 percent of the care recipients were still at home with no plans to move, 26 percent were awaiting nursing home placement, and 6 percent were already institutionalized. The caregivers were asked a series of ten questions about each recommendation made. These questions were designed to obtain the caregiver's perception of the

Table 3. Most Frequently Recommended Adaptations

1. Have copies of current photo available
2. Have patient wear ID bracelet
3. Store household cleaners and insecticides in locked closet
4. Install childproof cabinet locks
5. Install additional locks on exit doors
6. Post emergency numbers near telephone
7. Store medications in locked cabinet
8. Remove clutter
9. Notify police and offer photo
10. Double tape area rugs
11. Simplify clothing
12. Immobilize stove/Remove dials
13. Remove area rugs
14. Remove low furniture
15. Create and utilize signs for identification cues
16. Place ID information in patient's wallet
17. Notify neighbors
18. Install grab bars in bathroom
19. Use non-skid bathroom mats
20. Use night lights in bathroom
21. Use straws and finger foods
22. Keep furniture arrangement consistent

care recipient's susceptibility to and severity of the target problem; perceived barriers (expense, requirements for outside help, requirements for change in the caregiver behavior, and requirements for change in the household appearance); perceived effectiveness of the recommendation; and the likelihood of following through on the recommendation.

Table 5 illustrates that while caregivers perceived certain target problems as very serious, they did not perceive their family members as susceptible. For over half (53%) of the recommendations made, the caregivers perceived that the target problems were "very" serious; however, they only considered their family member "very" susceptible to the target problems addressed by 27 percent of the recommendations. The variability of behaviors over the course of the disease may make it difficult for caregivers to assess their family member's personal degree of susceptibility.

Caregivers did not perceive major costs associated with a majority of the recommendations made. In fact, for over 70 percent of the recommendations, the caregivers did not rate the adaptation as having a perceived "cost" (requiring

Table 4. Target Problems Addressed by Adaptation
Recommendations (Percent) (n = 501)[a]

Cognitive and behavioral impairments	45.4
Falling	22.4
Wandering	15.4
Reality orientation	4.0
Visual perception	1.8
Wayfinding	1.0
Hiding	0.6
Memory and coordination	0.2
Safety	30.9
Prevention of poisonous ingestion or choking	12.0
Fire prevention	10.0
Rapid response to crises	7.2
Prevention of injury due to sharp objects	1.8
Caregiver ease	19.8
Minimize rummaging	10.8
Increase caregiver coping strategies	4.4
Increase awareness of Alzheimer's disease	3.8
Prevent breakage of valuable items	0.8
Impairments in activities of daily living	3.4
Decrease incontinence	1.8
Decrease in fine motor coordination	0.8
Promote independence	0.6
Decrease fear and resistance in bathing	0.2

[a]Tables 4 and 5 reprinted from *Technology and Disability,* 2:4, N. M. Silverstein, J. Hyde, and R. Ohta, "Home Adaptation for Alzheimer's Households," pp. 58-68, 1993, with kind permission from Elsevier Science Ireland Ltd., Bay 15K, Shannon Industrial Estate, Co. Clare, Ireland.

outside help, change needed in caregiver behavior, change required in household appearance, or the inconvenience or unsightliness of the adaptation). Professionals have traditionally approached issues of implementation by assessing the associated costs. The level of implementation for the caregivers in this sample was affected by factors other than perceived costs.

Such a factor was the perceived effectiveness of the adaptation. Caregivers perceived that the adaptation was likely to be effective for just over half (55%) of the recommendations. Moreover, they reported that they were likely to implement just over half (53%) as well. If a caregiver perceived that an adaptation would be effective, he or she would be more likely ($r = .68, p < .001$) to implement the recommendation. Further, the "cost" of the adaptation in terms of difficulty

Table 5. Caregiver Perception of Target Problem and Recommended Adaptation at Time of Telephone Follow-Up

	Very	Somewhat	Not at All
Susceptibility to target problem (n = 616)	27.3	34.4	38.3
Seriousness of target problem (n = 616)	53.4	24.0	22.6
Expense of adaptation (n = 613)	7.8	21.7	70.5
Level of outside help required (n = 616)	9.1	16.9	74.0
Change required in caregiver behavior (n = 614)	6.2	22.1	71.7
Inconvenience of adaptation (n =613)	10.3	20.7	69.0
Change required in household appearance (n = 613)	8.2	21.5	70.3
Unsightliness of adaptation (n = 614)	4.4	11.2	84.4
Perceived effectiveness of adaptation (n = 611)	54.8	24.1	21.1
Likelihood of implementing adaptation (n = 640)	53.3	15.8	30.9

of installation, financial output, required changes in caregiver behavior, and unsightliness or institutional appearance when combined with the "perceived effectiveness" was correlated to the likelihood of implementation (r = .32, p < .001). Fifty-two percent of the recommendations were implemented by the time of the social worker's in-home visit.

The average number of recommendations implemented per household was thirteen. Table 6 depicts the adaptations that were most frequently recommended by the nurse practitioners and the percent of implementation by the caregivers. Of the adaptations that were most often recommended, only nine were implemented at a rate of 50 percent or greater:

- Post emergency numbers near telephone
- Keep care recipient's belongings together
- Lower hot water temperature to <120 degrees

- Double tape or remove area rugs
- Use night lights in bathrooms and hallways
- Remove low furniture
- Use sturdy chairs
- Use non-skid bathroom mats
- Regularly replace smoke detector batteries

Table 6. Adaptations Most Frequently Recommended by
Nurses and Implemented by Caregivers ($n = 31$)

	Recommendation (%)	Implementation (%)
1. Have patient wear ID bracelet	80.7	16.0
2. Store household cleaners and insecticides in locked cabinets	74.2	21.7
3. Have copies of current photo available	71.0	36.4
4. Post emergency numbers near telephone	64.5	100.0
5. Store medications in a locked cabinet	61.3	5.3
6. Simplify clothing	61.3	47.4
7. Remove clutter	58.1	38.9
8. Create and utilize signs for identification cues	58.1	11.1
9. Double tape or remove area rugs	54.8	88.2
10. Notify police and offer photo	51.6	18.8
11. Notify neighbors	51.6	43.8
12. Use non-skid bathroom mats	51.6	56.3
13. Immobilize stove/remove dials	48.4	26.7
14. Remove low furniture	48.4	60.0
15. Use night lights in bathroom and hallway	48.4	86.7
16. Install grab bars in bathroom	45.2	21.4
17. Keep furniture arrangement consistent	42.0	46.2
18. Limit rummage areas	42.0	23.1
19. Install additional locks on exit doors	42.0	15.4
20. Use straws and finger foods	35.5	45.5
21. Maintain clear pathways	35.5	45.5
22. Use sturdy chairs	35.5	63.6
23. Pad sharp corners	35.5	18.2
24. Use hand-held shower	35.5	36.4
25. Keep patient's belongings together	35.5	100.0
26. Lower hot water temperature <120°	32.3	100.0
27. Use tub seat	32.3	20.0
28. Remove small ingestible objects	32.3	30.0
29. Regularly replace smoke detector batteries	32.3	50.0
30. Keep sharp utensils in a locked cabinet	29.0	33.3
31. Use contrasting dishes	25.8	0
32. Keep valuables in a locked cabinet	25.8	25.0

The major reasons offered for not following through on recommended adaptations were that the care recipient was currently or would soon be institutionalized (49%) or that the caregiver did not agree that the adaptation was necessary (44%). The study also investigated whether at times caregivers partially implement adaptation recommendations; it seems that caregivers either followed through "completely" on implementing the recommendations or "not at all." This was true across all of the target problem areas.

How Adaptations and Recommendations Can be Made More Useful for People with Dementia and their Caregivers

While this analysis is based on a small sample, it does provide some interesting observations. First, caregivers may be receiving home adaptation recommendations too late in the disease process. For almost a third of this sample, institutionalization was expected in the near future and caregivers may have been reluctant to make short-term adaptations. Thus, timing may be a strong factor in implementation. Caregivers, however, tend to be crisis-oriented and may not access the service network earlier on. If agencies can encourage the use of supportive services earlier in the disease process, the challenge for providers will be to offer the recommendations in stages. That is, caregivers may be able to address current problems but be overwhelmed by recommendations that are designed to prevent problems in the distant future.

Further, caregivers are not likely to follow through with a recommendation unless they are convinced of its effectiveness, and their feedback in this regard is crucial. It was apparent during the telephone interviews that many caregivers did not understand why certain recommendations were made or did not think them necessary. One caregiver reported that she did not implement the recommendation to put visual cues or signs around the house because her husband is visually impaired. In other cases the caregiver understood the purpose of the adaptation but developed an alternative method, often a change in caregiving behavior, to accomplish the same purpose. For example, instead of removing the dials from the stove, the caregiver installed a switch to turn off the electricity when not in use. The rationality of these responses is clear only when the caregiver's point of view is clear.

More time may be needed to educate the caregiver about the importance of the recommendation as it relates to the disease process. Home adaptation assessments made over time may prove to be more effective than one-time visits. Moreover, the manner in which recommendations are made may also influence caregiver compliance. Caregivers need a chance to explore their feelings about the disease and may be hesitant to give up coping patterns that work, even for better solutions. Thus, one caregiver did not get a cane for his wife, stating "I am her cane." Ruth Gordon, RN, MS, of the Community Alzheimer's Specialist Program in Watertown, Massachusetts states that, "Unless the nurse educates the caregiver about the disease process and establishes trust, adaptation recommendations are not likely to be followed."

Following is a summary of the study's findings relevant to the unique characteristics of Alzheimer's home adaptation:

- Many caregivers do not seek help until late in the disease process. A home adaptation "audit" may be a good early service for agencies attempting to attract families earlier in the course of the disease.
- Recommendations are more likely to be implemented if practitioners elicit and consider caregiver concerns, experiences, and priorities when deciding which adaptations to recommend.
- Professionals' understanding of barriers to implementation of recommendations may be different from the caregiver's own assessment.
- Barriers such as financial cost or need for outside help when taken alone may not be significant deterrents to implementation if caregivers believe in the potential efficacy of the adaptation; however, the cumulative effect of "cost" factors does mitigate against the implementation of the adaptation.
- Agencies may be giving caregivers too many recommendations. Recommendations may need to be staged, addressing current problems now and listing recommendations to be implemented later.
- For those recommendations that are not in direct response to caregiver requests, practitioners may need to provide ongoing counseling and support. In this way they will be able to assist caregivers in understanding and accepting the progressive nature of the disease and to recommend adaptations more relevant to the care recipients' current or near-future problems.

CONCLUSIONS

The Need for Further Research

As discussed, home adaptation services for those with cognitive impairment may differ from those for adaptations that deal with purely physical impairments. The authors' research suggests, for example, that differences exist in caregivers' responses to adaptation recommendations and the need to educate caregivers about the progressive course of the disease and how some adaptations may work. The efficacy of particular interventions as they support cognitive functioning, enhance safety, and reduce caregiver burden remains to be fully documented. In addition, a better understanding is needed of the environment-behavior relationship of adaptations for the cognitively impaired as a basis for such research.

Recommendations for Future Practice

Across the United States, agencies increasingly offer in-home assessments that include home adaptation recommendations to families caring for someone with Alzheimer's disease or a related disorder. Practice implications for this type of analysis include the need for preparing assessment workers such as nurse practitioners, social workers, or other health care or housing professionals as to the caregiver's perspective when making recommendations. The next step would be to develop appropriate interventions to increase the likelihood of implementation. If providers are to include adaptation as an integral part of their services, it is important that they understand the caregiver's perspective as well as the factors that influence caregiver decision-making.

ACKNOWLEDGMENTS

An earlier version of this chapter was presented at the 44th annual meeting of the Gerontological Society of America, San Francisco, 1991. A related article also appears in *Technology and Disability* [23]. This research was funded in part by The Charles H. Farnsworth Trust Research Grant in Health Care of the Elderly of the Medical Foundation, Boston. The authors gratefully acknowledge Russell Ohta, Ph.D., project research consultant. We thank Francis Caro, Ph.D., and M. Powell Lawton, Ph.D., for their comments on the manuscript. We also appreciate the data collection contributions of Ruth Gordon, RN, MS (Community Alzheimer's Support Services, Watertown, Massachusetts); Marilyn Mulligan Stasonis, RN and Kathy Kilmartin, RN (Community Family, Everett, Massachusetts); and Elaine Silverio, RN and Judith Antonangelli, RN (formerly of Elder Care Connections, Holliston, Massachusetts).

REFERENCES

1. Alzheimer's Disease and Related Disorders Association of Eastern Massachusetts, *Alzheimer's Disease: The Facts*, Cambridge, Massachusetts, 1992.
2. L. Blume, N. A. Persily, and J. Mintzer, The Prevalence of Dementia: The Confusion of Numbers, *American Journal of Alzheimer's Care and Related Disorders Care and Research*, pp. 3-11, May/June 1992.
3. M. P. Lawton, Environmental Approaches to Research and Treatment of Alzheimer's Disease, *Alzheimer's Disease Treatment and Family Stress: Directions for Research*, U.S. Department of Health and Human Services, No. 344, 1989.
4. J. Pynoos, E. Cohen, and C. Lucas, *The Caring Home Booklet: Environmental Coping Strategies for Alzheimer's Caregivers*, Andrus Gerontology Center, University of Southern California, Los Angeles, 1988.
5. M. P. Calkins, K. H. Namazi, T. T. Rosner, A. Olson, and B. Brabender, *Home Modifications—Responding to Dementia*, Research Center of the Corinne Dolan Alzheimer Center at Heather Hill, Chardon, Ohio, 1988.

6. R. V. Olsen, E. Ehrenkrantz, and B. Hutchings, *Alzheimer's and Related Dementias: Homes that Help*, New Jersey Institute of Technology, Newark, New Jersey, 1993.
7. M. P. Calkins, *Caring for the Person with Dementia in the Community: Consequences and Coping Strategies*, unpublished paper and presentation to the Alzheimer's Association first annual caregiving conference, Chicago, 1992.
8. L. G. Hiatt, Design of the Home Environment for the Cognitively Impaired Person, in *Dementia Care*, N. L. Mace (ed.), Johns Hopkins University Press, Baltimore, pp. 231-242, 1990.
9. J. Pynoos, Toward a National Policy on Home Modification, *Technology and Disability*, 2:4, pp. 1-8, Fall 1993.
10. R. V. Olsen, E. Ehrenkrantz, and B. Hutchings, Creating Supportive Environments for People with Dementia and Their Caregivers through Home Modifications, *Technology and Disability*, 2:4, pp. 47-57, Fall 1993.
11. L. George and L. Gwyther, Caregiver Well-Being: A Multidimensional Examination of Family Caregivers of Demented Adults, *The Gerontologist*, 26:3, pp. 253-259, 1986.
12. L. Kapust, Living with Dementias: The Ongoing Funeral, *Social Work in Health Care*, 7:4, pp. 79-91, 1982.
13. P. Rabins, N. Mace, and R. Lucas, The Impact of Dementia on the Family, *Journal of the American Medical Association*, 248:3, pp. 333-335, 1982.
14. G. A. Hinrichsen and G. Niederhe, Dementia Management Strategies and Adjustment of Family Members of Older Patients, *The Gerontologist*, 34:1, pp. 95-102, 1994.
15. M. Stommel, C. E. Collins, and B. A. Given, The Costs of Family Contributions to the Care of Persons with Dementia, *The Gerontologist*, 34:2, pp. 199-205, 1994.
16. K. Hooker, L. D. Frazier, and D. J. Monahan, Personality and Coping among Caregivers of Spouses with Dementia, *The Gerontologist*, 34:3, pp. 386-392, 1994.
17. G. R. Hall, Case of the Patient with Alzheimer's Disease Living at Home, *Nursing Clinics of North America*, 23:1, p. 37, 1988.
18. D. Handler, *An Occupational Therapy and Social Work Approach to Dementia: A Binary Case Study*, thesis, Tufts University, Medford, Massachusetts, 1988.
19. J. Pynoos and R. Ohta, *Home Environment Management for Alzheimer's Caregivers: A Program of Research and Dissemination to Reduce Burden and Increase Safety and Functioning*, final report to the AARP Andrus Foundation, 1988.
20. R. Ohta and B. Ohta, *Factors Affecting the Acceptance and Use of Home Adaptation by the Elderly*, paper presented at the annual meeting of the Gerontological Society of America, Boston, 1990.
21. N. M. Silverstein, J. Hyde, and R. Ohta, *Home Adaptation for Alzheimer's Households: Factors Related to Implementation and Outcomes of Recommendations*, University of Massachusetts, Boston, Gerontology Institute, 1992.
22. J. M. Zarit, *Predictors of Burden and Distress for Caregivers of Senile Dementia Patients*, unpublished doctoral dissertation, University of Southern California, Los Angeles, 1982.

CHAPTER
7

Individualizing Home Modification Recommendations to Facilitate Performance of Routine Activities

Bettye Rose Connell and Jon A. Sanford

Most young, able-bodied people do not think twice about the routine household activities that structure daily life. However, everyday household activities, such as taking a bath, walking to a streetside mailbox, or even adjusting a thermostat, may create a variety of problems for older individuals who experience age-related loss of musculo-skeletal and sensory functioning. These individuals often report that, with functional loss, routine activities become more difficult, more time-consuming, and more hazardous.

The truism that older people are not a homogeneous group extends to characterizing their problems in the performance of routine household activities [1]. Older people differ in the activities that are problematic, in the type and severity of difficulties they experience, and in the reasons for their difficulty with a given activity. For example, some individuals who experience difficulty in bathing have problems with getting in and out of the tub, although others have problems adjusting the flow and temperature of the bath water. Of those individuals who experience problems in getting in and out of the tub, some may simply report that it takes more effort to get in and out than it did before, but others may report that this task is exhausting, time-consuming, and hazardous. Finally, older people also differ in the number of activities that are problematic. Some individuals experience, at most, minor inconveniences with a few routine activities, whereas other individuals find it difficult, if not impossible, to perform a wide range of routine activities of daily life.

Lawton and Nahemow's *Environmental Press* Model offers an important perspective for conceptualizing the problems that many older people experience with routine household activities [2]. The model describes these types of problems as resulting from the interaction between an individual's functional and sensory capabilities (*competence*) and the demands placed on the individual by the home environment (*environmental press*). When capabilities and environmental demands do not match, such as when an individual's functional status declines but the design characteristics of the home environment do not change, the model predicts that maladaptive behaviors and negative affect will result. The model predicts that the greater the severity of functional and sensory loss, the greater the impact of the environment on an individual's behavior. Thus, when *demand* exceeds *capabilities,* there are unmet housing needs.

Several types of strategies, such as medical or rehabilitation interventions, behavioral modification programs, training, and design modifications, might be adopted to ameliorate problems with routine household activities. Design modifications, the strategy of interest here, differ in a fundamental way from other strategies. Unlike strategies that target the individual and attempt to directly or indirectly modify his or her functional or sensory capabilities, design modifications are intended to reduce environmental demands.

The diverse problems that older people experience with household activities point to their diverse housing needs. Although one might expect to find a wide variety of design modifications in the homes of a large sample of older people, several studies [3-5] report that a limited repertoire of modifications are typically used. These include grab bars, ramps, wide doors, push bars, raised toilet seats, additional lighting, and lever faucet handles. Current practices of selecting modifications may result in stereotyping the problems that older people experience with routine activities. For example, grab bars will likely meet an important housing need of individuals with ambulatory problems. However, it is unlikely that they will address the problems experienced by individuals whose functional limitations are related to sensory impairments.

There are theoretical and practical justifications for individualizing home modification efforts to address specific housing needs. First, the environmental press model suggests that optimum behavioral and affective outcomes are achieved when the environment presents individuals with manageable demands. Thus, making modifications without attention to an individual's specific housing needs may unintentionally eliminate manageable demands and result in unanticipated consequences. Second, as most older people are living in homes they own and they often bear the cost of making modifications, it is reasonable to expect that they will be more willing to invest in modifications that are identified on the basis of individual need.

One difficulty in describing housing needs (and identifying appropriate home modifications to respond to those needs) has been the absence of a framework that provides practical, detailed links between problems with the performance of routine activities and specific aspects of housing design. Although there are some sources of information about home modifications that are helpful in diagnosing needs and personalizing decisions [6-16], they are not widely known. An illustrative example of how information on modifications is likely to be obtained by many elderly individuals and their families was shown several years ago on a segment of the PBS series *This Old House*. A middle-aged couple, whose renovation project included a bedroom-bathroom suite for an aging parent, turned to local accessibility building code requirements for guidance on bathroom design. The resulting space would likely be better suited for a younger person with paraplegia, and the couple's expectations that they had attended to a parent's future needs were probably unrealistic. Current code-based accessibility requirements will, at best, meet only some of the needs of some elderly people. (See also Chapter 4 of this book.)

This chapter describes the development and application of a conceptual framework to identify housing needs in order to individualize home modification for older people with a variety of disabling conditions. Data are presented for the elderly participants in a case study project based on the framework. Two of the case studies are presented in detail.

CONCEPTUAL FRAMEWORK

The Center for Accessible Housing at North Carolina State University, as part of its mandate to improve the appropriateness and availability of accessible housing, undertook a two-year study to identify the housing needs of people of all ages with a variety of disabling conditions, and to evaluate the responsiveness of their current housing to these needs [17]. This section describes two major considerations in the development of a conceptual framework to guide this research: design-relevant *routine activities* and task-relevant *design features*. In addition, it describes the methodological considerations involved in applying the framework.

Routine Activities

Scope of Activities

The extensive literature on functional assessment includes a large number of standardized assessment instruments. Many of these instruments were developed to characterize the functional independence of older people as the basis for medical and rehabilitative decision making. Despite the differences between the applications intended for these instruments and the purpose of the planned research, we anticipated that a careful review of the assessment literature would produce a comprehensive list of activities that could form the basis for the list of design-relevant routine activities for our framework.

Over twenty articles related to the assessment of independence in activities of daily living (ADLs) and instrumental activities of daily living (IADLs) were reviewed [18-39]. Although the review did not yield the expected list of activities, it was useful in clarifying the scope of activities to be differentiated as related (e.g., bathing, meal preparation) or not related (e.g., personal money management) to housing design. Activities incorporated into the conceptual framework included: 1) ADLs; 2) IADLs; 3) activities related to controlling ambient conditions, such as regulating temperature, lighting, and ventilation; and 4) other common household activities such as home maintenance (e.g., mowing the lawn) and communication (e.g., using the telephone, mailing a letter). The resulting list of activities was grouped to distinguish thirteen activity domains (e.g., personal hygiene) and forty-five specific activities (e.g., bathe/shower) that are included in the domains (see Figure 1).

Design-Relevant Tasks

Activity domains and specific activities represent complex events, particularly when one tries to relate functional difficulties with those events to housing design. Activities are constituted by tasks, which are readily understood in terms of the functional and sensory capabilities they require and which can be related to design features in the home. A task analysis procedure was used to identify a design-relevant task sequence for each activity. The tasks capture required functional capabilities such as body movements, positional changes, and sensory responses inherent in task performance. The task performances span an individual's ability to access (e.g., approach, locate), use (e.g., reach, grasp, manipulate, reposition, release, detect responses), and exit (e.g., safely leave) a particular room, appliance, fixture, or piece of hardware that is required to complete a task [40]. Representative tasks for selected activities are shown in Figure 2.

Focusing on tasks permits one to distinguish among possible functional problems in the performance of routine activities. Such distinctions are important in identifying housing needs. For example, bathing involves turning on the water, adjusting the temperature, getting into the tub, reaching for the soap, etc. An ambulatory individual who experiences difficulty with bathing may only have problems with the task of getting in and out of the tub. Other bathing tasks may pose no problems for this individual. In this case, there is a housing need to ameliorate problems in getting in and out of the tub.

The focus on tasks rather than activities as the "unit of analysis" is unusual, but not without precedent in the assessment and rehabilitation literature. Granger's typology of rehabilitation orientations described *disability*, as distinct from *impairment* or *handicap*, as "difficulty with tasks" that are assessed through "selected performance (behavioral) descriptors" [22, p. 20]. Weber and Czaja used sub-activity sets of ADLs in the development of human factors demand profiles for selected ADLs [41]. Kuriansky and Gurland's performance test of

Activity Domain	Activity
Personal Care	
Hygiene	Bathe/shower
	Use toilet
Health Care Management	Brush/floss teeth/dentures
	Wash face/hands
	Taking medications
Appearance	Shave/apply makeup
	Comb/style hair
	Hand/foot care
Household Activities	
Clean House	Vacuum, sweep, mop
	Scrub
	Dust/polish furniture
	Clean walls/windows
	Clean appliances/fixtures
	Make/change bed
	Put away clothes, groceries, etc.
	Take out trash
	Write (letter, pay bills, grocery list)
Garment Care	Wash/dry clothes
	Iron clothes
	Mend clothes
Eating	Meal preparation
	Cooking/baking
	Set table/eat
	Wash dishes (automatic or manual)
	Clean work/eating area
Exterior Maintenance	Yard work (e.g., mow lawn)
	Upkeep house (e.g., paint exterior)
Control Ambient Conditions	
Thermal Comfort	Regulate temperature
	Light pilot
	Change filter
Light/Ventilation	Open/close window
	Change screen/glass in storm door
	Open/close curtains, shades, etc.
	Turn lights on/off (overhead or lamp)
	Change light bulb
	Reset breaker/change fuse
General Safety	
Response	Respond to fire/burglar alarm
	Answer phone, doorbell
Systems Maintenance	Change batteries in fire/burglar alarm
Communication	
Initiate Action	Use telephone or intercom
	Send/receive mail
Motor Activities	
Ambulation	Get in/out of home or room
	Moving around house
	Changing levels (stair/ramp, elevator)
Transfer	Get in/out of bed

Figure 1. Activity domains and activities included in the
conceptual framework.

	Design Relevant Tasks			Task Relevant Design Features		
Activity Domain	Activity	Tasks		Space	Product	Controls/Hardware
Personal Care Hygiene	Bathe/Shower	Dress/Undress Turn water on/off Regulate water temperature Transfer	Reach/Grab soap, shampoo, etc. Wash self Reach/Grab towel Transfer	Bathroom	Tub/Shower	Seat, drain, faucet, shower head, soap dish, shelves
					Grab bars Towel rack	
	Use toilet	Transfer Dress/Undress Reach toilet paper Wipe self	Flush Use personal hygiene products Transfer		Toilet Grab bars Toilet paper holder Storage cab or drawer	Seat, handle Toilet paper holder Handle, door/ drawer pulls
Health Care Management	Brush/Floss teeth/dentures	Use mirror Turn water on/off Reach/Grab brush, toothpaste Apply toothpaste Brush teeth/dentures	Reach/Grab dental floss Use floss Rinse mouth Reach/Grab towel Put things away/ Dispose of floss		Mirror Medicine/Storage cabinet Sink Cup holder Towel rack Trash can	 Faucet
	Wash face/ hands	Use mirror Turn water on/off Regulate water temperature	Reach/Grab soap Wash face/hands Reach/Grab towel Put soap/towel away		Sink Towel rack Soap dish Mirror	 Door/Drawer pulls
	Taking medications	Select appropriate medication Reach medicine Reach/Grab cup Turn water on/off Put medicine/cup away			Medicine/Storage cabinet or drawer Cup holder Sink	Door/Drawer pulls, plug Faucet

Figure 2. Conceptual framework.

activities of daily living (PADL), developed for use with institutionalized elderly individuals, is one of the few standardized tests that assess functional capability in terms of the task components of activities [28].

Housing Design

Scales of Design

Three scales or levels of design features in housing place demands on the functional capabilities involved in task performance [42]. These scales or levels include the design of spaces, products, and controls/hardware. Space includes interior spaces such as rooms, hallways, and closets. It also includes exterior spaces associated with use of and access to a dwelling (e.g., porch, deck, parking area, and grounds). Products are located in rooms or other spaces and include: appliances such as stoves, refrigerators, and microwave ovens; plumbing fixtures such as toilets and sinks; and building elements such as doors and windows. Controls and hardware are typically located on products and include: handles, knobs and locks on doors; levers and faucets on toilets or tubs; and electronic or mechanical controls on stoves or washing machines. Nonoperable, fixed hardware (such as handrails and grab bars) is often installed in a room and is not part of a product.

Task-Relevant Design Features and Design Characteristics

The task analysis procedure and expert input were used to identify design features at the three scales of design that impact task performance. Characteristics of design features that create functional demands also were described (see Figure 3). For example, the height of a tub determines how high an ambulatory individual must lift his/her feet to get into the tub. Similarly, the size and contrast of text on digital display panels help determine its readability. Design characteristics of spaces, products, and hardware/controls that impact task performance are described below.

- *Spaces.* The physical characteristics of rooms and other spaces place demands on older people that can determine accessibility, require maneuvering, or affect the ability to locate products or controls. The layout of fixtures in a bathroom determines if a lateral wheelchair-to-toilet transfer is possible. Light levels impact the ability of an individual with low vision to read the label on a bottle of medicine. Categories of spatial characteristics that determine demand include:
  - Size and spatial configuration and layout
  - Entry (doorway width and threshold height)
  - Systems locations (location of switches, outlets, fixtures, and appliances)
  - Floor materials and finishes
  - Ambient conditions (illumination and noise)

Space	Product	Controls/Hardware
Bathroom Entry: doorway width, threshold height Size Layout Systems locations: plumbing, electric, lighting, ventilation Floor materials/Finishes Ambient conditions	Tub/Shower Type (description) Size/Dimensions Hardware configuration (location of hardware) Lighting Materials/Finishes	Faucet Type (description) Size Approach: distance and angle Force required Operational charac- teristics: direction, distance, calibration Materials/Finishes Door/Curtain Type (description) Size Approach: distance and angle Force required Operational charac- teristics: direction, distance, calibration Materials/Finishes Drain Type (description) Size Approach: distance and angle Force required Operational charac- teristics: direction, distance, calibration Materials/Finishes Seat Type (description) Size Approach: distance and angle Force required Materials/Finishes Soap Dish, Grab Bars, Toilet Type (description) Size Approach: distance and angle Materials/Finishes

Figure 3. Characteristics of design features
(that impact demand on tasks related to the activity of bathing/showering).

- *Products.* Products create demands for users, including requiring them to bend, reach, or lift to use a control or piece of hardware. For example, locating controls at the rear of an electric range requires an individual using a wheelchair to reach across the burners to operate the appliance. The product characteristics of interest include:
  - Type
  - Size
  - Force required (specifically to open and close doors and windows)
  - Materials and finishes (type, texture, and color contrast)
  - Auditory and visual signals (intended to alert user to take further action)
  - Location of operable parts
- *Controls and hardware.* Controls and hardware typically create demands that require the user to grasp, twist, rotate, push, or pull an object in order to accomplish a task. For example, round doorknobs must be grasped and rotated to open a door. The color contrast between a control and the product on which it is mounted affects an individual's ability to locate and operate the control with precision. Important product characteristics that influence demand include:
  - Type of control/hardware
  - Minimum approach distance and angle
  - Hardware configuration
  - Size
  - Force of activation
  - Operational characteristics (direction and distance to be moved, calibration)
  - Materials and finish (type, texture, and color contrast)

Application of the Framework

The initial application of the conceptual framework was in a case study project of forty individuals with a variety of disabling conditions. Four aspects of implementing the conceptual framework in the case study project are described below: scope of activities studied; outcome variables; procedure for collecting data on activity performance; and procedure for collecting data on design characteristics.

Scope of Activities

In order to keep the time commitment required of subjects to a reasonable length, twenty-seven design-related activities were selected from the forty-five identified in the framework (see Figure 4). The protocol utilized the same twenty-seven activities regardless of an individual's type or severity of disability or housing situation. The activities selected for the protocol represented at least one activity from each of the thirteen activity domains included in the framework.

- Regulate temperature
- Answer door when doorbell rings
- Open and close windows and shades
- Answer the telephone
- Make a telephone call
- Respond to the smoke detector
- Write a letter
- Get a sweater and go outside
- Mail a letter
- Mow the lawn
- Prepare a lunch
- Eat lunch
- Clean the dishes
- Sweep the floor

- Put away the groceries
- Do the laundry
- Clean teeth
- Wash face and hands
- Shave or apply makeup
- Take medicine
- Simulate showering or bathing
- Simulate toileting
- Get in and out of bed
- Move around the house
- Get in and out of a room
- Get in and out of the house
- Change levels

Figure 4. Activities included in the case study protocol.

Measuring Housing Needs

An individual's performance of routine activities could be assessed in terms of *independence* or *difficulty*. Although most assessment efforts use dependence as an outcome measure, two studies suggest that difficulty is the preferred outcome variable for defining housing need and evaluating the impact of housing design on the performance of routine, household activities.

Nieuwenhuijsen, Frey, and Crews examined the effects of disability scale construction on assessing small functional gains among blind older people who participated in blindness rehabilitation programs [43]. They concluded that the practice of rating dependence (defined as performance aided by use of an assistive device) and difficulty (how well, how efficiently a task was performed) on the same scale biased assessment of the effect of interventions on functioning in routine activities. Traditional scale construction assumed individuals were "more disabled" if task performance was aided by an assistive device or other modifications, even if the task could be performed more easily. They demonstrated that dependence, "how," and difficulty, "how well," could be meaningfully treated as separate constructs in characterizing disability and rating the effects of design change on functional performance.

Windley obtained measures of dependence (personal or mechanical assistance) and difficulty (cost-benefits of effort) on ADLs and IADLs from a sample of older people [44]. His analysis revealed that activity dependence is distributed hier-archically, as would be expected, across ADLs and IADLs. However, activity difficulty is not. Difficulty with all ADLs occurred at a much higher frequency than did dependence in ADLs. In contrast, the percentage of this sample that was dependent in IADLs was greater than the percentage that experienced difficulty with IADLs. Windley speculated that the cost-benefits of completing an activity independently, but with difficulty, may be more acceptable for personal activities, such as bathing, dressing, toileting, transferring, and feeding, than they are for less personal activities, such as housekeeping, shopping, and transportation. He argues that

> design . . . interventions should address difficulty before dependence. Individuals who are activity dependent . . . may become independent if difficulty could be reduced. Interventions aimed at reducing difficulty will likely have their most immediate impact on the individual level when addressing ADLs [44, pp. 6-7].

Activity Performance Protocol

Data on difficulty in the performance of routine activities were obtained using a video-based, naturalistic observation protocol. A nondirective approach, "Show me how you do . . . ," was used in which the individual was requested to complete or simulate, as appropriate, the routine activities listed in Figure 4. Individuals were not prompted to demonstrate component tasks unless specific tasks were omitted. If an individual did not typically undertake a particular activity for reasons of choice, the subject was asked to demonstrate how he/she would do that activity. The protocol took approximately two hours to complete.

The protocol was completed in each participant's home, rather than in a laboratory setting with standardized design features. Individuals used the spaces, products, and hardware they normally used in conjunction with routine activities. No props were used. Thus, the activity performance data were obtained in a familiar setting using design features that participants had had some choice in selecting or modifying. This choice of a research setting for applying the conceptual framework enhanced the richness of the case study data by providing the study with an opportunity to obtain multiple data points about design characteristics as well as about functional difficulties in activity performance.

Observed, reported, and inferred problems with task performance were identifiable through an analysis of the videotapes. Observed problems were captured on the videotapes and identified by the tape coder. Self-reported problems were related by the subjects during the course of completing a task and were recorded on the audio portion of the videotapes. Inferred problems were presumed to exist when a modification was present in an individual's home. Examples of the three types of problems are as follows: Mr. A was observed having difficulty locating the thermostat; Ms. B reported having difficulty reading the calibrations on the thermostat, although this was not observable on the videotape; and Mr. C's thermostat had tactile markings, from which it was inferred that the modification was necessitated by a problem in seeing the thermostat calibrations.

Design Characteristics Protocol

A housing inventory was used to obtain accurate measures of the physical characteristics of the task-relevant design features in each participant's home. Initially, the videotaped data for each participant was reviewed to identify the spaces, products, and hardware/controls that each participant used or had been unable to use in completing the activity protocol. The characteristics of each design feature were described in as much detail as possible from the videotapes. Subsequently, a walk-through inspection of each residence was made to obtain physical measures for each task-relevant design feature identified in the videotape analysis. These data resulted in measured drawings of room layouts, fixtures, and hardware installations.

CASE STUDIES

This section reports the findings of case studies of seventeen older people with visual, mobility, and/or hearing impairments. In addition, the detailed case studies of two of the participants are presented—Mr. T, who was totally blind, and Mr. P, who was hemiplegic and clinically depressed. Both case studies illustrate the benefit of diagnosing an individual's housing needs as a basis for determining the most appropriate home modifications.

Findings

Sample of Older Individuals

Older participants ranged from fifty to eighty years of age. The sample included seven people with orthopedic impairments, five with visual impairments, and five with hearing impairments. The group with orthopedic impairments included nonambulatory and ambulatory individuals. The group with visual impairments included individuals with low vision as well as individuals who were totally blind. All of the subjects lived in single-family homes, usually suburban tract-built or multi-family retirement housing in the Atlanta, Georgia area. Although a few minor modifications had been made in some of the homes, none of the housing was built to be, or would be considered, accessible.

Problems with Activities and Tasks

A total of sixty-three problems, fewer than four per participant, were identified involving twenty different activities and thirty different tasks. Five activities— bathe/shower (12.7%), use telephone (11.1%), regulate temperature (9.5%), wash/dry clothes (7.9%), and answer doorbell (7.9%)—accounted for almost one-half of the total number of activity-related difficulties encountered by the seventeen participants (see Table 1).

These data suggest that this group of older people experienced few problems in performing routine, daily activities, and that the problems they did experience were distributed across a fairly large number of activities and tasks. However, when problems were examined for each disability group (i.e., vision, orthopedic, and hearing impairments), a different pattern emerged.

The groups differed regarding the activities and tasks that were problematic (see Table 1). The most problematic activities and tasks for visually impaired participants were: regulate temperature (locate thermostat and adjust settings), wash/dry clothes (set cycles), and use telephone (dial number and hang up phone). The most problematic activities and tasks for orthopedically impaired participants were: bathe and shower (transfer in and out and wash self), change levels (up and down stairs and up and down ramp), and prepare meals (open a jar). The most problematic activities and tasks for hearing-impaired participants were: answer doorbell (respond to ring), answer telephone (respond to ring), and use telephone (carry on conversation). When the same activity was problematic for more than one group, it was due to difficulties with different tasks.

Housing Needs

Another perspective on the disability-specific nature of the participants' problems can be seen when the sixty-three problems are aggregated by type of functional or sensory capability required (see Table 2). All five visually impaired participants had problems seeing text and symbols on products, such as thermostats, telephones, mailboxes, washers, and dryers. These problems made it difficult for the visually impaired participants to operate dials and knobs with reasonable precision and for apartment dwellers to identify their mailbox in a bank of boxes. One individual had difficulty locating objects in space, such as a thermostat on a wall. Only individuals with vision impairment experienced these types of difficulties. Participants with orthopedic impairments encountered a variety of problems related to reaching, repositioning, balancing, grasping, lifting, and maneuvering. The most pervasive difficulty for this group involved getting in and out of the tub and shower. Participants with hearing impairments had problems using products that required detecting and responding to auditory signals. These problems involved products that are used in emergency and routine communications (e.g., fire alarm, telephone, and doorbell).

Home Modifications

In homes occupied by individuals with vision impairments, few modifications had been made to address the types of problems typically encountered by this group. One individual with a vision impairment had a telephone with large print

Table 1. Performance Difficulties by Activity and Task

| Activity Task | Number of Difficulties | | | |
	Visually Impaired	Ortho-pedically Impaired	Hearing Impaired	Total[a] (n)
Mail a Letter				2
locate mailbox	2			
Regulate Temperature				6
locate thermostat	1			
reach controls		1		
adjust settings	4			
Wash/Dry Clothes				5
setting cycle	4	1		
Put Away Groceries				2
organizing items	1			
putting items on shelves		1		
Prepare Meal				3
open can/jar		3		
Cooking				2
setting temp on stove	2			
Wash Dishes (Automatic)				1
select setting—dishwasher	1			
Clean House				1
sweep floor	1			
Use Telephone				7
dial the number	3			
hang up phone	1			
carry on conversation			3	
Answer Telephone				3
respond to auditory signal			3	
Answer Doorbell				5
respond to auditory signal			5	
Respond to Fire Alarm				1
respond to auditory signal			1	
Bathe/Shower				8
transfer in/out of tub	1	6		
wash self		1		
Use Toilet				1
transfer on/off commode		1		
Shave				1
look in mirror	1			
Open/Close Window				4
push window up		2		
locate window	1			
locate window hardware	1			
Get In/Out of Home				1
move through doorway		1		
Moving Around House				4
finding one's way	1			
moving through a space	1	2		
Changing Levels				4
get up/down stairs		3		
get up/down ramp		1		
Get In/Out of Room				2
move through doorway		2		
Total	25	26	12	63

[a]Total number of problems per activity

Table 2. Types of Functional and Sensory Difficulties by Design Feature

Design Feature	Seeing Text/ Symbols[a]	Locating Finding	Reaching For/Into	Pulling Lifting	Grasping Twisting Turning	Maneuvering Navigating	Repositioning[b] Balancing	Hearing Auditory Signals
Thermostat	4(vi)	1(vi)	1(oi)	—	—	—	—	—
Window/Treatments	—	2(vi)	—	2(oi)	—	—	—	—
Telephone	3(vi)	1(vi)	—	—	—	—	—	6(hi)
Mailbox	2(vi)	—	—	—	—	—	—	—
Oven/Stove	2(vi)	—	—	—	—	—	—	—
Can/Jar Opener	—	—	—	—	3(oi)	—	—	—
Dishwasher	1(vi)	—	—	—	—	—	—	—
Kitchen Storage	1(vi)	—	1(oi)	—	—	—	—	—
Washer/Dryer	4(vi)	—	—	—	1(oi)	—	—	—
Tub/Shower	—	—	1(oi)	—	—	—	6(oi) 1(vi)	—
Toilet	—	—	—	—	—	—	1(oi)	—
Doorbell	—	—	—	—	—	—	—	5(hi)
Fire Alarm	—	—	—	—	—	—	—	1(hi)
Thresholds	—	—	—	—	—	1(oi)	—	—
Door	—	—	—	—	—	2(oi)	—	—
Flooring	—	1(vi)	—	—	—	1(oi)	—	—
Stairs/Handrails	—	—	—	—	—	3(oi)	—	—
Ramp	—	—	—	—	—	1(oi)	—	—
Spatial Layout	—	—	—	—	—	1(oi) 2(vi)	1(oi)	—
Total	17(vi)	5(vi)	3(oi)	2(oi)	4(oi)	9(oi) 2(vi)	8(oi) 1(vi)	12(hi)

[a]vi = visual impairment, oi = orthopedic impairment, hi = hearing impairment
[b]Repositioning refers to lateral movement as in transferring.

numbers, one had a programmable telephone, and a third had paint drops to mark settings on the thermostat.

There are many products that, in principle, can ameliorate the types of functional difficulties experienced by older people with vision impairments. These products improve the legibility of text and symbols or provide auditory and tactile information in addition to visual information. For example, stove controls that have preset stops or tactile calibrations would provide nonvisual information for controlling temperature. Although there are a wide variety of technologically-sophisticated, commercially-available home modification products, the people with vision impairments in this sample seemed to prefer simple, sometimes "homemade" modifications.

The modifications most frequently found in the homes of the participants with orthopedic impairments were off-the-shelf products such as grab bars and shower and tub seats. Most of these products addressed functional difficulties in getting in and out of the tub. Participants' maneuvering difficulties were usually the result of inadequate space, a problem most effectively addressed by architectural modifications, such as enlarging rooms and widening doorways. These types of modifications were not commonly found in the participants' homes. One-half of the architectural modifications were observed in the home of one participant who had severe disabilities. There were no housing modifications to compensate for functional difficulties with reaching, lifting, or grasping. These types of problems could be addressed by design changes such as lowering cabinets or replacing existing appliances (see also Chapters 3 and 4 in this book). In general, the types of modifications that were found addressed problems that could be dealt with quickly, easily, and inexpensively. In contrast, the functional problems that were not addressed through home modifications would be relatively more expensive and disruptive to implement.

In contrast to the other disability groups, the types of modifications found in the homes of the subjects with hearing impairments involved more sophisticated, commercially-available technology that required expertise to install and/or use. Although modifications were limited to telephones or doorbells, four of the five participants with hearing impairments had at least one modification. None of the participants with hearing impairments had a modified fire alarm, which presents a potentially life-threatening situation.

For older people with orthopedic impairments, certain modifications may not be perceived as spatially or economically practical. For example, renovating a bathroom to create enough space for wheelchair access may not be perceived to be worth the disruption and cost. In other cases, the alternatives may not be perceived as needed, such as the installation of grab bars when a towel bar has served the purpose in transferring. Participants with vision impairments may not perceive high-tech modifications as being any better than the homemade ones; or alternatively, they may not be aware that commercially available modifications exist. For people with hearing impairments, typical modifications may be perceived as "high tech," although that is an overgeneralization. Many older people are not familiar with technology that younger individuals take for granted and may not readily adopt modifications involving technology for a number of reasons. Such modifications may require a change in the habits of a lifetime. From the older individual's perspective, the costs may simply outweigh the benefits.

Mr. T

Background

Mr. T was a sixty-seven-year-old retired financial manager who lived with his wife in their suburban single-family home. He developed a pituitary tumor and lost his vision two years prior to the study. His vision loss was sudden and complete.

Mr. T purchased his residence approximately four years earlier as a retirement home. The 2,100 square-foot, one-story residence also included a finished room above the attached garage. No major modifications had been made to the home subsequent to Mr. T's loss of vision.

The home had three bedrooms and two and a half baths (see Figure 5). The fifty square-foot master bathroom was accessed through the master bedroom. The bathroom included a sink, toilet, and walk-in shower. There was no bathtub. The kitchen and dining area was a 265 square-foot room. The living and dining rooms were visually open to each other. Narrow hallways led to both the front and garage entrances to the home. The stairs to the finished space above the garage were located in the hallway next to the garage entry door. A large wooden deck, accessible from the living room and the master bedroom, was built across the rear of the house.

Mr. T did not appear to have developed techniques to allow him to move around the familiar environment of his home with ease, efficiency, and safety. He did not attempt many routine household activities, apparently content to allow his wife to complete them instead. Some of these were domestic activities that he likely had done infrequently prior to losing his sight; according to his wife, after his vision loss, he was unable to do them without "making a mess." He had not received any orientation and mobility instruction, nor any rehabilitation instruction in activities of daily living. He did not use any mobility aids, such as a long cane, although he did use a walking stick to assist him in going to his mailbox, which was at the end of a long driveway. On the Folstein Mini-Mental State Examination screening for cognitive function that was administered prior to videotaping, he scored highly, but initially gave the present year as 1961. When asked to repeat the names of three objects, he named only two. He indicated no difficulties or disabilities except his blindness. He reported having some arthritis, but did not believe it limited his activities.

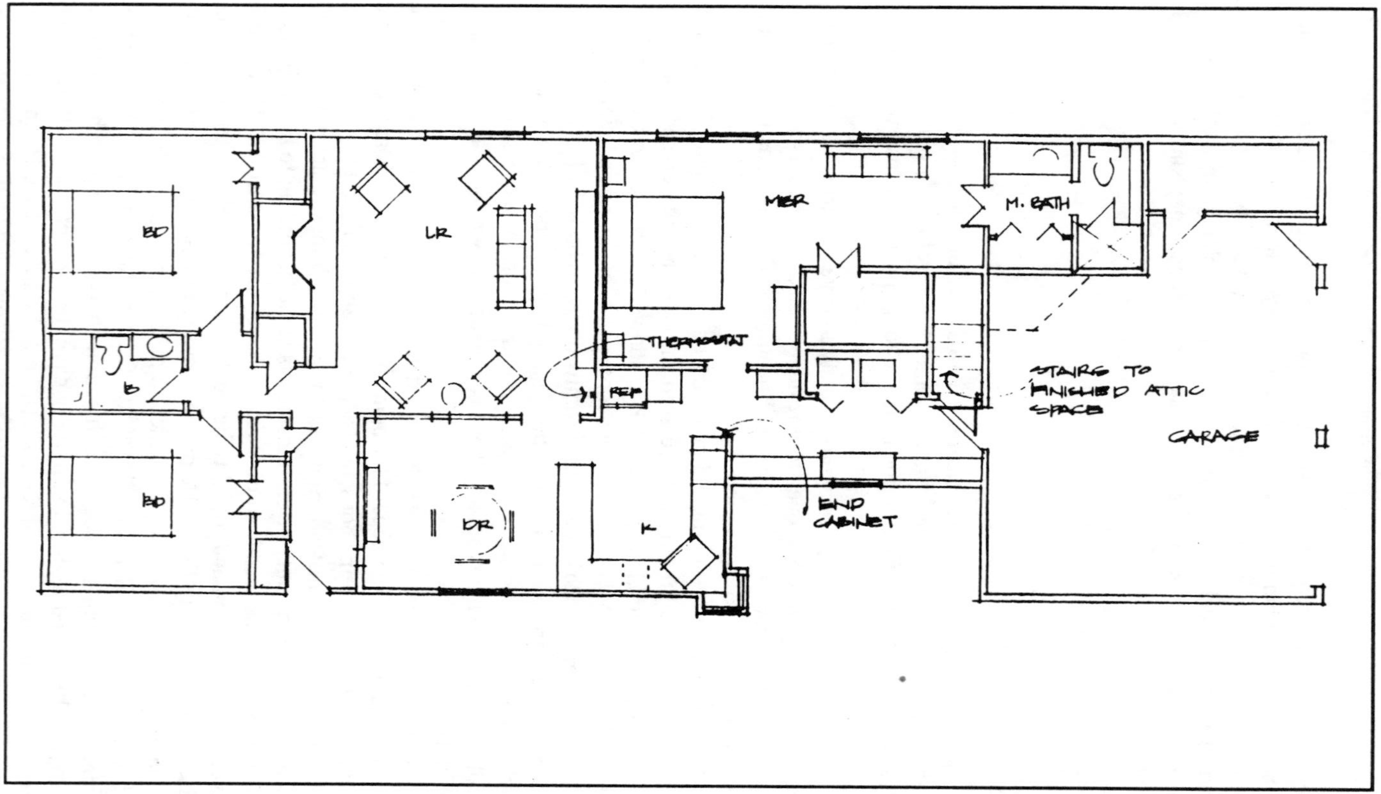

Figure 5. Existing floor plan of Mr. T's residence.

130

On a self-report questionnaire of abilities, Mr. T reported that he had "no difficulty" cleaning house, bathing, showering, washing his face and hands, using the toilet, using the telephone, dressing or undressing, getting into and out of his home, and getting into and out of bed. He reported that he had "moderate difficulty" adjusting the thermostat and answering the door, and that he "could not" switch the lights on and off, wash and dry clothes, or prepare meals.

Performance

There were a number of inconsistencies between self-reported and observational data on Mr. T's abilities. He reported no difficulty with cleaning the house, using the telephone, dressing and undressing, and getting in and out of the home. However, when asked to demonstrate these activities, Mr. T was either partially or totally dependent on his wife. Mr. T was able to complete only half of the activities included in the protocol. He demonstrated the ability to independently complete six activities without difficulty and he was able to complete five additional tasks with considerable difficulty. He did not or could not complete the remaining activities. It is likely that some of these activities were ones that he did not undertake prior to his vision loss (see Table 3).

Mr. T's housing needs were complicated by the "excess disability" he experienced as a result of his lack of rehabilitation training and the extent to which he appeared satisfied with his dependency on his wife. With regard to those activities he attempted, his problems were related to: moving around the house and yard, regulating the temperature in the home, opening and closing windows, and using the telephone.

1. *Moving around the house and yard* (Photos 1 and 2). Although Mr. T ultimately reached his intended destinations, his gait was consistently awkward and slow. He did not seem to have a problem with general direction of travel, but estimating distance or location was quite difficult. He used his hands and arms to

Table 3. Observed Performance of Mr. T

Completed without Difficulty	Completed with Difficulty	Did Not Attempt/ Could Not Complete
Wash dishes manually	Move around the house	Mow the lawn
Shave	(e.g., answer door and	Prepare lunch
Eat lunch	mail letter)	Set the table
Get in/out of shower/bath	Regulate the temperature	Wash dishes (dishwasher)
Use toilet	Open/close windows	Sweep the floor
Get in/out of bed	Use the telephone	Put away groceries
Get a sweater		Wash/dry clothes
		Brush teeth
		Take medication

Photo 1.
There are no clear, straight
pathways in many of the rooms.

Photo 2.
Long, curved driveway
leading to mailbox.

grope for furniture and walls and he did not appear to readily recall the route from one place to another. He often did not know where to expect or how to avoid furniture, walls, or doors. He frequently walked into walls, hit his head, stumbled over furniture, and nearly fell down the stairs. In the finished attic he bumped into the low-sloped ceiling as well as the furniture, and he questioned his wife as to how the furniture got there. When attempting to answer the doorbell, Mr. T had extreme difficulty negotiating his way to the door (e.g., he bumped into the wall and he tripped over several pieces of furniture). When walking down his fairly long, curved driveway to mail a letter, Mr. T's movements were awkward, slow, and unsafe. Despite his use of a walking stick to try to follow the edge of the driveway, he stepped into the flower beds and almost fell several times. Upon returning to the house, Mr. T would have walked into the brick garage wall had one of the researchers present not intervened. At the end of the activity protocol, Mr. T wiped his brow and stated that if he were ever to build a house, he would be sure it had round corners so that he would not hurt himself.

2. *Regulating temperature* (Photo 3). Although Mr. T did not experience difficulty in adjusting the thermostat, he had extreme difficulty in locating the thermostat on the wall. He groped around the wall for several minutes before locating the thermostat. He was able to adjust the temperature because he knew the direction in which the dial should be turned.

Photo 3.
Mr. T trying to locate the thermostat.

3. *Opening and closing windows.* All but one window in Mr. T's house had been nailed shut and had not been operable for several years. One window in the finished attic, a place that Mr. T had not been in since losing his sight, remained operable. He was unable to locate this window on the wall without a great deal of searching. When he located the window, it took additional searching to find the crank handle for the casement window.

4. *Using the telephone.* Mr. T reported being unable to locate the correct numbers on the keypad. However, he was able to make calls with relative ease to those individuals whose numbers were programmed for speed dialing. In addition, the design of his telephone required that the receiver be placed precisely in the cradle. Mr. T had great difficulty trying to align the receiver to the telephone base in order to hang up the phone.

Modifications

Mr. T had two pervasive problems: navigating safely in his house and yard, and locating objects in space. These two problems affected his ability to complete a number of routine activities such as answering the door, mailing a letter, and regulating the temperature. A number of possible changes (see Figure 6) could be made to Mr. T's home to ameliorate the impact of these problems.

A basic modification strategy could be used to accommodate Mr. T's inability to locate wall-mounted objects. Objects mounted in undifferentiated space, such as the thermostat, could be relocated beside a door frame. Alternatively, a large piece of furniture, such as a bookcase, could be moved closer to the thermostat to help define its location. A similar approach could be used to make controls, such as light switches and outlets, easier for Mr. T to find.

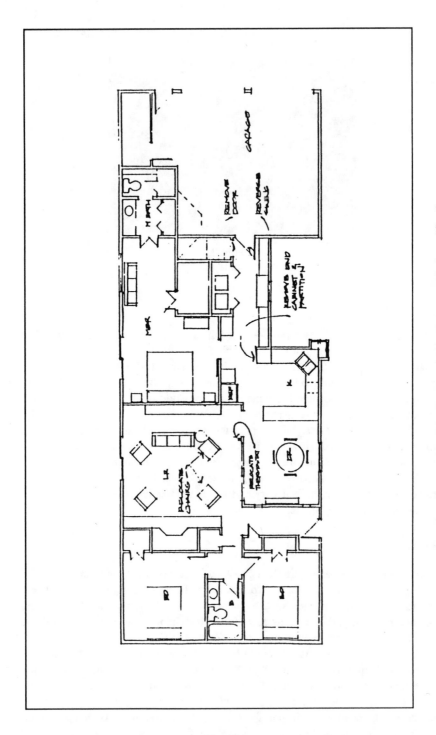

Figure 6. Floor plan of Mr. T's home with recommended modifications.

Several things could be done to help Mr. T to navigate more safely. Inside his home, clear pathways within and through rooms were needed. These pathways could be created and their edges defined by relocating furniture in the living room and by an existing cabinet in the kitchen. He also needed a pathway to the outdoors that would not be obstructed by doors that opened into the path of travel. To address this need, the door to the finished attic space could be removed and the door swing on the garage door reversed.

In the yard, landscaping could be used to define the edges of exterior pathways more clearly. For example, the split-rail fence along the front of his property could be continued up the driveway, or a low hedge could be planted close to the driveway. This approach would be more effective in helping Mr. T stay on the driveway than the edge that currently exists. If the fence were extended, he could use the top rail as a guide in navigating to the mailbox.

If Mr. T were to obtain orientation and mobility training, many of these types of modifications would likely be useful, but not as necessary. Instead, he might benefit from more sophisticated interventions. However, Mr. T has shown little motivation or family support to obtain training.

Mr. P

Background

Mr. P was a sixty-five-year-old former building contractor who lived with his wife in their suburban single-family home. At the age of sixty-two, Mr. P had a stroke that left him wheelchair-bound, hemiplegic, and suffering from severe depression. Following the stroke, Mrs. P was forced to go to work for financial reasons. As a result, Mr. P spent his days alone in the house.

Mr. P built his own home and had lived there for twelve years. The residence was a 2,100 square-foot, one-story ranch house with four bedrooms and three baths (see Figure 7). Several modifications had been made to the house and the yard. In the backyard, ramps had been added to provide access to the driveway, sidewalk, and back door. Modifications also had been made to one bathroom. The doorway had been widened to four feet, but the size and layout of the room (5 feet × 8 feet) did not permit Mr. P to position the wheelchair parallel to the toilet or tub for a side transfer. A raised seat with integral grab bars had been added to the toilet, and a seat and grab bars had been added to the bathtub.

Despite his hemiplegia, Mr. P used a manual wheelchair to get around his house. He moved and guided the chair by pushing one wheel and pulling with one foot. Mr. P's functional capabilities had declined following his recovery from the stroke. His wife attributed this decline to the effect of his mental state on his physical functioning. He had lost strength and the ability to complete activities that he could complete shortly after the stroke. He could only use the toilet when his wife helped him transfer. In addition, because of his weight and the limited

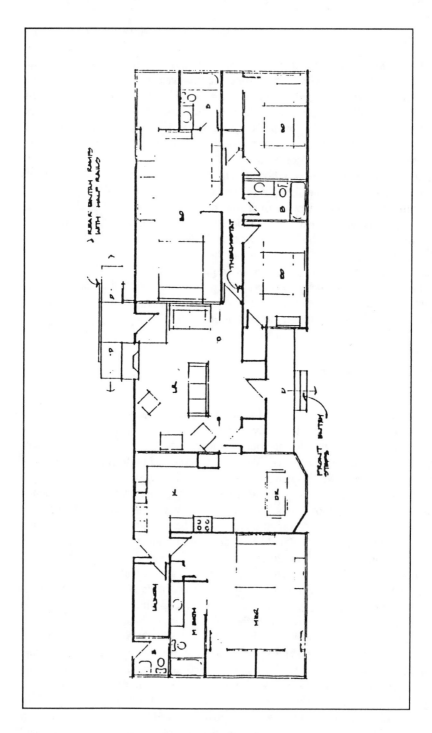

Figure 7. Existing floor plan of Mr. P's residence.

space between the toilet and tub, his wife was unable to transfer him to the tub seat. He could only tub bathe when his son was there to transfer him. Minor adaptive devices have helped Mr. P function. They included a jar opener, reach extender, specialized cutting board, portable urinal, and portable phone.

On a self-report questionnaire of functional abilities, Mr. P reported that he was able to clean house, adjust the thermostat, wash and dry clothes, use the toilet, dress and undress, and get in and out of the home. He reported "extreme difficulty" in preparing meals and bathing/showering; "moderate difficulty" in getting in and out of bed; "little difficulty" in washing his face and hands; and "no difficulty" switching lights on and off, answering the door, and using the telephone.

Performance

There were only two discrepancies between self-reported and observational data on Mr. P's functional abilities. Despite reporting that he could not clean his house, he was able to sweep the floor, although he was not able to pick up the dirt. In addition, he reported that he could bathe with difficulty. During the videotaping, Mr. P was not able to transfer into the tub. Overall, Mr. P completed less than half of the activities included in the protocol. He demonstrated the ability to independently complete five activities without difficulty, and an additional five activities with considerable difficulty. He could not toilet or bathe without personal assistance in transferring. He did not attempt to complete any of the remaining activities (see Table 4).

Mr. P's functional abilities were complicated by the effect of his depression on his motivation to be more independent. As his functional abilities declined, his housing needs increased. For those activities that Mr. P attempted, his

Table 4. Observed Performance of Mr. P

Completed without Difficulty	Completed with Difficulty	Did Not Attempt/ Could Not Complete
Answer the door	Without Assistance	Move around parts of the
Use the telephone	Open/close blinds	house (impacts regulating
Prepare lunch (warm a roll)	Set the table	temperature)
Eat lunch	Sweep the floor	Open/close windows
Brush teeth	Shave	Mow the lawn
	Get in/out of bed	Prepare lunch (open a can)
		Wash dishes
	With Assistance	Put away groceries
	Get in/out of shower/bath	Wash/dry clothes
	Use toilet	Get a sweater
		Take medication

functional problems were related to: moving around the house, opening and closing windows, using the toilet, shaving, and getting in and out of the shower/bath.

1. *Moving around the house and yard* (Photos 4 and 5). Mr. P was able to move through part of his house and negotiate around obstacles without difficulty. However, half of the house was not accessible due to a narrow doorway in the hall that prevented his wheelchair from passing through. As the thermostat was located in the section of the house that Mr. P could not access, he could not regulate the temperature in the house. The front entry to the house was located at the top of a flight of stairs and was not wheelchair-accessible.

Ramps had been added at each of the two rear entrances. However, one ramp was steep, was covered with artificial grass which was slippery when it got wet, had no curb, and had a side rail that did not extend to the bottom of the ramp. When Mr. P went down the ramp, a rear wheel of his wheelchair slipped off the side of the ramp where there was no railing. In addition, he could not ascend the ramp without assistance. Finally, he had difficulty maneuvering the wheelchair in the one bathroom that was accessible to him.

2. *Opening and closing windows.* Mr. P was unable to open and close windows. The location of furniture prevented him from reaching the windows, and he also lacked the strength to open them with only one arm.

3. *Using the toilet* (Photo 6). The layout of the bathroom to which Mr. P had access required him to perform a front transfer to the toilet. Although a raised toilet seat with integral grab bars had been added, Mr. P lacked the strength and balance to complete a front transfer by himself.

Photo 4.
A narrow doorway
prohibited Mr. P from
getting to the thermostat.

Photo 5.
The ramp was too steep
for Mr. P. The discontinuous
rail was hazardous.

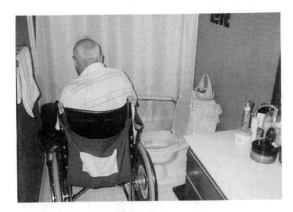

Photo 6.
The bathroom was too narrow for a
typical front or side transfer.

4. *Getting in/out of the bath.* Although Mr. P had added a tub seat to aid in transferring to and from the bathtub, the location of the toilet obstructed wheelchair access to the tub. As a result, Mr. P required assistance to get in and out of the bathtub. Despite reporting that he needed assistance from his son to transfer into the tub, during the simulation his wife helped him to transfer from the toilet to a seat in the tub where he was able to simulate bathing with a hand held shower. Mrs. P reported that the space between the toilet and bathtub was too large. She worried that Mr. P would fall between the two fixtures while transferring.

5. *Shaving.* Mr. P had great difficulty shaving as he could only view the left side of his face in the bathroom mirror. This limitation was the result of the bathroom being too small to maneuver the wheelchair.

Home Modifications

Mr. P experienced a variety of functional difficulties and was activity-dependent on his wife in a number of areas. The degree of difficulty and dependence he experienced was exacerbated by the spatial characteristics of his house. Although it is clear that Mr. P had serious functional problems, it is likely that the extent of these problems would be reduced by a number of design modifications (see Figure 8). Additionally, modifications would make it easier for his wife to assist him without risking injury to herself.

The two most prevalent functional problems experienced by Mr. P involved activities that required maneuvering and repositioning. Maneuvering affected his ability to move around parts of his house, get up and down ramps, and shave. Problems with repositioning were most evident in bathing and toileting

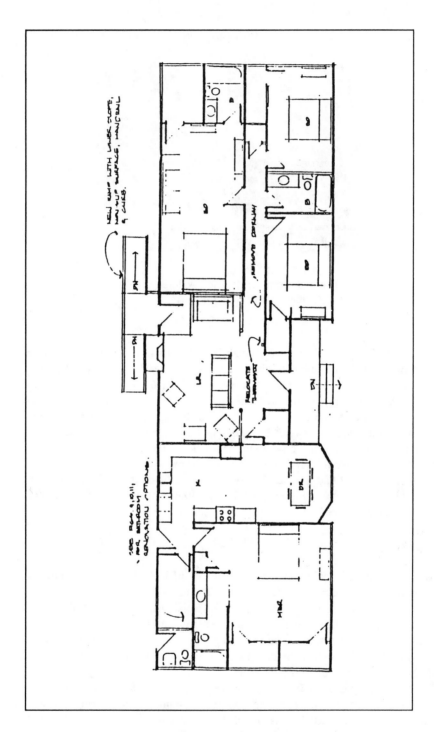

Figure 8. Floor plan of Mr. P's residence with recommended modifications.

activities. These difficulties were compounded by maneuvering problems in the bathroom.

Mr. P had widened the doorway to the bathroom to provide wheelchair access, and added grab bars and a raised toilet seat. These modifications had done little to improve his ability to function independently or without difficulty in the bathroom. The small size and layout of the room were the underlying design problems that impacted Mr. P's maneuvering and transferring. Mr. P needed a larger bathroom, laid out to be more responsive to his functional abilities and disabilities.

Several possible bathroom modifications are shown in Figures 9-11. Figure 9 shows a bathroom modification that could be accommodated in the space of the existing bathroom. In this alternative the tub would be replaced with a roll-in shower, Linido™ grab bars added at the toilet, and knee space provided at the lavatory. Figure 10 shows a modification that utilizes the existing bathroom space as well as part of the existing laundry room. This plan would provide the same accessible features as those included in Figure 9, but in a larger, easier-to-maneuver space. The modification shown in Figure 11 includes a conventional tub as well as a roll-in shower in a master bath that is approximately twice as large as the existing master bath. This plan utilizes most of the existing laundry room space as well as an existing bathroom for the outdoor pool.

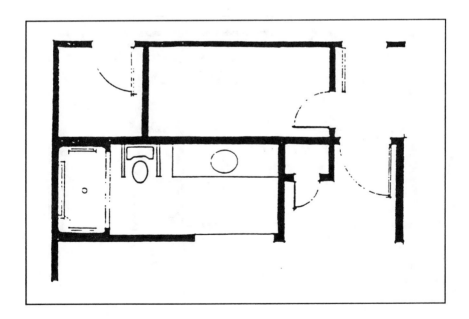

Figure 9. Modifications within the existing bathroom.

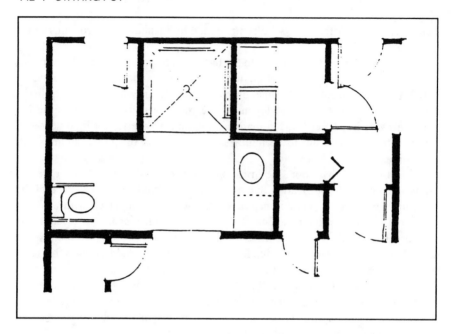

Figure 10. Using part of the laundry room to enlarge the bathroom.

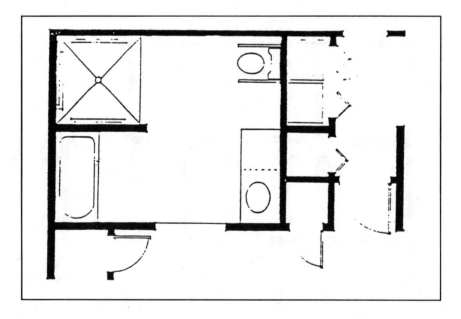

Figure 11. A spacious master bath with tub and roll-in shower.

Mr. P's ability to use only one hand and one foot to propel and guide his manual wheelchair made it difficult for him to maneuver safely on a ramp. Several modifications would improve Mr. P's ability to use his existing ramp. A railing or curb should be installed the full length of the open side of the ramp to ensure that the wheels of the chair do not slip off when he is descending the ramp. Mr. P's ramp was built of treated wood that becomes slippery when wet. It is likely that the artificial grass was installed on the ramp in an effort to reduce its slipperiness. However, this material has few slip-resistant qualities whether wet or dry. The artificial grass should be removed and a new slip-resistant surface, such as deck paint or self-adhesive safety strips, added. Alternatively, a new ramp that incorporates the previous features as well as a shallower slope would likely be easier for Mr. P to use.

Mr. P's problems with depression clearly affected his motivation to function independently. However, the modifications described above should enable Mrs. P to assist Mr. P with less difficulty, as well as help make Mr. P more independent.

CONCLUSIONS

The case study data illustrate that it is beneficial to diagnose an individual's housing needs as a basis for identifying the most appropriate home modifications. It is not hard to imagine how little the commonly used home modifications (grab bars and ramps) would help Mr. T. In fact, Mr. P had these modifications and they did little to improve his ability to function either by himself or with assistance. However, decisions about home modifications cannot be made solely on the basis of need.

In practice, several factors will likely affect whether older people will undertake home modifications. First, there may or may not be a perceived need for a change or awareness of alternatives. For example, individuals who have been using the side of the lavatory to assist in transferring to the toilet may view this arrangement as adequate or may not be aware that a variety of commercially available grab bars would likely work better. Second, some modifications are more expensive than others, and the initial cost may not be affordable to individuals. Third, modifications may have a real or perceived "useful life." Individuals with progressive disabilities or those who are likely to relocate to an assisted living or long-term care setting in the foreseeable future may not judge the useful life of a modification to make it worthwhile. Fourth, there may be a concern that the costs of modifications, particularly a major home modification such as adding a bathroom, will not be realized in the market value or marketability of a house. Fifth, individuals may want to avoid the disruption and "mess" that is inevitable with a renovation project.

An important aspect of the dissemination mission of the Center for Accessible Housing at North Carolina State University is to educate housing consumers and housing producers about the inherent merits of *universal design*—designing in a way that makes housing work better for all people of all ages. When universal design is more widely practiced, the need to modify existing housing for older people will be greatly reduced. However, we are a long way from that day. In the interim, it is important to recognize that older people with disabling conditions are heterogeneous with regard to their housing needs. Although there are fairly predictable, disability-specific needs, individual capabilities and motivations must be considered in planning effective and appropriate home modifications.

ACKNOWLEDGMENTS

The work reported in this chapter was supported by a grant from the National Institute on Disability and Rehabilitation Research, Grant #4133B90003.

The authors gratefully acknowledge the contributions of staff at the Rehab R&D Center on Aging, Atlanta Veterans Affairs Medical Center for their assistance in collecting the functional capabilities data reported in this chapter; Richard G. Long, Eliece Gifford, Connie Archea, Beth Sharon, and Gale Watson. Chris Butler completed the site inspections and prepared the architectural drawings used in this chapter.

REFERENCES

1. W. C. Mann, D. Huerren, M. Tomita, M. Bengali, and E. Steinfeld, Environmental Problems in Homes of Elders with Disabilities, *Occupational Therapy Journal of Research, 14*:3, pp. 191-211, 1994.
2. M. P. Lawton, *Environment and Aging* (2nd Edition, reprint), Center for the Study of Aging, Albany, New York, 1986.
3. P. H. Mutschler and J. R. Miller, *Staying Put: Adapting to Frailty in Owner Occupied Housing,* paper presented at the annual meeting of the Gerontological Society of America, Minneapolis, Minnesota, 1989.
4. M. P. LaPlante, G. E. Hendershot, and A. J. Moss, Assistive Technology Devices and Home Accessibility Features: Prevalence, Payments, Needs, and Trends, in National Center for Health Statistics, *Advance Data, 217*, pp. 1-12, 1992.
5. American Association of Retired Persons, *Understanding Senior Housing for the 1990's*, #PF4522 (593) D 13899, Washington, D.C., 1993.
6. *Handbook for Design: Specially Adapted Housing*, VA Pamphlet 26-13, Department of Veterans Benefits, U.S. Veterans Administration, Washington, D.C., 1978.
7. *Building Design Requirements for the Physically Handicapped* (Rev. Edition), Eastern Paralyzed Veterans Association, Jackson Heights, New York, n.d.
8. Adaptive Environments Center, *A Consumer's Guide to Home Adaptation*, Adaptive Environments Center, Boston, 1989.
9. R. Statham, J. Korczak, and P. Monaghan, *House Adaptations for People with Physical Disabilities: A Guidance Manual for Practitioners*, U.K. Department of the Environment, 1988.
10. A. Sverdlik, Safety for Seniors: Graying Generation Continues to Seek Security at Home, *Atlanta Journal*, pp. C1-C4, June 19, 1990.

11. M. P. Calkins, K. H. Namazi, T. T. Rostner, A. Olson, and B. Brabender, *Home Modifications: Responding to Dementia: A Manual Describing Changes Families Can Make to Homes to Ease the Demands of Caregiving*, Research Center of Corrine Dolan Alzheimer Center, Chardon, Ohio, 1990.

12. R. J. Struyk and J. P. Zais, *Providing Special Dwelling Features for the Elderly with Health and Mobility Problems*, Urban Institute, Washington, D.C., 1982.

13. L. M. Rickman, C. E. Soble, and J. M. Prescop, *A Comprehensive Approach to Retrofitting Homes for a Lifetime*, NAHB Research Center, Upper Marlboro, Maryland, 1991.

14. R. V. Olsen, E. Ehrenkrantz, and B. Hutchings, *Alzheimer's and Related Dementias: Homes that Help*, New Jersey Institute of Technology, Newark, New Jersey, 1993.

15. J. Pynoos and E. Cohen, *The Perfect Fit: Creative Ideas for a Safe and Livable Home*, American Association of Retired Persons, #PF 4912 (992): D14823, Washington, D.C., 1992.

16. R. V. Olsen, E. Ehrenkrantz, and B. Hutchings, Creating Supportive Environments for People with Dementia and Their Caregivers through Home Modifications, *Technology and Disability, 2*:4, pp. 47-57, 1993.

17. J. Sanford, B. R. Connell, and R. G. Long, Housing Design and Disability: The Relationships between Typical Design Features and Performance of Routine Activities, in *Healthy Environments*, J. U. Soria (ed.), Environmental Design Research Association, Washington, D.C., pp. 189-199, 1991.

18. W. B. Applegate, J. P. Blass, and T. F. Williams, Instruments for the Functional Assessment of Older Patients, *New England Journal of Medicine, 322*:17, pp. 1207-1214, 1990.

19. L. G. Branch and A. R. Meyers, Assessing Physical Function in the Elderly, *Clinics in Geriatric Medicine, 3*:1, pp. 29-51, 1987.

20. M. D. Brown, Functional Assessment of the Elderly, *Journal of Gerontological Nursing, 14*:5, pp. 13-17, 1988.

21. G. G. Fillenbaum, Screening the Elderly: A Brief Instrumental Activities of Daily Living Measure, *Journal of the American Geriatrics Society, 33*:10, pp. 698-706, 1985.

22. C. F. Granger, Goals of Rehabilitation of the Disabled Elderly: A Conceptual Approach, in *Aging and Rehabilitation: Advances in State of the Art*, S. J. Brody and G. E. Ruff (eds.), Springer, New York, 1986.

23. J. M. Guralnik and L. G. Branch, Direct Assessment of ADL in Alzheimer's Disease, *Journal of the American Geriatric Society, 37*:2, pp. 196-197, 1989.

24. J. M. Gulalnik, L. G. Branch, S. R. Cummings, and J. D. Curb, Physical Performance Measures in Aging Research, *Journal of Gerontology, 44*:5, pp. M141-146, 1989.

25. B. J. Gurland and D. E. Wilder, The CARE Interview Revisited: Development of an Efficient, Systematic Clinical Assessment, *Journal of Gerontology, 39*:2, pp. 129-137, 1984.

26. J. M. Heath, Comprehensive Functional Assessment of the Elderly, *Primary Care, 16*:2, pp. 305-327, 1989.

27. E. Helmes, K. G. Csapo, and J. A. Short, Standardization and Validation of the Multidimensional Observational Scale for Elderly Subjects (MOSES), *Journal of Gerontology, 42*:4, pp. 395-405, 1987.

28. J. Kuriansky and B. Gurland, The Performance Test of Activities of Daily Living, *International Journal of Aging and Human Development, 7*:4, pp. 343-351, 1976.

29. M. S. Lachs, A. R. Feinstein, L. M. Cooney, M. A. Drickamer, R. A. Marottoli, F. C. Pannill, and M. E. Tinetti, A Simple Procedure for General Screening for Functional Disability in Elderly Patients, *Annals of Internal Medicine, 112*:9, pp. 699-739, 1990.

30. M. Law and L. Letts, A Critical Review of Scales of Activities of Daily Living, *American Journal of Occupational Therapy, 43*:8, pp. 522-528, 1989.

31. F. I. Mahoney and D. W. Barthel, Functional Evaluation: The Barthel Index, *Maryland State Medical Journal, 14*:2, pp. 61-65, 1965.

32. E. Pfeiffer, T. M. Johnson, and R. C. Chifolo, Functional Assessment of Elderly Subjects in Four Service Settings, *Journal of the American Geriatrics Society, 29*:10, pp. 433-437, 1981.

33. E. M. Pinholt, K. Korenke, J. F. Hanley, M. J. Kussman, P. L. Twyman, and J. L. Carpenter, Functional Assessment of the Elderly: A Comparison of Standard Instruments with Clinical Judgement, *Archives of Internal Medicine, 147*:3, pp. 484-488, 1987.

34. A. R. Potvin, W. W. Tourtelotte, J. S. Dailey, J. W. Albers, J. E. Walker, R. W. Pew, W. G. Henderson, and D. N. Snyder, Simulated Activities of Daily Living Examination, *Archives of Physical Medicine and Rehabilitation, 10*, pp. 476-486, 498, 1972.

35. R. A. Pruchno, M. H. Kleban, and N. L. Resch, Psychometric Assessment of the Multidimensional Scale for Elderly Subjects (MOSES), *Journal of Gerontology, 43*:6, pp. P164-169, 1988.

36. M. E. Tinetti and S. F. Ginter, Identifying Mobility Dysfunctions in Elderly Patients: Standard Neuromuscular Examination or Direct Assessment? *Journal of the American Medical Association, 259*, pp. 1190-1193, 1988.

37. M. E. Tinetti, Performance-Oriented Assessment of Mobility Problems in Elderly Patients, *Journal of the American Geriatrics Society, 34*, pp. 119-126, 1986.

38. M. E. Williams and J. C. Hornberger, A Quantitative Method of Identifying Older Persons at Risk for Increasing Long Term Care Services, *Journal of Chronic Diseases, 37*:9/10, pp. 705-711, 1984.

39. M. E. Williams, N. M. Hadler, and J. A. L. Earp, Manual Ability as a Marker of Dependency in Geriatric Women, *Journal of Chronic Diseases, 35*, pp. 115-122, 1982.

40. M. Feuerstein, E. Steinfeld, J. Sanford, and G. Shiro, Hands On Architecture: A Typology for Designers and Researchers, in *Proceedings of 18th Annual Environmental Design Research Association Conference,* J. Harvey and D. Henning (eds.), pp. 115-120, 1987.

41. R. Weber, S. Czaja, and R. Bishu, Activities of Daily Living of the Elders—A Task Analytic Approach, in *Proceedings of the Human Factors Society 33rd Annual Meeting,* pp. 182-186, 1989.

42. J. Sanford, *Hands On Architecture: Vol. 1, Part Two—Field Research,* final draft report submitted to the Architectural and Transportation Barriers Compliance Board, 1987.

43. E. R. Nieuwenhuijsen, W. D. Frey, and J. E. Crews, *Measuring Small Gains Using the ICIDH Severity of Disability Scale: Assessment Practice among Older People Who are Blind,* unpublished paper, 1990.
44. P. G. Windley, *Autonomy in the Residential Setting: The Role of ADL Dependence and Difficulty,* paper presented at the annual scientific meeting of the Gerontological Society of America, Boston, 1990.

CHAPTER
8

The Effects of Income on
Home Modification:
Can They Afford to Stay Put?

Phyllis H. Mutschler

Scant notice has been taken of how important housing is to elders' ability to stay put. As noted in earlier chapters, the search for ways to help frail elders remain in their homes rather than move to institutions has focused primarily on in-home and community services. The few major housing-related policy initiatives have concentrated on design and construction of (or rent subsidies and other incentives for) multiple-unit senior housing. These policies do not address the needs of the majority of elders who are homeowners, most of whom want to age in place and remain in their communities.[1] As this chapter will document, many of them, due to low income, have difficulty affording the adaptations they need.

There are many reasons why elderly homeowners want to "stay put." Equity in a home is the primary asset of most elders; for many, this illiquid form of wealth provides the assurance of shelter in familiar surroundings, a repository of personal and family history, and a bequest to their heirs. Yet disabling conditions may compromise continued residence, particularly if help is unavailable. With some exceptions [1-15] research and policy analyses of this issue assume that moving to a more sheltered environment or bringing formal or informal caregivers into the

---

[1] Lawton [1] cautions that research findings showing owners' preferences to remain in their homes may be misleading because so few feasible alternatives exist; or as Golant [10] sums it up in the title of his book: *Housing America's Elderly: Many Possibilities, Few Choices.*

existing home are the only options when frailty increases. But another important strategy is modifying the home.

To put this strategy in context, it is necessary to consider the individual decision maker. Rounding out the decision-making discussion begun in Chapters 5 through 7, this chapter presents the findings of an analysis examining whether low incomes keep elderly homeowners with disabling conditions from making such modifications. These data confirm the common-sense expectation that disabled elders who have more money and own their own homes are more likely to have adaptations. They suggest further that poor or marginally poor households face real constraints in making such housing adjustments. This chapter also highlights other characteristics of those most likely to reside in homes containing devices or features to help them perform daily activities.

BACKGROUND

Until recently, little information was available about factors related to the use of home modifications by frail or disabled elders. During the last ten years, however, several studies have begun to address which elders are likely to use adaptations, what structural elements support or serve as barriers to the implementation of modifications, and what relationships exist between modifications and use of other services.

The most important of these are based on the data from the U.S. Department of Health and Human Services National Long Term Care Surveys (NLTCS), three rounds of interviews with a large sample of community-dwelling elders with at least one limitation in activities of daily living (ADL) or instrumental activities of daily living (IADL). According to Manton and his colleagues,

> the NLTCS were designed to measure: a) the 1982, 1984, and 1989 prevalence of chronic disability and institutionalization in the U.S. elderly Medicare-enrolled population; and b) changes (both improvements and decline) in chronic disability (and institutionalization) in individuals [16, p. 168].

Their studies of the three surveys show an encouraging decrease over time in the level of chronic disability, despite an increase in the numbers of older people. They attribute this change to improvements in health care and—pertinent to our analysis—to the use of home modifications and adaptive equipment. Also pertinent is their finding that higher incomes are associated with lower levels of disability [17, p. S163].

The analysis in this chapter uses the 1982 data. Although the Manton et al. findings suggest important changes in some areas of concern from 1982 to 1989, change is not expected in the relationship between income and home modifications, especially since no sufficiently major new home adaptation assistance programs were implemented during the 1980s.

It is also useful to look at other studies that give considerable information regarding home adaptations. For example, Struyk [9, 18-21] described and estimated the scope of dwelling problems for older people; Reschovsky and Newman [2, 22] examined how elders may support continued independence through repairing, maintaining, or altering their current residence or through relocating; and Hereford [23] and Pynoos [24] examined elders' preferences with respect to repairing or modifying their homes. More recently, the American Association of Retired Persons [11], LaPlante et al. [25], and Norburn et al. [26] have added to our knowledge of individual use of home modifications.

Struyk divides dwelling problems into two types [9, 18-21]. *Dwelling-specific* problems are associated with habitability (structural design or maintenance) and housing costs (including rents) that exceed 30 percent of a household's monthly income. *Dwelling-use* problems result from housing features that may threaten the well-being of those with functional limitations, even though they are appropriate for persons without such disabilities. Stairs, for example, or controls on stove units that are difficult to see or reach, pose risks for elders with (respectively) heart conditions or vision problems. Dwelling-specific difficulties may be ameliorated by repairs, reduced overcrowding, or lower housing or maintenance costs (e.g., through subsidies). Dwelling-use problems may be addressed by providing human assistance or through modifying housing design or structure to allow elders to accomplish necessary activities. Some dwellings, of course, may be substandard, overpriced, *and* difficult for someone with functional limitations to use. As noted in Chapter 1 and elsewhere [10, 12, 13], it is often necessary to address dwelling-specific problems before dwelling-use problems can be solved.

Dwelling-specific problems affect substantial numbers of elders. Estimates range from 6 percent to over 8 percent, or from 1.1 to over 1.5 million [20, 27]. Among elderly homeowners, 180,000 had multiple housing problems, such as paying more than 30 percent of household income to occupy dwellings that were also physically inadequate [20]. These problems, as expected, are more prevalent among poorer individuals, members of minority groups, women, and residents of rural areas.[2] Struyk estimates that 64 percent of elder-headed households below the poverty line have at least one dwelling-specific problem [9].

Exactly how many elders are affected by dwelling-use problems is unknown,[3] but Struyk calculates that, of 8.6 million households in which at least one person had health problems or activities limitations, only 10 percent had any dwelling

---

[2] As noted in [7], about half of elders with very high levels of impairment and living alone lacked any type of supportive environmental elements.

[3] Struyk estimated that 12 percent of persons age sixty-five and older or about 3.5 million people—7 percent of those under seventy-four and 21 percent of those seventy-five and over—need supportive services in their homes, and 750,000 households require formal support service provision [9].

modification in 1979. He estimates that one million units occupied by elder-headed households need to be modified to address functional limitations [9]. Our own analysis of the 1982 NLTCS found that less than 5 percent of the elderly respondents (all of whom had at least 1 ADL or IADL limitation) lived in special housing units for elderly or handicapped and only 25 percent of the remainder resided in housing that had been modified by adding ramps, elevators, grab bars, or railings [28].

With respect to elders' behavior concerning their housing, Reschovsky and Newman found repair or maintenance activities quite common among older homeowners and renters and among those both with and without functional impairments [2, 22]. The elderly are no less likely than younger householders to make repairs or perform upkeep chores, especially on critical systems, although elders undertake fewer jobs and spend fewer dollars on them [22]. Findings of particular interest with respect to this chapter are that:

- "Frail non-repairers" were poorer than those who performed repairs.
- "Income has sizable effects on the quality of home upkeep conducted" [16, p. S228][4]
- Ten percent of frail elders, compared to only 1 percent of those who were not frail, had altered the size, layout, or features of their housing units.

In market surveys conducted at the beginning of the Supportive Services Program for Older Persons,[5] many elders ranked home repair services first among a list of possible services [23]. In fact, 45 percent of elders across eight demonstration sites said they would purchase home handyman services if given the opportunity; more than one-third said they would pay for yard and chore services. Surprisingly, even elders with very low incomes indicated their willingness to pay for these home maintenance services, and a disproportionate number did in fact purchase services.

Similarly, in another study, older focus group members—regardless of income level—indicated that they would undertake and pay for repairs or modifications to their homes [24]. AARP has found that 53 percent of older Americans had performed at least one home modification (using a broad definition, including behavioral strategies as well as physical modifications) [11]. La Plante et al. found that less than one-fourth of those with home accessibility features benefited from third-party payments for those features [25]. The rest paid for them themselves or with their families' help.

---

[4] Struyk and Devine also found income a key influence on the likelihood of elders' making repairs [19].

[5] The goal of this Robert Wood Johnson Foundation national demonstration program (see Chapter 10) was to promote the expansion of "consumer-driven" nontraditional health and health-related services to the elderly.

Finally, analyzing data from the first wave (1990-91) of the National Survey of Self-Care and Aging, Norburn et al. found that

> the most frequent type of self-care practice (75.4%) involves modification in patterns of behavior [such as] doing things less often and more slowly, avoiding lifting heavy objects, and stocking up when going to the store. Less than half use various forms of equipment or adaptive devices in dealing with these limitations. About one-third make adaptations in their living environments [26, p. S105].

Norburn et al. did not find a consistent relationship between income and self-care (including modifications).

In summary, the research to date suggests that modifications make a difference, that the need for both modifications and repair is significant, that older people do undertake (and are willing to pay for) repairing, maintaining, and modifying their homes, and that the association between income and modifications is variable.

WHO MAKES MODIFICATIONS?
FINDINGS OF THE NLTCS

Much of the rest of this chapter focuses on the association between income, homeowner status, and selected other factors and the use of home modifications as reflected in the first NLTCS. The data set contains information about housing, income, housing modifications, functional limitations, chronic conditions, living arrangements, and other characteristics of about 6,300 frail elders living in the community. Although the modification survey items are far from exhaustive—they focus on mobility-oriented modifications such as grab bars, ramps, wide doors, push bars, and raised toilets—they do permit an analysis of the relationship between the presence of home modifications and other respondent characteristics.

The first comparison to be discussed is that between homeowners and renters. Frail elderly renters differ from homeowners in numbers (less than one-fourth of respondents were renters), circumstances, and characteristics. Although levels of functional impairment are comparable—about one in five elders in both groups are severely disabled—homeowners have higher household incomes as well as having the asset of home equity, and are less likely to live alone. For the following reasons, they also have more incentive to modify their homes:

- Homeowners are freer to make modifications at will. Although the Fair Housing Act requires landlords to allow tenants to make accessibility modifications at their own expense, it also allows landlords to require the tenant to restore the unit to its original condition before moving. The option is practical, moreover, only if the law is known and enforced.
- Homeowners, unlike tenants, may realize a return on an investment in modifications.
- Homeowners are less likely than renters to move.

As we see in Table 1, renters tend to be older, less educated, poorer, and more likely to be single and female than homeowners. What is perhaps surprising is that renters have more modifications in their homes than homeowners at lower levels of disability (see Figure 1).

Even more surprising is the high percentage (42%) of renters with impairments in one or two key activities of daily living (ADLs) who have modifications in their units, compared to only 30 percent of similarly impaired older homeowners. However, as levels of disability rise, homeowners have more modifications than renters. Similarly, in the presence of a disease or condition (Table 2), homeowners are much more likely to have adaptations than renters. This suggests that many older renters live in housing designed specifically for seniors, especially in low- and moderate-income, government subsidized housing, which often includes grab bars and other adaptive devices in all or most units, regardless of the needs of the particular tenant.

Homeowners at the highest levels of disability are more likely to have modifications than those at lower levels—just under half at the highest levels, compared to one in six at the lower. These relationships between mobility problems and modifications are not observed among renters, again suggesting that many renters live in buildings designed to be more accessible.

Table 1. Characteristics of Homeowners and Renters

	Homeowners (n = 3556)	Renters (n = 1425)
Mean Age	76	77
Mean Education (yrs.)**	10	9
Mean Income****	$10,320	$6,739
Mean Value of Home	$34,000	—
Males****	39%	27%
Race****		
White	85%	80%
Black	11%	15%
Hispanic	2%	4%
Marital Status****		
Currently married	50%	29%
Previously married	46%	63%
Never married	4%	8%

*$p < .05$
**$p < .01$
***$p < .001$
****$p < .0001$
Source: Author's tabulation of the National Long Term Care Survey, 1982.

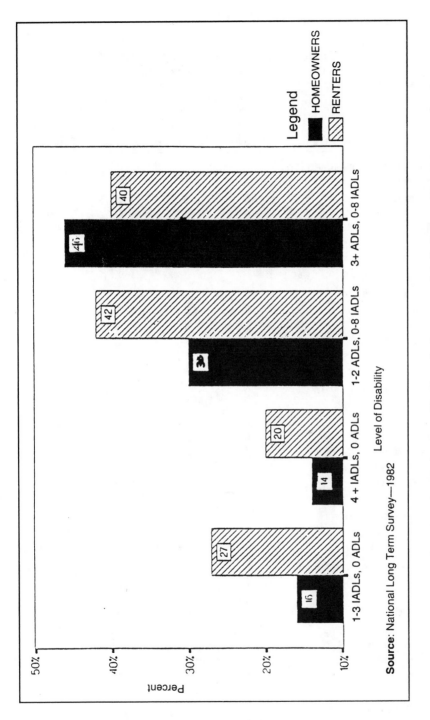

Source: National Long Term Survey—1982

Figure 1. Frail elders whose homes have modifications that accommodate limitations: homeowners and renters.

Table 2. Elders With or Without Certain Chronic Conditions Whose Homes Have Modifications (Percent)

Condition/Modification	Homeowners		Renters	
	With Condition	Without Condition	With Condition	Without Condition
Amputated Leg or Broken Hip				
Grab bars	25	20	29	27
Ramps	15	3****	5	5
Wide doors	6	2***	6	9
Push bars	—	—	3	3
Raised toilet	15	5****	6	12*
Asthma or Bronchitis				
Grab bars	16	21**	28	26
Ramps	2	3	5	3
Wide doors	3	3	9	9
Push bars	—	—	3	2
Raised toilet	6	4	7	5
Arteriosclerosis or Circulatory Problems				
Grab bars	21	19	29	23*
Ramps	4	2**	5	5
Wide doors	3	2	8	10
Push bars	—	—	3	3
Raised toilet	6	5	7	6
Arthritis, Rheumatism, Stiffness				
Grab bars	22	14****	28	22
Ramps	4	2*	5	5
Wide doors	3	2	9	8
Push bars	—	—	3	3
Raised toilet	6	4*	7	6
CP, MS, Parkinson's				
Grab bars	30	20**	29	27
Ramps	3	3	2	5
Wide doors	5	2	7	9
Push bars	—	0	3	5
Raised toilet	8	5	4	7

Table 2. (Cont'd.)

Condition/Modification	Homeowners		Renters	
	With Condition	Without Condition	With Condition	Without Condition
Vision Problems				
Grab bars	20	20	27	26
Ramps	4	3	5	4
Wide doors	3	2	10	9
Push bars	—	—	3	3
Raised toilet	5	6	8	6
Stroke				
Grab bars	24	20	34	26
Ramps	7	3*	9	5
Wide doors	3	2	9	9
Push bars	0	—	3	3
Raised toilet	7	5	8	7
Emphysema				
Grab bars	16	21*	30	26
Ramps	3	3	6	5
Wide doors	4	2	11	3
Push bars	0	—	5	3
Raised toilet	6	4	6	7

*$p < .05$
**$p < .01$
***$p < .001$
****$p < .0001$
Source: National Long Term Care Survey—1982.

However, at first glance, neither income nor renter status appears to be a major determinant of adaptation use. Indeed, a previous study suggested that economic factors do not significantly influence the likelihood of making dwelling modifications (although analyzing economic factors was not the primary purpose of this study) [21]. In addition, several studies reported earlier found that many elders want home repairs or modifications even when incomes are limited. Despite these indications, however, it seems likely that poverty often will prove an insurmountable barrier to obtaining the home modifications needed. Other research would seem to support this assumption [2, 6, 16, 17, 22, 24, 28, 29]. To explore it further, the analysis that follows assesses specifically whether poor elderly homeowners are significantly disadvantaged in adapting their environments to help them cope with limitations. As already described, lower income elders are far less likely to be homeowners; more than eight out of ten elders with incomes exceeding 200 percent of the poverty level are homeowners compared with just over half of those who are poor. This pattern is true for all four disability groups, although the most severely impaired who are poor are slightly less likely to own their own homes (see Figure 2).

When poor elders do own homes, however, does having that asset improve their ability to make needed modifications? As we see from Table 3, poorer older homeowners' homes are worth less than the homes of those with higher incomes.

No poor elders own homes valued at $150,000 or more, and only 5 percent own homes valued at $75,000 or more. (These figures are in 1982 real dollars.) Nearly half of poor elders own homes worth $20,000 or less, while only 10 percent of those with higher incomes have homes with such low values. Housing values can affect elders' willingness or capacity to make home modifications in two ways. First, because a home with lower market value represents less collateral, lenders may charge higher interest rates or make less money available for home equity loans. Poorer individuals are also less likely to have good credit ratings and more likely to live in areas affected by discriminatory banking practices. Thus, since the poor own homes worth far less than those with incomes above the poverty line, poor homeowners have neither income nor home equity readily available for home modifications. Second, elders may view homes with lower market values as less attractive investments and believe that they will not be able to recover the investment in modifications if and when they move.

It therefore comes as no surprise that poor elderly homeowners are far less likely to have home modifications that with those with incomes over the poverty line. This contrast is especially dramatic among those with severe impairments. As can be seen in Figure 3, only 29 percent of the poor with high levels of limitations have any modifications, while nearly 50 percent of those with higher incomes and high levels of limitation reside in homes that have been modified.

Although not shown in the figure, this finding holds true for particular chronic conditions as well. For example, among arthritis sufferers, 19 percent of the poor versus 32 percent of those with incomes greater than $20,000 have modifications.

Table 4 displays the actual differences in household incomes between those who have modifications and those who do not. The table presents these figures for elders in different household types and varying levels of functional impairment to control for the effect of household size on income. In all but three cases, those with modifications have higher household incomes than those whose homes are not modified. Among the severely impaired, except for married couples who live by

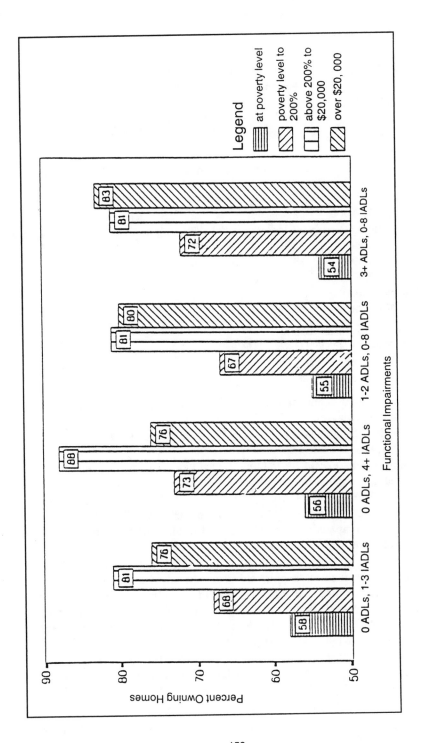

Figure 2. Functional impairment, income status, and home ownership among frail elders.

159

Table 3. 1982 Housing Values for Elders of Differing
Household Income Levels[a]

	Total	Poor	Poverty to 200% Poverty	200% Poverty to $20,000	$20,000 or more
Numbers (in 000s)	3011	578	1074	567	792
Home value:	(%)	(%)	(%)	(%)	(%)
Less than $20,000	22	48	22	12	11
$20,000-34,999	23	27	28	21	13
$35,000-49,999	22	14	24	28	18
$50,000-74,999	18	6	18	22	23
$75,000-99,999	7	3	4	8	14
$100,000-149,999	5	2	2	6	12
$150,000-or more	3	0	1	3	8

$\chi^2 = 666.9^7$, $df = 18$, $p = .000$
[a]Percentages may not add to 100 due to rounding.

themselves, $2,000 in annual income separates those who don't have modifications from those who do.[6]

As expected, those owning homes with higher market values are more likely to have modifications (Table 5).

Not surprisingly, except for mildly disabled elders, more than twice as many elders residing in homes worth at least $150,000 have modifications as those in homes worth $20,000 or less. Among the severely disabled, where the need would be greatest, less than one in three elders with homes worth $20,000 or less have modifications, compared with more than two in three whose homes are worth $150,000 or more.

Given these results showing the disadvantages faced by poor elders, particularly those with high levels of impairment, we may ask whether higher levels of informal support compensate for this shortfall in modifications. Do greater numbers of helpers provide additional assistance to elders who do not have home adaptations? As Table 6 shows, however, the answer is "No." Severely disabled elders have higher numbers of helpers than those who are less impaired. But, across the board, those *with* modifications have the same or greater numbers of helpers, on average, than do those whose homes are not modified. Modifications,

---

[6] These figures also reveal the very limited incomes available to those living alone or as two unmarried individuals.

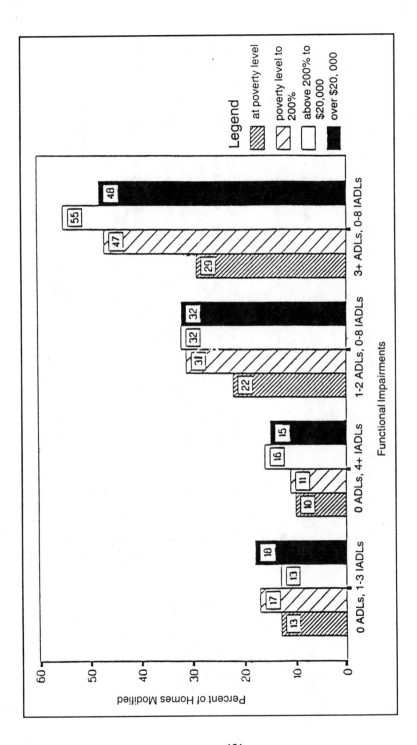

Figure 3. Home modification among elderly with varying levels of functional impairment and income.

Table 4. Mean Household Income of Elderly Homeowners With and Without Home Modifications by Functional Impairment and Household Composition

Level of Functional Impairment	Total		Mild No ADLs 1-3 IADLs		No ADLs 4+ IADLs		1-2 ADLs 0-8 IADLs		Severe 3-4 ADLs 0-8 IADLs	
Modifications?	None	Some	None	Some	None	Some	None	Some	None	Some
Household Composition:										
Lives alone	$ 5,034	$ 7,108	$ 5,118	$ 7,605	$ 4,085	$ 6,567	$ 5,090	$ 7,011	$ 4,510	$ 6,421
Married couple	10,652	11,582	10,906	12,412	10,088	16,049	10,321	11,554	10,861	10,734
Two unmarried individuals	7,965	10,178	7,964	7,756	7,937	11,582	8,331	9,954	7,453	11,689
Couple plus others	13,738	17,550	14,807	21,080	7,652	29,218	12,435	11,403	15,636	19,377
Three or more individuals	17,149	20,407	14,925	20,378	17,220	12,253	19,136	24,722	16,296	18,212
Total	9,648	11,132	9,216	10,323	10,162	14,147	9,705	10,992	10,629	11,558

Note: Main Effects: F = 53.7***, Modifications: F = 19.5***, Functional Impairment: F = 4, Household Composition: F = 101.8***
***p < .001

Table 5. Percentage of Elderly Homeowners with Home Modifications
by Severity of Functional Impairments and 1982 Home Values

Functional Impairment	Total	Mild No ADLs 1-3 IADLs	No ADLs 4+ IADLs	1-2 ADLs 0-8 IADLs	Severe 3+ ADLs 0-8 IADLs
Numbers (000s)	3,560	1,348	261	1249	702
Percentage	100%	38%	7%	35%	20%
Less than $20,000 (n = 686)	20	12	14	22	31
$20,000-34,999 (n = 712)	24	15	11	28	40
$35,000-49,999 (n = 689)	29	18	10	29	54
$50,000-74,999 (n = 570)	28	16	13	31	53
$75,000-99,999 (n = 233)	32	20	16	43	45
$100,000-149,999 (n = 173)	30	15	32	39	42
$150,000 or more (n = 108)	44	19	36	52	69
Total	26	16	14	30	46

rather than substituting for personal care, may be indicators that the disabled person is marshalling all available resources: for example, in Table 6 more modifications are almost always associated with "more helpers."

Moreover, those with incomes exceeding $20,000 have greater numbers of helpers than the poor, or those just above poverty. Thus, poor elders appear to lack both assistance and modifications.

As noted earlier, the Manton et al. studies [16, 17] found a decrease in the level of disability from 1982 to 1989, although "the declines do not wholly compensate for population aging" [17, p. S164]. They also found that "reliance on personal

Table 6. Mean Number of Helpers for Frail Elderly Homeowners Who
Have or Do Not Have Home Modifications by Household Income Status

	Total ($n = 3,054,000$)	1-2 ADLs 0-8 IADLs ($n = 1,098,000$)	3+ ADLs 0-8 IADLs ($n = 655,000$)
Average Number of Helpers	2.1	2.1	2.6
Poor			
No modifications	2.1	2.3	2.5
Some modifications	2.3	2.5	2.4
Above Poverty up to 200% Poverty			
No modifications	1.8	1.8	2.3
Some modifications	2.2	2.0	2.5
200% Poverty to $20,000			
No modifications	1.8	1.9	2.0
Some modifications	2.2	2.1	2.6
Above $20,000			
No modifications	2.2	2.2	2.9
Some modifications	2.4	2.2	2.9
Total			
No modifications	1.9	2.1	2.4
Some modifications	2.3	2.2	2.7

assistance only declined. Dependence on equipment—by itself or in combination with personal assistance—increased" [16, p. 175]. As in our review of the 1982 data, they found that use of modifications among the severely disabled was positively correlated to homeownership and income. They also suggest that higher levels of education (which are also associated with higher income) may influence the use of modifications and assistive devices [16, p. 176].

DISCUSSION

The goal of providing "a decent home and suitable living environment for every American family" became part of the United States Code (Title 42, Subchapter 1 S & 1441) in 1949. Decency and suitability may be elusive for frail elders attempting to stay put, however: insufficient numbers of housing units exist to meet their needs, and programs to help them make housing modifications are inadequately funded and coordinated.

In this analysis we have seen a significant relationship between homeowners with certain chronic conditions and greater functional impairments and the presence of certain home modifications. The more severe the respondents' impairments, the more likely they are to have grab bars, ramps, wide doors, push bars, or raised toilets. Only 16 percent of elderly homeowners with mild limitations, compared to 46 percent of those with severe limitations, live in homes that have been modified. Poor homeowners and those who own less expensive homes, however, regardless of their level of disability, are far less likely than those at higher income levels or with higher-value homes to have modifications. Not surprisingly, these two groups—poor homeowners and those who own less expensive homes—overlap, and face double jeopardy with respect to home modifications: they neither have sufficient income to pay for them, nor sufficient home equity on which to draw.

As noted above, although homeowners who have particular disabling conditions are more likely to have housing modifications, the number with housing modifications is small. To be sure, this survey measured only certain identifiable modifications—primarily grab bars, ramps, wide doors, push bars, and raised toilets. Information is needed about a much wider variety of modifications. As we have seen in other chapters, home modifications may include a wide variety of changes to dwellings—some easily accomplished and inexpensive, others involving major outlays of time, expertise, and money. Currently, however, elders' choices and plans may be constrained by the services or products available through agencies. Even elders who can afford to make more expensive modifications may find it hard to obtain technical information to help them make the most effective changes. Further research is needed, but a system of technical assistance is equally important to enable frail elders to benefit from the information that is already available, and to help them achieve their desire to stay put.

Most elders in the NLTCS own their own homes, and over 90 percent are satisfied with their neighborhoods. Like elders in countless other surveys, they do not wish to move. To the extent that home modifications allow these elders to remain in their homes, they should be worthy components of public policies that aim to deter or prevent premature institutionalization or to provide real independent living choices to elders. Although extensive analysis of longitudinal data is required to establish the impact of home modifications on continued community residence, the study reported here provides initial evidence of the links between disability and housing modifications. Moreover, as Soldo and Longino have discovered, these changes may also provide important benefits in relieving caregiver burdens [7].

The findings of this study also support those of prior research showing that home repairs and alterations are influenced by elders' income and housing values.

Although many modifications are relatively inexpensive, elders who are poor or near-poor cannot afford even moderately expensive changes to help them live safely or function independently. Given the evidence of income barriers to undertaking home modifications presented here, policies offering subsidies or vouchers may prove useful in helping frail elders who are poor or near-poor remain in their homes. The results suggest that further analysis in this area would yield important information about the ways in which housing modifications may be combined with other service strategies to raise the opportunities for all elders to successfully age in place.

ACKNOWLEDGMENTS

Support for the research reported here was generously provided by the Hartford Foundation and the Brookdale Foundation group.

REFERENCES

1. M. P. Lawton, Housing Preferences and Choices: Implications, in *Housing an Aging Society*, R. J. Newcomer, M. P. Lawton, and T. O. Byerts (eds.), Van Nostrand Reinhold, New York, pp. 65-68, 1986.
2. J. D. Reschovsky and S. J. Newman, Adaptations for Independent Living by Older Frail Households, *The Gerontologist, 30*:4, pp. 543-552, 1990.
3. S. J. Newman, Housing and Long Term Care: The Suitability of the Elderly's Housing to the Provision of In-Home Services, *The Gerontologist, 25*:1, pp. 35-40, 1985.
4. S. J. Newman, The Shape of Things to Come, *Generations, 10*:1, pp. 14-17, 1985.
5. S. Newman, The Frail Elderly in the Community: An Overview of Characteristics, in *Aging in Place: Supporting the Frail Elderly in Residential Environments*, D. Tilson (ed.), Scott, Foresman, Glenview, Illinois, pp. 3-24, 1989.
6. J. Pynoos, E. Cohen, L. Davis, and S. Bernhardt, Home Modifications: Improvements that Extend Independence, in *Housing the Aged*, J. Pynoos and V. Regnier (eds.), Elsevier, New York, pp. 277-304, 1987.
7. B. J. Soldo and C. F. Longino, Jr., Social and Physical Environments for the Vulnerable Aged, in *The Social and Built Environment in an Older Society*, Institute of Medicine and the National Research Council, Committee on an Aging Society, National Academy Press, Washington, D.C., pp. 103-133, 1988.
8. B. J. Soldo and H. B. Brotman, Housing Whom? in *Community Choices for Older Americans*, M. P. Lawton and S. L. Hoover (eds.), Springer, New York, pp. 36-55, 1981.
9. R. J. Struyk, Current and Emerging Issues in Housing Environments for the Elderly, in *The Social and Built Environment in an Older Society*, Institute of Medicine and the National Research Council, Committee on an Aging Society, National Academy Press, Washington, D.C., pp. 134-168, 1988.
10. S. M. Golant, *Housing America's Elderly: Many Possibilities, Few Choices*, Sage, Newbury Park, California, 1992.

11. American Association of Retired Persons, *Understanding Senior Housing for the 1990s*, #PF4522 (593) D 13899, Washington, D.C., 1993.

12. P. Porter, Facilitating Aging in Place through Home Repairs, *Long Term Care Advances: Topics in Research, Training, Service & Policy, 6*:2, 1994.

13. J. Pynoos, Toward a National Policy on Home Modification, *Technology and Disability, 2*:4, pp. 1-8, Fall 1993.

14. H. D. Kiewel, Serving Community Needs for Home-Accessibility Modifications, *Technology and Disability, 2*:4, pp. 40-46, Fall 1993.

15. E. Steinfeld and S. Shea, Enabling Home Environments: Identifying Barriers to Independence, *Technology and Disability, 2*:4, pp. 69-79, Fall 1993.

16. K. G. Manton, L. Corder, and E. Stallard, Changes in the Use of Personal Assistance and Special Equipment from 1982 to 1989: Results from the 1982 and 1989 NLTCS, *The Gerontologist, 33*:2, pp. 168-176, 1993.

17. K. Manton, L. Corder, and E. Stallard, Estimates of Change in Chronic Disability and Institutional Incidence and Prevalence Rates in the U.S. Elderly Population from the 1982, 1984, and 1989 National Long Term Care Survey, *Journal of Gerontology: Social Sciences, 48*:4, pp. S153-166, 1993.

18. R. J. Struyk and H. M. Katsura, *Aging at Home: How the Elderly Adjust Their Housing without Moving*, Haworth Press, New York, 1988.

19. R. J. Struyk and D. Devine, Determinants of Dwelling Maintenance Activity of Elderly Households, in *Community Housing Choices for Older Americans*, M. P. Lawton and S. L. Hoover (eds.), Springer, New York, pp. 221-244, 1987.

20. R. J. Struyk, M. A. Turner and M. Ueno, *Future Housing Policy: Meeting the Demographic Challenge*, Urban Institute, Washington, D.C., 1987.

21. R. J. Struyk, Housing Adaptations: Needs and Practices, in *Housing the Aged*, J. Pynoos and V. Regnier (eds.), Elsevier, New York, pp. 259-270, 1987.

22. J. D. Reschovsky and S. J. Newman, Home Upkeep and Housing Quality of Older Homeowners, *Journal of Gerontology, 46*:5, pp. S288-S297, 1991.

23. R. Hereford, The Market for Community Services for Older People, *Pride Institute Journal, 8*:1, pp. 44-51, 1989.

24. J. Pynoos, Strategies for Home Modifications and Repair, *Generations, 16*:2, pp. 21-26, 1992.

25. M. P. La Plante, G. E. Hendershot, and A. J. Moss, Assistive Technology Devices and Home Accessibility Features: Prevalence, Payment, Need, and Trends, in National Center for Health Statistics *Advance Data, 217*, pp. 1-12, 1992.

26. J. E. K. Norburn, S. Bernard, T. Konrad, A. Woomert, G. H. DeFriese, W. D. Kalsbeek, G. G. Koch, and M. G. Ory, Self-Care and Assistance from Others in Coping with Functional Limitations among a National Sample of Older Adults, *Journal of Gerontology: Social Sciences, 50B*:2, pp. S101-S109, 1995.

27. M. Mikelsons and M. Turner, *Housing Conditions of the Elderly in the 1980s: A Data Book*, Urban Institute, Washington, D.C., 1991.

28. P. Mutschler and J. Miller, *Staying Put: Adapting to Frailty in Owner-Occupied Housing*, paper presented at annual meeting of the Gerontological Society of America, Boston, 1989.

29. U.S. General Accounting Office, *Elderly Americans: Health, Housing, and Nutrition Gaps between the Poor and Nonpoor*, GAO/PEMD-92-29, Washington, D.C., 1992.

PART III

IMPLEMENTING HOUSING ADAPTATION PROGRAMS

Introduction

The first two parts of this book describe the characteristics of home adaptations, the characteristics of the groups and individuals who use them, and the relationship between adaptation and user. They document that the number of people who require adaptations is growing, and that the fit between adaptation and person is the key to the adaptation's usefulness. This part of the book focuses on those agencies and groups that bring adaptation and user together to make home adaptation possible. Over the past ten years, hundreds of non-profit and proprietary groups have developed home adaptation programs of various sorts. Information about some of these programs and projects is presented in this section with the dual purpose of informing other groups that seek to provide similar services and raising related policy issues.

Pynoos, Liebig, Overton, and Calvert present the first thorough overview of the home adaptation industry. Their national survey of approximately 300 agencies providing home adaptation and repair services found that home adaptation is an "add-on" service to the agencies' primary mission. With funding limited and eligibility restricted, the number of people these agencies are able to serve is modest. However, this chapter offers invaluable information on the history of home adaptation services, the general characteristics of programs and clients, a thorough review of funding sources, the types of professionals providing adaptation assessment, coordination with other agencies, training of workers, and the types of services agencies are providing. Particularly valuable is an analysis of service delivery methods, as the advantages and disadvantages of in-house versus contracted staff and the use of volunteers are issues often debated by home adaptation groups.

In Chapter 10, based on a major study conducted as part of a Robert Wood Johnson demonstration project, Russell Hereford focuses on the functioning of home adaptation and repair services. The lessons learned from the home health agencies that participated in this study have broad application. Discussed are issues agencies must face, such as defining the size and types of home repair and adaptation services they offer, market definition, including targeting those who can pay privately, setting prices, putting management systems into place, and dealing with outside factors such as worker availability.

Finally, in Chapter 11, Susan Lanspery discusses the initiatives some subsidized housing sponsors have taken with respect to home adaptation. Since 6 percent of all elders live in subsidized housing, operators of these buildings can play a significant role in the provision of adaptations. This chapter shares the results of a demonstration project which established and evaluated supportive services in subsidized elderly housing in ten states, with special attention to what the housing sponsors did in the area of physical plant changes.

If the first section of the book is the skeleton, and the second section is the nervous system, this section is the muscle of the book, focusing as it does on how providers actually are getting home adaptation services to their client. Or, as Mrs. R might say: "Everyone is always talking about home adaptation, but who is actually going to do it?"

CHAPTER
9

The Delivery of Home Modification and Repair Services

Jon Pynoos, Phoebe Liebig, Julie Overton, and Emily Calvert

As noted in earlier chapters, home modifications and repairs are key elements in supporting aging in place for frail older persons and mainstreaming for younger persons with disabilities [1-6]. They can make it easier to carry out activities for both age groups and their caregivers. Despite the growing importance of these services, home modifications and repairs have been generally overlooked in housing and social service/community-based long-term care policy. Housing has tended to focus on "bricks and mortar" construction while social services and community-based long-term care have emphasized personal care, leaving home modification and repair in limbo between the two domains.

Over the last fifteen years, awareness of the benefits of home modifications and repairs has been increasing. Small amounts of public funds have been made available to provide limited subsidies for these services, and expertise regarding accessibility and assistive devices has matured. As a result, a small but growing number of modification and repair programs have developed. They range from Area Agencies on Aging with chore, repair, or weatherization programs to multi-service agencies that perform major modifications and include needs assessment. A recent survey of AAAs revealed that home modification and repair services and weatherization programs are the housing areas in which these agencies have been most active and have expended their greatest effort [7].

Despite the greater recognition of the importance of home modifications and repairs, prior to this study, information about the modes and mechanisms for delivering these services has been limited. Very little analysis has been conducted on how these service programs are organized, whom they serve, how they are funded, what services they provide and how, the level and type of needs assessments performed, the types of education and training provided, and the extent to which activities are coordinated among agencies. Of particular interest is the extent to which these programs meet the needs of an increasing number of older, frail persons for more supportive and suitable living environments.

Better understanding of how these service programs operate can help to improve existing service delivery and can provide information that can be used to develop new programs. To expand our understanding of how these programs meet the needs of an increasing number of older, frail persons for more supportive and suitable living environments, we need to have a more complete picture of the nature of these services and how they are provided to clients. This chapter addresses some of these knowledge gaps by reporting on the first national survey of home modification and repair programs.

The survey was conducted in 1990-1991. To identify programs, nominations were sought from area agencies on aging, state units on aging, and state departments of rehabilitation. About half of the 600 nominated programs responded to a structured mail survey. A basis for several of the questions was the Department of Housing and Urban Development (HUD) seven-city home maintenance demonstration, which was created because of concerns that older persons' fixed or declining income, coupled with their difficulty in making repairs themselves, was leading to major problems over time and precipitating similar neglect by neighbors [8, 9].

Because the survey was sent to programs nominated by publicly funded agencies, the increasing activity in home modification and repair among private-sector contractors is probably not well reflected in the sample. While such contractors may not specialize in home modification and repair, and thus may not be known to community agencies, many contractors have become interested in these areas as new construction has declined and demand for modification and repair has increased. It is thus much less surprising than it would have been a decade ago that the First National Invitational Conference on Home Modifications Policy was held in conjunction with the 1993 National Association of Home Builders' Remodelers' Show (see the Epilogue).

The findings of the survey suggest that much work remains to be done before all persons who need to adapt, maintain, or upgrade their dwelling units can readily do so.

HISTORY

In the late 1940s and 1950s, housing policy focused on new construction programs such as public housing and urban renewal. The emphasis was on tearing down dilapidated sections of cities, including individual housing units, and replacing them with new structures. By the early 1970s, these programs had lost much of their political support, in part because of their high costs and their deleterious effect on neighborhoods. During the 1970s and 1980s, programs such as Community Development Block Grants (CDBGs) began to emphasize neighborhood rehabilitation, aspects of which were preservation of property values and the upgrading of homes of lower-income persons living in deteriorating areas. The energy crisis of the late 1970s added weatherization to the agenda of improvements that needed to be made to existing housing stock. Department of Energy (DoE) programs that provide services such as installing storm windows and insulation frequently targeted the dwelling units of elderly persons.

In the 1980s, housing suitability began to emerge as another problem related to existing housing stock. Research indicated the very strong preference of frail older persons to "age in place," and to stay as long as possible in the dwelling units in which they had resided for many years. However, evidence suggested that many elders, especially those who are poor or members of minority groups, live in housing that needs substantial repair [2, 10] and that most housing lacked features such as grab bars, ramps, and handrails that could improve accessibility, prevent accidents and make it easier to carry out daily tasks ([1, 11]; see also Chapter 8 in this book). While the recognition of housing suitability as a factor in successful aging in place did not result in any large federal program such as weatherization, many agencies at the local level began to use programs such as the Older Americans Act (OAA) to adapt homes while others extended their service menus to include home modifications.

Concerns about housing conditions, weatherization, and housing suitability have generated considerable activity at the local level. A 1982 study of twenty-five cities across the country found that twenty-three of them had some form of publicly assisted home repair program that served low-income homeowners [12]. Another study of a 10 percent random survey of metropolitan areas in the country found that 68 percent of them had a maintenance and repair program serving low-income elderly households [13].

General Characteristics of Programs and Clients

The goals of programs in this study range from broad concerns such as upgrading the housing stock and keeping older persons in the community to more specific missions such as reducing energy expenditures. Since the goals of a program affect the scope of activities that it undertakes, some programs provide a range of services that include modification, upkeep, and safety and security, while others focus on specific improvements such as repairs or energy conservation.

Auspices can influence program goals, activities, and target populations. According to the survey, the great majority (86%) of home modification and repair programs are part of larger organizations; only 14 percent report being stand-alone programs. This organizational arrangement may provide advantages in terms of spreading administrative costs, securing funds, gaining referrals, and securing access to other services. The respondents were primarily not-for-profit: 38 percent were nonprofit agencies, 19 percent community action agencies, and 27 percent county and city agencies. The remaining 3 percent were profit-making organizations. Sixty-nine percent of the programs indicated that aging/social services are the primary orientation of their agency, while 24 percent reported that they are connected with housing agencies.

Auspices can also have important consequences for practice. For example, aging/social service agencies are much more likely to conduct functional assessments of clients than housing-oriented programs, suggesting that they are more concerned and responsive to the needs of frail older persons. Housing agencies are more likely to focus on dwelling repairs and remodeling while aging/social service agencies are more likely to carry out modifications, maintenance, and security as single or joint activities.

In accord with their primarily public auspices, programs serve predominantly low-income clients: 43 percent of clients have incomes below $6,000 and 41 percent between $6,000 and $11,999. While 64 percent of clients are Caucasian, programs report serving a substantial number of minority clients: 27 percent African-Americans, 5 percent Latino, 4 percent Native Americans, and 1 percent Asian/Pacific Islanders. In terms of tenure, 84 percent of clients are owners and 16 percent are renters. Programs also serve a predominantly older population: in fact, 42 percent of programs serve only persons over age sixty. Twenty-eight percent of all clients are over seventy-five years of age and 53 percent are between sixty and seventy-four. Programs assist a relatively large percentage of frail persons: 25 percent of clients are very frail and 43 percent are moderately frail. A substantial proportion of clients have mobility impairments: 11 percent use wheelchairs, while 23 percent use either a cane or a walker.

Programs vary considerably in the numbers of clients they serve, from a low of five to a high of 7,250. The average number of clients served per year is 281; the cost of services per client averages $1,074. Program budgets average $80,000 and range from zero dollars for those run entirely by volunteers to $1,000,000 for a large weatherization program.

Issues and Implications

The evolving concern over the home environment has spawned a large number of programs that deliver home modification and repair services. While these programs differ considerably in terms of their overall mission, the services they provide, and their size, they all are involved in modifying and repairing the home environment and serve primarily low-income persons, a large proportion of whom are frail older persons. The overwhelming proportion of the programs surveyed are nonprofit. An issue for the future is whether a viable role exists for the profit-making sector in this field or whether the low-income status of prospective clients or other factors make that difficult.

Funding

Funding can determine what programs offer, to whom and under what circumstances. No single national policy or entitlement program exists that addresses modifying and repairing the homes of older Americans. Consequently, as Table 1 indicates, a variety of categorical programs and other public and private funding sources support home modification and repair efforts.

Federal Sources

Federal funding sources include block grants and the Older Americans Act (OAA). Block grants, which have generally been used to pay for major repairs and renovation, are the major source of funds for the programs surveyed. Community and Social Services Block Grants were used by 38 percent of the programs, providing just under two-fifths of all funding for home modification and repair services. By far, CDBG funds, authorized by the Housing and Community Development Act of 1974, are the type that programs used most often. Block grant amounts range from $2,000 to $2 million, with an average amount of $231,000. Programs also utilize two DoE programs to weatherize the homes of older persons: the Low-Income Home Energy Assistance Program (LIHEAP) (see [7]) and

Table 1. Funding Sources for Home Modification/
Repair Programs

Source	Percent of Programs Using These Funds	Percent of Total $	Amount From This Funding
CDBG, CSBG, SSBG	38	39	$20,590,704
State Funds	23	16	$8,410,300
Dept. of Energy	18	16	$8,249,045
Client Payment/Donations	32	5	$2,509,393
Title III, Title V Older Americans Act	39	5	$2,481,433
Foundations	15	4	$1,889,225
City, County	19	3	$1,818,339
Charitable Contributions	18	2	$888,257
Fundraising	14	1	$438,676
Other Sources	25	11	$5,833,582
Total amount from all sources			$53,108,954

Source: Long Term Care National Resource Center at UCLA/USC, 1990.

the Weatherization Assistance Program (WAP). Together, these funds were used by 18 percent of programs and make up 16 percent of total program budgets.

Thirty-nine percent of programs receive funds under the OAA. The U.S. Administration on Aging (AoA) allocates these funds to states which, in turn, make allocations to area agencies on aging and local governments. OAA resources range from a low of $500 to a high of $171,207 with most of the money coming from Title III, which funds a variety of services to help older persons remain in the community. The demand for Title III funds is usually highly competitive; consequently, many home modification and repair programs use Title III money as start-up funding rather than on-going support. Title III program data (FY 1990) indicate that $2,289,000 was spent on repairs, maintenance, and renovation on homes of 36,365 older persons [14], suggesting the overall modest nature of expenditures and the greater likelihood that these funds pay for minor repairs and modifications. Title V funds, used far less frequently, help pay for low-income senior workers to deliver home repair services. Overall, survey respondents reported that only about 5 percent of their total expenditures came from OAA funds.

State and Local Sources

Because CDBG, DoE, and OAA appropriations did not grow much over the last decade, programs also rely on state and local government revenues. In some cases, cities and counties fund such programs for a limited period, by providing revolving loans or the local match needed to obtain federal funding. State funds in the form of grants for home modification and repair service are usually administered through a state unit on aging or a department of housing and community affairs. State revenues financed 16 percent of overall program budgets, in contrast to 3 percent provided by cities and counties. State funding ranges from $300 to nearly $2 million.

State-sponsored home modification and repair programs seem to have increased during the period of the 1980s and early 1990s. For example, Ohio allocated $4.1 million in 1990 to create and expand innovative housing options, including home modification and repair services. In that same year, Maryland began awarding grants to local organizations, including area agencies on aging, to provide minor repairs and maintenance of properties occupied by low-income elderly and handicapped individuals. Similarly, state housing finance agencies, such as the Rhode Island Housing Mortgage Finance Corporation and the Minnesota Housing Finance Agency, have provided low-interest loans for home repairs and improvements.

Non-Government Sources

In addition to government sources, programs are supported by client payments, foundations, local charitable groups, and fundraising. Thirty-two percent of programs receive client payments. On average, however, client payments contribute only 5 percent to program budgets. This low proportion is understandable, given that most programs serve low- and moderate-income persons. Nevertheless, a number of programs expect client payments to expand, particularly if they plan to serve moderate- and middle-income persons. Foundations and charitable organizations together are sources of funding for 33 percent of programs, but, as in the case of client payments, they make up only a small percentage of total expenditures (4%). Foundations usually do not provide ongoing resources to programs, but rather help start new programs or fund demonstration projects.

Issues and Implications

Funding remains a major impediment to increased activity in the area of home modification and repair. Many programs had minuscule budgets and report that they are able to address only a limited number of area households with needs for home modification and repair. To maximize the amount of dollars spent on clients, to provide clients with more services, and to provide a broad range of services, two-thirds of programs surveyed had multiple funding sources. Such a strategy, however, also can create coordination problems due to different eligibility and program requirements.

Funding sources often dictate what services programs provide and to whom. Most programs operate with fixed budgets that limit the number of clients served per year. Many programs also report restrictions as to: 1) spending per person or dwelling unit per year; 2) providing certain types of modifications (e.g., locks, weatherization); and/or 3) serving particular geographic areas. These limitations can lead to large gaps in service delivery and make it difficult to solve specific problems. For example, home modification programs relying on sources such as the OAA often report that they can repair small plumbing leaks and install hand-held showers but are unable to repair basic underlying deficiencies such as worn-out pipes or metal pans underlying shower floors. On the other hand, programs funded exclusively by DoE often cannot install grab bars or hand-held showers. Consequently, older persons who need weatherization and modifications may find themselves dealing with several different agencies. This specialization can make it difficult for clients, family members, and even intermediaries such as case managers to organize home modification services.

Methods of Service Delivery

Home modification and repair programs differ from more traditional social service agencies in the types of persons involved in service delivery, the skills that are necessary to carry out the work, and the ways in which service delivery is organized. There are four basic models of service delivery: on-staff work crew, subcontractors, use of volunteers, and an integrated approach. Among the survey respondents, while the subcontractor and crew models are frequently used, a majority of programs use an integrated model of service delivery. All generally utilize a program director to plan, coordinate, and monitor activities.

On-Staff Crew

In this model, an on-staff crew is directly supervised by a program director or service coordinator. The crew often consists of semi-skilled/skilled handymen and/or carpenters. The semi-skilled crew members primarily focus on non-licensed work involving minor modifications, minor repairs, and safety and security measures, typically the type of work that skilled subcontractors are not willing to do. Nearly two-fifths of the programs reported having an on-staff handyman, while one-fourth employed their own carpenters.

Programs with their own work crews reported being able to ensure high quality services and reliability. They perceive an advantage in sensitizing their staff to the needs of older persons and providing the flexibility to shift crew members from one job to another, depending on need. This flexibility is especially useful in making minor modifications and in meeting emergencies. However, a number of programs reported that recruiting and retaining crew members with a working knowledge of many diverse crafts was difficult. Generally, because of budget restrictions, programs often paid lower than prevailing wages. Some programs tried to overcome such problems by providing competitive pay, benefits, job training, and a guaranteed work week. Moreover, exclusive reliance on this model required keeping an inventory of supplies and tools.

Subcontracting

Subcontractors are most often used by programs whose main objectives include eliminating health and safety code deficiencies and increasing accessibility—activities often requiring substantial repairs and/or major modifications. In general, such jobs require licensed professionals (e.g., electricians, general contractors, and plumbers). In order to overcome the reluctance of such subcontractors to take on small jobs, some programs have arranged predetermined working agreements, bids for an annual contract, and agreements with small contracting firms.

Some programs indicated that hiring subcontractors saves time and money over the other methods of service delivery as it keeps downtime to a minimum. According to many, however, the lack of quality control is a major disadvantage of the subcontracting approach, especially when funding sources require awarding the contract to the lowest bidder, who is not necessarily the most qualified. To promote quality work, programs have tried strategies such as continually monitoring work, conducting pre- and post-inspections, and withholding payment for services until completion and inspection of the job. Several programs conducted training sessions for subcontractors on working with elderly clients and/or educated clients on how to deal with subcontractors.

Volunteers

The volunteer model is an increasingly common method of service delivery for home improvements as programs seek low or no cost methods to meet client needs. Among the surveyed programs, 43 percent used volunteers. Approximately 18 percent used senior volunteers such as retired handymen, electricians, and plumbers. A number of programs used youths from places such as trade schools. Programs also turned to employees and retirees of utility companies, corporations, unions, trade associations, and job banks to obtain skilled volunteers and donated materials.

The reported disadvantages of using volunteers were problems with reliability, recruitment, retention, and liability. As skills range widely, depending on volunteers means that certain skills might not be available when needed. Some programs found it necessary to hire a volunteer coordinator to match the skills of the volunteers to the jobs. Programs have dealt with the liability problem by purchasing their own insurance, utilizing volunteers already insured, or reducing the risks by limiting the type of work assigned to volunteers.

Integrated Delivery System

Many of the more mature and comprehensive programs use a combination of approaches to provide services. This enables them to respond to the multi-faceted needs of their clients, to overcome some of the disadvantages of the models noted above, and to become less dependent or reliant on other programs. For example, a number of programs utilized an on-staff crew for specific categories of jobs such as minor repairs and modifications, while subcontracting for major repairs and using volunteers for upkeep and chore services.

Issues and Implications

Depending on the nature of the program, the delivery of home improvement services can be a complex undertaking. Programs that provide major repairs are likely to require supervisors who have a broad knowledge of construction and can manage different trades; the ability to schedule, manage, and oversee complex jobs; the resources to absorb a certain amount of downtime; and space to store equipment and materials. Consequently, major repair programs are found most frequently in housing agencies. Meeting the needs of frail older persons may require similar skills, but it also requires specialized expertise concerning adaptations for accessibility, a supportive environment, and safety. This type of work may be more demanding than straightforward repair work in terms of providing clients with advice, tailoring adaptations to the particular needs of clients, and counseling.

Assessments

The assessment process is a critical component in the identification of service needs and interventions. Key issues are what to assess, who should do the assessment, how to collect information, and the role of assessments in determining needs. Programs used two basic types of assessments: functional and environmental. Functional assessments identify limitations in an older person's ability to carry out tasks such as bathing, cooking, climbing stairs, and housework. Environmental assessments identify aspects of the physical environment that need repair or modification. Fifty-three percent of respondents used functional assessments of individual clients and 82 percent carried out environmental assessments. Auspices make a significant difference in the type of assessment: two-thirds of the programs under the auspices of an aging/social service agency carried out functional assessments in comparison to only one-third of programs that were part of a housing agency. Seventy-seven percent of the programs conducting functional assessments used their own staff.

As indicated in Tables 2 and 3, various types of personnel conduct assessments. Case managers most frequently carry out functional assessments, followed by social workers and nurses. Environmental assessments are conducted most often by home inspectors, followed by family and friends and case managers. Occupational therapists, the professionals trained to analyze person-environmental interactions, are used relatively infrequently in functional or environmental assessments.

The survey respondents reported considerable variation in what was evaluated and the emphasis given to the environment. For example, staff who worked for housing repair, weatherization, or home security programs generally only concerned themselves with dwelling unit attributes for which their agencies had responsibility and in which they had training. They usually did not assess the home's suitability in terms of its supportiveness for frail residents, although many programs reported that their staff referred clients to other services.

Methods of assessment varied as widely as the types of persons who carried them out. Weatherization programs used a fairly standardized format, as did programs that operated under Medicaid waivers. Some assessments were based on a comprehensive examination of features, while others were more open-ended, relying on the professional judgment of the assessor. The more comprehensive methods included an assessment of the older person's ability to carry out activities of daily living and instrumental activities of daily living independently. An evaluation of the home's ability to support the person was

Table 2. Persons Responsible for
Functional Assessments[a]

Case Manager	43.6%
Social Worker	27.8%
Visiting Nurse	19.5%
Client	17.4%
Family/Friends	17.0%
Occupational Therapist	15.8%
Handymen	12.0%
Volunteer	9.8%
Home Inspector	9.0%

[a]Adds up to more than 100 percent because of multiple persons conducting assessments.
Source: Long Term Care National Resource Center at UCLA/USC, 1990.

Table 3. Persons Responsible for
Environmental Assessments[a]

Home Inspector	53.7%
Family/Friends	30.0%
Case Manager	26.6%
Social Worker	21.2%
Handymen	20.2%
Occupational Therapist	17.0%
Client	14.0%
Visiting Nurse	12.8%
Volunteer	11.9%

[a]Adds up to more than 100 percent because of multiple persons conducting assessments.
Source: Long Term Care National Resource Center at UCLA/USC, 1990.

then made using a checklist of areas and features. Typically, such an assessment was conducted using a questionnaire and visual inspection of the home. In only a few cases did respondents indicate that clients were asked to demonstrate how they carried out a particular task, a procedure more likely to provide an accurate sense of both personal capabilities and interaction with the environment (see Chapter 7).

Issues and Implications

The assessment process is a weak link in the delivery of home modifications and repair services. Because many "assessors" only examine the specific aspects of the environment they are responsible for changing, it seems likely that many problems may be overlooked, especially by programs focusing on repairs and weatherization. The important role of case managers, social workers, and nurses also raises issues of how well they are trained in assessing the environment. Of particular concern is the limited use of occupational therapists, which may be due to expense or reimbursement policy. In addition, older persons and/or their family members were actively involved in assessments, especially in programs in which client payments played an important role. While such involvement may help to insure that the changes made are the ones that clients wanted, studies suggest that older homeowners are least likely to provide valid reports of housing conditions when repairs are needed, either because of their lack of knowledge of housing systems or their low expectations regarding housing quality [15]. It is not known to what extent under-reporting may also apply to supportive features. The specialized nature of many assessments, the variability in what assessments cover, and the potential for under-reporting problems all underscore the need for standard assessment instruments, strong referral mechanisms, and the training and education of assessors in identifying and solving environment-related problems.

Types of Services

Services can be divided into four main categories: repairs, modifications, maintenance and upkeep, and safety and security. Of the programs surveyed, the largest expenditures were for repairs (52%), followed by modifications (20%), upkeep (15%), and safety and security (13%). Most programs provided at least two types of services; the most common combination was repairs and modifications.

Repairs

Repairs include minor repairs (e.g., fixing a leaking faucet), emergency repairs (e.g., plumbing problems), and major repairs (e.g., re-roofing). Programs reported that repairs, which generally require a high degree of skill and know-how, were the most frequently provided service. The most common repairs reported were heating and cooling (48% of programs), electrical (46%), roofing (45%), plumbing (45%), and exposed wiring (44%).

Modifications

The purpose of modifying the home environment of functionally impaired individuals is to make activities such as bathing, cooking, walking, navigating steps, and opening doors easier and safer. Minor and major modifications are intended to improve individual functioning and the home's accessibility and to prevent accidents. According to the survey, the most common modifications were ramps (36%), handrails (35%), grab bars (33%), and electrical outlets (33%).

Maintenance and Upkeep

The goals of maintenance and upkeep are generally to prevent deterioration of the physical environment and increase energy efficiency. Weatherization, aimed at protecting the dwelling occupants from the effects of inclement conditions, conserving energy, and reducing utility bills, was the most common home maintenance service (37%). Other common services were installing storm windows (27%), rubbish removal (27%), cleaning gutters (27%), and tree removal (27%). Chore services constituted the second major component of upkeep services. Chore services refers to more ongoing indoor and outdoor services such as heavy cleaning, lawn mowing, snow removal, and yard work.

Safety and Security

Safety and security measures are aimed at avoiding accidents and preventing crime. Fewer programs were involved in safety and security measures than any of the other categories of services. The most common safety and security service was installing locks/deadbolts, followed by a variety of other adaptations such as installing smoke detectors and securing loose flooring to improve safety.

Issues and Implications

The emphasis on repairs has several possible explanations. First, most clients have low to moderate incomes and may live in dwelling units in poor condition. Because repairs tend to be the most costly of home improvements, they are likely to consume the largest percentage of program budgets. Second, repairs are often necessary before other alterations can be made. Third, major funding sources such as CDBGs are oriented toward repairs.

The amount of resources devoted to repairs raises the question as to whether other areas such as modifications, safety and security, and upkeep receive enough attention. As indicated earlier, the most likely combination of services offered is repairs and modifications, suggesting that when repairs are made, it is also possible for such programs to carry out modifications. Many of the programs that undertake major repairs do not carry out minor repairs, modifications, upkeep, or safety/security as separate activities but only in conjunction with repairs. However, despite the high level of expenditures on repairs, programs most often reported repairs as the greatest unmet need of clients.

Coordination

A major issue in the delivery of human services is the extent to which any one service is linked to other services needed by a particular client group. This is especially true for the frail aged, who often require multiple services to maximize their independent functioning in their homes and communities or to prevent premature institutionalization. Because numerous organizations and agencies provide programs and services for the elderly, service providers and planners must undertake actions to overcome fragmentation [16, 17].

Better coordination can ensure that clients receive both appropriate and available services and can promote optimal use of existing resources, thereby reducing unwarranted duplication and its costs and improving the quality of service delivery [16]. Agencies may undertake a wide range of coordination actions to create and maintain community-based care systems. These can include integrating activities, such as information sharing and cross-referrals of clients, and integrated or consolidated activities such as co-location of services and joint funding [18, 19].

Coordination actions can be grounded in different kinds of organizational arrangements. For example, agencies may provide a service cluster, such as housing finance and housing finance counseling, or they can involve a single "umbrella" agency that acts as a gatekeeper or entry point for existing services, such as an area agency on aging. A program may also work frequently and closely with a specific network of agencies, or develop standard strategies for interacting with external organizations.

The home modification and repair programs in the survey were asked to identify their characteristic referrals to and working arrangements with other agencies; the three major organizations with which they work most closely; and the coordination methods and strategies they find to be most effective. Of particular interest was their collaboration with and assistance from area agencies on aging (AAAs) and state units on aging (SUAs).

Referrals to Other Agencies

Referrals are clearly the most common coordinating mechanism, which is fairly typical of most aging services delivery. Nearly all (96%) of the programs made referrals to multiple agencies. More than 75 percent and 66 percent, respectively, referred clients to weatherization agencies and AAAs; more than half referred their elderly clients to transportation, home care, and housing rehabilitation agencies. They were far less likely to steer clients to tax abatement, housing finance counseling, and handyman repair programs. Home modifications and repair programs made referrals in roughly equivalent proportions to agencies offering services related to the physical environment and social service organizations, probably reflecting both service availability and client need.

Coordination Activities

Programs were engaged in several working arrangements with other agencies, with slightly more than half (54%) using interagency agreements. It is not known, however, if these were formal written agreements or informal "handshake" arrangements. Other coordination activities included meetings of advisory committees or service providers and subcontracting or purchase of service agreements.

Few programs engaged in more programmatic consolidation such as joint assessments, joint funding or sharing staff specialists, and co-location of services, although a majority have relatively small, defined target areas (e.g., county-wide). Additionally, nearly 90 percent were part of larger organizations that are more able to promote and provide integrated services under that umbrella, without requiring unusual staff time and effort.

Types of Working Arrangements with Partner Agencies

The programs in the survey tended to be part of a "parent" agency with a social services orientation. Nearly two-thirds of the programs identified their primary orientation as aging and/or social services; about one-quarter were oriented toward housing. Nearly three-fifths of the partners of these programs were social services agencies, about one-third were aging-related organizations, and one-quarter were housing-related. Less than 10 percent were charitable organizations, such as United Way, or health care agencies.

These programs were also more likely to work with their "own kind." That is, programs imbedded in aging/social services agencies were far more likely to work with other agencies like themselves; the same was true for programs located in housing-related agencies. Shared concerns and missions make it easier to collaborate, but delivering the services needed by a client may require partnerships with unlike and unfamiliar agencies.

The dominant working arrangement of nearly all the programs (almost 90%) with their major partners was a system of cross-referrals. Others included grantor-grantee subcontracting for services; sources of volunteer labor; and shared assessments, inspections or surveys. About 10 percent cost-shared some aspect of service delivery with their customary partners. It would appear that the administrators of these programs were more comfortable with looser ties to their partner agencies.

Effective Methods or Strategies of Coordination

Programs identified enhancing communication and knowledge and improving the interagency referral system as the two most effective types of strategies. The first focuses on networking and outreach activities, such as meeting regularly with community forums or councils and making presentations to various organizations, and the second focuses on such activities as defining the roles and functions of agencies in the community, helping clients with paperwork from other agencies, or assisting other agencies with client follow-up.

Two other areas were mentioned less frequently: improved utilization of private sector resources, such as establishing relationships with contractors, suppliers, and inspectors or working closely with organizations that are sources of volunteer labor; and creating joint activities, such as careful scheduling and joint assessments.

Relationships with the Aging Network

Most programs were not part of AAAs, but a significant proportion (81%) worked with the aging network, primarily with AAAs. For those programs that did work with the network, client referrals were the most important tie (77%), followed by funding (67%)—usually at very low rates—and technical assistance (37%), primarily related to program administration. Program staff are not very likely to serve on AAA advisory committees; the reverse was also true.

Issues and Implications

The home modifications and repair programs responding to the survey employed integrating rather than integrated activities that focus on improving communication and initiating planning—in short, on developing a *process* for working together, rather than on facilitating changes in the *structure* of service delivery. In this regard, these programs are not different from the majority of human service agencies. The idea of coordination, while highly desirable, is often difficult to put into practice due to issues such as professional territoriality, the lack of incentives or support (especially from funding sources), and the expenditure of time and energy, which can be particularly difficult for small agencies providing home modification and repair programs.

For home modification and repair programs to take their rightful place among core services for the frail elderly, however, means undertaking a more aggressive educational campaign targeted on the public, the AAAs and SUAs, and a wide range of funding sources; it also requires more structured advocacy and consultation to other agencies serving the elderly. Systematic information sharing, periodic problem-solving sessions, and case management activities are but a few mechanisms that could help integrate these programs more firmly into community-based service systems for the frail aged.

Education and Training

In addition to educating and training program staff to assess person-environmental relationships correctly, home modification and repair programs can raise the awareness of the public and professionals about the importance of the home environment, and can provide technical information concerning how to assess the environment and make changes. In this study, approximately 30 percent of programs were involved in education, with a major focus on providing information to clients on energy conservation.

Housing agencies tended to provide the most information about home modification and repair issues such as how to hire a contractor, construction techniques, and sources of funds for needed changes. A number of programs also reached out to the broader community such as health care professionals, legislators, and business professionals concerning the importance of home modifications for aging in place. Thirteen percent of programs trained professionals such as the housing community and contractors. Several aging and social service-based programs also indicated that they trained medical professionals. However, with the exception of weatherization programs, few made systematic efforts to educate the wider public or to train professionals about environmental modifications or assessments.

Issues and Implications

An increased emphasis on education and training could help raise the skill level of staff involved in assessments. If programs do not make increased use of occupational therapists (see [20]), then it would seem especially important to train case managers and other staff on the use of better assessment instruments. The small number of staff, limited budgets, and the need of their own staff for training impinge on the ability of programs to provide education and training to other groups, including the general public. These constraints suggest the need for a wider educational role for professionals such as occupational therapists; the creation of video and slide programs that can be used in group settings such as senior centers and day care centers to educate older persons and their families about how to assess the environment; the development of resource centers that include displays of attractive ways to modify homes; and more products and information available in building supply and drug stores.

THE FUTURE

With the expected increase in the number of older frail persons who desire to age in place, home modifications and repair should be seen as a more integral component of long-term care policy rather than a "stepchild" of current housing or social services programs. In order to maximize the potential of the home environment to support the independence and functioning of older persons, existing programs need to be improved, additional research carried out, public policy barriers overcome, and universal housing created.

Improving Existing Programs

Over the last decade a large number of nonprofit and governmental agencies have become involved in home modification and repair. As this study suggests, these programs are relatively small and highly dependent on public funds to serve low- and moderate-income persons. Many programs have evolved over time to address the multiple needs of clients while others provide more specialized services. Even though most programs coordinate their efforts with those of other agencies, the current system remains highly fragmented, inadequately funded, and full of gaps.

While a large percentage of clients are older and frail, many programs, especially those connected with housing agencies, do not carry out functional assessments. Even among those programs that assess the home environment and the functional abilities of residents, methods and procedures vary considerably. These practices suggest the importance of developing more standardized methods of assessment and client referral. It seems important to coordinate home repair, modification, and weatherization and link them to in-home services, especially when these tasks are carried out by separate agencies. In situations in which only one type of need is being met, consideration should be given to expanding program scope or developing new initiatives to address client needs comprehensively.

The market for home modifications and repairs is likely to grow as a result of the increase in the number of frail older persons, demand by young persons with disabilities who are seeking more accessible and functional housing, and the accelerating demand of older homeowners because of the increased availability of reverse annuity mortgages which can provide funds for home modification and repair. This larger market for modifications and repairs could allow non-profit providers to serve a wider group of persons and draw in the private sector, including remodelers. Such an emphasis could result in the growth of a specialized group of providers who are proficient in assessing the needs of frail and disabled persons, identifying products suited to their needs, making changes, and following up to insure that the adaptations achieve the desired results.

Need for Research

This study was based on a sample of home modification and repair programs that were nominated primarily by the aging network. As such, it includes neither an analysis of private-sector programs nor the perspective of older persons who carry out their own adaptations and interact with home modification and repair programs. Moreover, it leaves unanswered a number of key questions which should be the focus of future research. For example, it would be useful to understand the influence of such factors as targeting, staffing, auspices, service menu, and method and type of assessment on the effectiveness of programs in delivering home modification and repair. Most importantly, more knowledge is needed about the effects of adaptations on such client outcomes as life satisfaction, activity level, ease of caregiving, the ability to "age in place," and the use of services.

Overcoming Policy Barriers

Home modification and repair would benefit if it were viewed as a mainstream component of both housing and long-term care policy. The majority of program funds are spent on repairs. These expenditures are in accord with the goals of major funding sources such as CDBG to prevent the housing stock from deteriorating and to stabilize property values. There has been less emphasis on adapting the environment for safety and supportive functioning to keep frail older persons in their homes, prevent accidents, and reduce the need for personal care services. A number of strategies could make modifications more available in the future: pass legislation that provides funding for modifications on a more widespread basis; expand the types of assistive devices, adaptations, and occupational therapy visits funded by Medicare and Medicaid; include home modification and repair in needs assessments and statewide housing and long-term care plans; expand funds authorized under the 1990 National Affordable Housing Act to test and develop new models of home modification and repair programs; create programs and training to sensitize remodelers and builders to the needs of the elderly for home modification and repair; and insure that conditions of the home are included in health histories taken by physicians and in assessments conducted by professionals such as case managers and home health workers.

Universal Housing

In the long run, problems that the home presents for disabled and older frail persons need to be addressed by a broader approach that builds more supportive, adaptable, and accessible housing in the first place. In this regard, concern over how well the existing physical environment meets the needs of disabled persons has spawned a worldwide movement toward universal housing (see also Chapter 4 in this book). Universal housing meets the needs of users throughout their life span or adapts to their needs if they become more frail or disabled. Principles underlying such housing include accessibility, safety, low maintenance, and control by the resident. Universal housing incorporates such special features as wheelchair-accessible entryways, kitchens and bathrooms; single-lever faucets; nonslip flooring; easy-to-reach temperature controls; water temperature mixers that prevent scalding; and grab bars by tubs and toilets. A step in this direction is the Fair Housing Act of 1988, which requires that buildings of over four units provide basic accessibility and provisions for adding features such as grab bars. However, new units add only about 2 percent to the housing stock each year and single-family housing, our most prevalent form, is not included in the Act's provisions. Consequently, efforts to improve the delivery of home modification and repair services need to remain high on the public agenda.

ACKNOWLEDGMENTS

This chapter is based on a study supported, in part, by award number 90AT0386 from the Administration on Aging, Department of Health and Human Services, Washington, D.C. 20201. Grantees undertaking projects under government sponsorship are encouraged to express freely their findings and conclusions. Points of view or opinions do not, therefore, necessarily represent official Administration on Aging policy.

REFERENCES

1. M. P. Lawton, Housing the Elderly, Residential Quality and Residential Satisfaction, *Research on Aging, 2,* pp. 309-328, 1980.
2. J. Pynoos, Strategies for Home Modification and Repair, *Generations, 16*:2, pp. 21-26, 1992.
3. P. Porter, Facilitating Aging in Place through Home Repairs, *Long Term Care Advances: Topics in Research, Training, Service & Policy, 6*:2, 1994.
4. R. D. Lynch, Karl's House: *Technology and Disability, 2*:4, pp. 30-39, Fall 1993.
5. H. D. Kiewel, Serving Community Needs for Home-Accessibility Modifications, *Technology and Disability, 2*:4, pp. 40-46, Fall 1993.
6. E. Steinfeld and S. Shea, Enabling Home Environments: Identifying Barriers to Independence, *Technology and Disability, 2*:4, pp. 69-79, Fall 1993.
7. National Eldercare Institute on Housing and Supportive Services, *Area Agencies on Aging Efforts in Housing, 1992,* NEIHSS, Los Angeles, 1994.
8. D. Greenstein, Home Repair Programs, *Generations, 10*:2, pp. 52-54, 1985.
9. U.S. Department of Housing and Urban Development, *The Seven City Home Maintenance Demonstration for the Elderly: Final Report, Vol. 1,* unpublished report, Washington, D.C., 1983.
10. S. M. Golant and A. J. LaGreca, Housing Quality of U.S. Elderly Households: Does Aging in Place Matter? *The Gerontologist, 34*:6, pp. 803-814, 1994.
11. R. Struyk, Housing Adaptations: Needs and Practices, in *Housing the Aged: Design Directives and Policy Considerations,* V. Regnier and J. Pynoos (eds.), Elsevier, New York, pp. 259-275, 1987.
12. P. Myers, *Aging in Place,* Conservation Foundation, Washington, D.C., 1982.
13. U.S. Department of Housing and Urban Development, *Preliminary Evaluation Design for a Home Maintenance and Repair Demonstration for Low Income Elderly Homeowners,* unpublished report, Washington, D.C., 1979.
14. U.S. Administration on Aging, *Fiscal Year 1990 National Summary of State Program Reports for Title III under the Older Americans Act,* Washington, D.C., 1991.
15. A. Chen and S. Newman, Validity of Older Homeowners' Housing Evaluations, *The Gerontologist, 27*:3, pp. 309-313, 1987.
16. R. S. Azernoff and J. S. Seliger, *Delivering Human Services,* Prentice-Hall, Englewood Cliffs, New Jersey, 1982.

17. D. E. Gelfand, *The Aging Network: Programs and Services* (3rd Edition), Springer, New York, 1988.
18. R. J. Agranoff, *Intergovernmental Management,* State University of New York Press, Albany, New York, 1986.
19. R. J. Agranoff, W. F. Anderson, B. F. Frieden, and M. J. Murphy, *Managing Human Services,* International City Managers Association, Washington, D.C., 1977.
20. Aging Design Research Program, *Design for Aging: Strategies for Collaboration Between Architects and Occupational Therapists,* AIA/ACSA Council on Architectural Research, Washington, D.C., 1993.

CHAPTER
10

Establishing Home Modification, Maintenance, and Repair Programs in Community-Based Agencies

Russell W. Hereford

While public policy has long emphasized the importance of health care and social services in helping elders to accomplish their usual goal of living independently in their own homes for as long as possible, the key role of adequate, supportive housing is also increasingly recognized. Although greater policy emphasis needs to be placed on adaptations, as noted in earlier chapters, it is also important to address home upkeep and repair ([1-3]; see also Chapter 9, in this book). Housing adaptations will be less than successful in homes that need repair:

> Frail homeowners will need assistance with major and minor repairs, with routine chores such as changing light bulbs and putting up storm windows [as well as with accessibility or safety modifications]. In addition . . . older people, not surprisingly, tend to live in older homes. Older homes often require not only more maintenance but also replacement of major items like roofs, furnaces, and hot water heaters [4, p. 35].

In fact, "housing occupied by nearly half the elderly is over 40 years old and thus both poorly insulated and subject to high maintenance costs" [5, p. 6].

Repairs and maintenance not only enhance safety and improve the supportive nature of the housing environment; they also help older people to feel secure, to take pride in their homes, and to feel comfortable about visits from guests or even people hired to help with household activities. This effect on emotional health may be as important as the physical effects of repairs, maintenance, and modifications. Many older people perceive a loss of control over their physical environment as a part of losing control over other aspects of their lives: "For the more impaired, remaining at home may have the additional significance of being the one constant in an emotional world threatened by losses" [6, p. 1]. It is worth noting that three-fourths of those with supportive housing features paid for these features themselves or with their families' help [7], suggesting the importance of these features to consumers.

This chapter distills the experience of several community-based service providers in offering home repair, maintenance, and modification services. Such providers are often in a good position to help older people maintain their homes. Their success in delivering health, nutritional, and social services to seniors makes them a logical choice to consider for other services necessary to help people to age in place. By expanding their array of services to include home maintenance and modification, these organizations can fill a void in the array of services available to older people. At the same time, these organizations can often establish revenue-generating, self-sufficient services, and may even be able to generate an operating surplus. This not only enhances their organizational capacity, it also serves as a foundation for further growth: as government funds become more restricted, community-based agencies that have "answers and strategies will be in a favorable resource-attracting situation" [8, p. 325].

Estimates of the need for modification and repair services appear to be about 20 percent to 30 percent of the elderly's housing units [2, 9]. While the number of older people living in extremely substandard housing is low [9], this number probably underestimates the actual maintenance and repair challenges many older people face, especially those faced by poor, minority, and frail elderly [4, 6, 9-11]. These challenges include the difficulty of getting someone to do the work: "Many older people do not trust the remodeling industry and many remodelers do not want to work with the elderly, particularly the frail elderly" [4, p. 36]. Further, while analysts have estimated need based on measurable factors—such as housing condition, older homeowners' ability to carry out activities of daily living, and older homeowners' income—it is difficult to estimate the size of the probably substantial group of elders who are fairly healthy and independent, but are neither wealthy nor able to do all the maintenance they used to do.

The capacity of community agencies, specifically home health agencies, to provide services such as these was tested in the Supportive Services Program for Older Persons (SSPOP), a national initiative supported by the Robert Wood Johnson Foundation. This program funded home health agencies to expand the range of service options available to seniors through a private market for nontraditional health and health-related services. Market research covering a wide range of services from case management to shopping assistance showed an unexpectedly strong demand among older homeowners for home repair and maintenance services. Hence, most participating agencies initiated such services. Examples include routine upkeep that has become difficult for older homeowners, such as interior and exterior painting, repairing leaky faucets, replacing worn sash cords, strengthening and replacing banisters and steps, yard work, and snow removal. Many of those interviewed were also interested in modifications to the physical structure, such as installation of wheelchair ramps or grab bars, moving and replacing electrical outlets and fixtures, and replacing doorknobs with lever handles.

Early in the implementation of the Supportive Services Program, it became clear that there was a strong demand for housing and home maintenance services. At that time, the program staff joked that the participating home health agencies should develop a special logo depicting a nurse carrying a ladder and hammer. In retrospect, the logo would have been even more appropriate than we anticipated at the time. Offering home maintenance and modification pushes the margins and creativity of even the most ambitious home health and community agency. To be sure, these agencies' expertise in dealing with a senior clientele gave them a certain advantage, including familiarity with older people, access to referral sources, and a degree of credibility among consumers and in the community. Nevertheless, this business differs from any they have conducted before, and presents a number of daunting challenges.

This chapter discusses how these agencies met the challenges, so that others considering such ventures can benefit from their experience (see also Chapters 9 and 12 in this book and [12-18]). While the project participants (see Table 1) were home health agencies, the lessons they learned are useful for other community agencies and groups as well.

Table 1. Organizations Participating in the
Supportive Services Program for Older Persons
(November 1990)

Visiting Nurse Association of Delaware
    New Castle, Delaware
Kennebec Valley Regional Health Agency
    Waterville, Maine
Michigan Home Health Care
    Traverse City, Michigan
MCOSS Foundation
    Manasquan, New Jersey
Smile Independent Living Services
    Albany, New York
Visiting Nurse Association of Texas
    Dallas, Texas
Visiting Nurse Service Affiliates
    Seattle, Washington

THE SCOPE OF WORK

The nature of the work that a home modification program undertakes will affect directly every other aspect of program operations. Defining the limits on the type of services that will be offered depends on the agency's *realistic* capacity to carry out the job in a high-quality manner. The decision on what services to offer also must take into account any regulations relating to licensure, bonding, or other legal considerations.

An agency may be tempted to undertake large jobs, due to the potential for high cash flow. Inexperienced agencies, however, are probably well advised to resist this temptation until their skills more closely match their ambitions. Rather than trying to replace roofs or put on a second story, successful SSPOP participants concentrated on maintenance and simple repair and modification projects. Some agencies defined their scope of work with an upper dollar limit on jobs (e.g., $500). Most SSPOP participants that attempted large jobs too soon had to scale back; some found their entire program was faltering.

For agencies getting into this field, the important point is that an agency *must* stay within its capacity and capabilities to deliver a quality product. The SSPOP agencies found ample demand for home repair services among seniors, and these services are easier to offer and manage. Revenues from home repair services, as well assss from others offered according to consumer demand, can be substantial, as illustrated in Table 2.

DEFINING THE MARKET

A target market of people who can pay for services is the only way to ensure financial self-sufficiency in the long run. If this group is large enough, or if

Table 2. Revenues Generated by Supportive Services Program Agencies
March 1, 1998–August 31, 1990

Service	Revenue	Percent of Total
Home Repair/Handyman	$1,683,159	48.4
Housekeeping	$1,278,485	36.7
Yard and Chore	$269,710	7.8
Emergency Response	$75,321	2.2
Case Management	$19,138	0.6
Other	$153,439	4.4
Total Revenue	$3,479,252	100.0

Source: Data are from Management Information System Reports submitted to SSP National Program Office at Brandeis University.

third-party support (e.g., a grant program or a bequest left to the agency) is available, the agency will also be able to serve at least some lower-income people. It is also worth noting that, compared to the overall U.S. elderly population, the SSPOP clients tended to be older, poorer, more often female, somewhat less healthy, and far more likely to have difficulty performing chores (see Tables 3 and 4). Most participants had not expected so many lower-income people to purchase their services.

Agencies must also decide whether to market to the population at large, or to focus on seniors as was done in the Supportive Services Program. Other likely service users include individuals with disabilities, a target population that is consistent with a home health or elder service agency's mission. There is also, however, a demand for home maintenance and repair services among the broader population. The resources of the latter group provide a potential subsidy for services to lower-income seniors and others.

Table 3. Demographic Characteristics
Clients of Supportive Services Program for Older Persons[a]

Population	Percent of Supportive Services Clients	Percent of U.S. Elderly
Annual Household Income		
Less than $10,000	32.5	15.1
$10,001 to $30,000	51.9	56.1
Greater than $30,000	15.6	18.8
Living Arrangement		
Live Alone	55.4	53.3
Live with Spouse	31.1	30.6
Live with Other	13.4	16.1
Age		
65 to 74	41.2	59.4
75 to 84	39.0	31.0
85 and Older	19.8	9.5
Sex		
Male	18.6	40.4
Female	81.4	59.6

[a]Data are from eight of eleven original Supportive Services Sites for January-November 1988.
Data Source: National Evaluation of Supportive Services Program, Center for Health Policy Studies, Georgetown University.

Table 4. Functional and Health Characteristics
Clients of Supportive Services Program for Older Persons[a]

Population	Percent of Supportive Services Clients	Percent of U.S. Elderly
Self-Reported Health		
Excellent	21.5	35.9
Good	40.5	31.0
Fair to Poor	38.0	32.6
Hospitalized in Last Three Months	16.1	4.3
Has an Activity Limitation	54.0	39.6
Difficulty Performing		
Heavy Chores	84.8	23.8
Light Chores	24.4	13.4
Personal Tasks	13.3	12.7

[a]Data are from eight of eleven original Supportive Services Sites for January-November 1988.
Data Source: National Evaluation of Supportive Services Program, Center for Health Policy Studies, Georgetown University.

A second market-related decision is how to advertise and sell the product. The SSPOP agencies found the most success in local community newspapers. (They reported very little success, however, from the free newspapers frequently distributed through local senior organizations.) These advertisements, of course, should target towns with a high proportion of likely buyers.

Radio talk shows targeted at a particular audience proved to be another useful advertising medium in the SSPOP. For example, a Saturday morning "Senior Talk" radio show had a large local following in one SSPOP city; a guest appearance on the show worked wonders for the agency's business. Feature articles in newspapers or magazines or on radio or TV were effective. The unusual combination of home health and home maintenance services piqued the interest of some media representatives. Other advertising sources—for example, radio, television, metropolitan newspapers, or even the Yellow Pages—yielded mixed results. These media are expensive and tended not to be cost-effective for smaller SSPOP agencies.

SETTING PRICES

Direct Costs

In a home repair business, direct costs contain three essential elements: personnel, material, and travel costs. The most successful SSPOP participants made accurate projections of these costs a high priority.

Personnel costs cover the wages and fringes of the people who are actually doing the work. While wages must be competitive with similar local industries, an organization may be able to find part-time personnel who will do this type of work for less than general market wages. The agency must project fringe benefits accurately, paying particular attention to workers' compensation and liability insurance costs. These are likely to be higher for construction-type workers than for nurses or social workers, so the full cost of coverage must be recognized and included in personnel costs.

For *material costs,* the agency should be able to negotiate a discounted price with suppliers, which it then marks up in the customer's bill. It is important to remember that marking up supplies is not "ripping off the elderly consumer," but a way for the agency to recover the costs associated with travel and time necessary to go to the hardware store, lumberyard, or supplier to obtain the materials. This material cost and markup also applies to any one-time equipment that must be rented or purchased for the job.

Travel costs are a direct expense that must be covered in the pricing scheme. The agency may pay mileage to workers as they travel from job to job, or it may purchase fuel and oil for agency-owned vehicles. In either case, the agency must recognize the expenses associated with this cost of doing business.

Indirect Costs

Indirect costs are the overhead expenses of running a program. Among them are administrative staff (secretarial, management, billing), utilities, rent, photocopying, telephone, postage, and advertising/sales. In addition, the costs of any one-time equipment (e.g., computers) or capital investment (e.g., a van or truck) purchases must be amortized through the pricing structure.

Prices must include a profit margin (more properly called an "operating surplus" in nonprofit organizations) sufficient to cover these indirect costs. Failure to recognize these overhead costs as true expenses was a leading cause of difficulty for some SSPOP participants. Consider, for example, an agency with an overhead of $60,000 per year—a modest amount if the costs of a director, part-time secretary, and the other elements listed above are calculated—and direct costs of $240,000. This organization needs to generate $300,000 per year in revenue, a profit margin of 25 percent over direct costs, just to cover expenses.

Other SSPOP participants ran into difficulty because of overhead costs that were too high for them to be able to set competitive prices.

DATA NEEDS

The management information system (MIS) requirements for a home maintenance program present unique challenges to traditional home health agencies. Their existing MIS tools are likely to be inappropriate because they are clinically based, an unsuitable characteristic for a demand-driven system such as home repair.

In designing an MIS, home repair providers need to keep in mind how the information will be used. Before commencing services, the most successful SSPOP agencies evaluated thoroughly the necessary data elements, and, if necessary, revised them as the program proceeded. At a minimum, the data system should address the following:

- *Pricing.* Do prices cover the true and ongoing cost of the program?
- *Billing and Accounts Receivable.* Especially for smaller agencies, cash flow is critical. The agency should bill frequently and follow up on outstanding bills to maintain a strong cash flow position. An accrual-based accounting system that considers outstanding as well as current debts and revenues is a must for this type of business.
- *Accounts Payable.* The MIS must contain accurate and up-to-date information on materials purchased in order to recover these costs through the pricing system.
- *Cost Control and Productivity Monitoring.* Holding direct costs as low as possible is a constant struggle. Information on actual performance versus estimated bids will measure productivity and efficiency. One supportive services program provided an example of the usefulness of this type of information. A highly-skilled construction worker based his estimates of the time required for particular jobs on the amount of time it would take *him* to do the job. Less skilled workers, who actually carried out the job, required more time. By having this information available, the agency was able to adjust future estimates to reflect its actual costs in the prices charged.
- *Outstanding Jobs.* Accurate information on jobs for which the agency has submitted bids, but has not received a response, lets the staff follow up, leading to more business for the program.

Additional uses of the MIS include payroll management, scheduling workers, and measuring the cost-effectiveness of advertising. A personal computer system should easily be able to meet the data requirements for most programs.

ADMINISTRATIVE STRUCTURE

Overall Management

Often when agencies implement a new initiative such as this, the task is headed up by the one person in the agency who seems always to take on special projects. The new job is added to the existing workload with a commensurate reduction in other duties. Because a home modification program is such a radical departure from traditional operations, however, this new business demands a full-time manager to oversee the range of necessary developmental activities. The SSPOP participants found that an ideal candidate is someone who knows and understands the home maintenance and repair business (e.g., a retired carpenter with a small business background). It is important that the manager be business-oriented. The most successful agencies recognized that home repair is not simply an extension of traditional activities, but a business that requires complex—and often new— management skills. Rather than the traditional hierarchical management structure found in most community agencies, the supportive services programs found the best results from a shallow staffing pattern that emphasizes flexibility and accessibility.

Supervisor

A worker supervisor will be needed in the field to estimate jobs, oversee workers, and assure quality. Supportive services projects found it useful to have the supervisor in the field earning money at least 50 percent of the time. This position cannot be desk-bound, due to the high overhead costs. The supervisor must be active in the field, generating billable time on the job.

Direct Work Staff

Finding, hiring, and retaining quality staff is one of the major challenges for minor home repair programs. SSPOP agencies tried three approaches: per diem workers, independent contractors, and salaried staff.

By far the most successful approach used by the supportive services agencies was reliance on per diem staff, for example, a pool of workers who are hired on an as-needed basis. The agency pays only for time actually worked and avoids the fixed costs of a permanent work force. SSPOP participants, as home health agencies, are often familiar with personnel issues related to per diem workers since it is a common staffing arrangement for home health aides, nurses, and other personnel.

A second option, arrangements with independent contractors, also eliminates fixed overhead costs, but SSPOP participants found that this option left them with little direct control over the contractor. In addition, several programs report that contractors have "stolen" customers by offering to do the same job without paying the referral markup to the agency.

The third staffing option, full-time salaried workers, has the benefit of a permanent work force, but the major disadvantage of carrying high fixed costs when work is slow (e.g., in the winter months). SSPOP agencies that did not limit their full-time salaried staff ran serious deficits.

Differences in the Work Force

SSPOP participants often found many differences between the personnel with whom they usually work (e.g., nurses, home health aides, or social workers) and those employed in a home maintenance program. Handymen, for example, appeared to be motivated less by altruistic concerns than by financial considerations. Construction workers tend to be independent, and many have difficulty working in a large organization with the accompanying paperwork and levels of supervision. Finally, and not insignificantly, the mere mingling of (predominantly) male handymen with a (predominantly) female nursing staff sometimes caused a good deal of friction, especially if the offices were housed together.

EXTERNAL FACTORS

A number of events beyond the immediate control of the agency affected the SSPOP agencies' prospects for success. Three factors are quite important.

The Local Economy

In a booming economy, home repair and modification programs can do well. The biggest difficulty facing a program may be the need to find workers. The construction industry will have plenty of work, employment will be high, and the demand for "small jobs" will be strong because workers are not available to do these jobs. In an economic slump, however, competition from laid-off construction workers is likely to increase, as these individuals look for any available work to earn money. In addition, potential customers have more options and will be more selective in their choice of service provider.

Competition

Whatever the state of the local economy, agencies face competition from an underground economy. In many areas, the independent handyman or home modification worker is able to offer lower prices due to lower overhead costs (i.e., an answering machine and a pickup truck compared to agency overhead). In addition, an independent handyman who works "under the table" can lower prices even further, since taxes and other business costs are not included in the price.

State and Local Regulations

These affect the cost of doing business. Examples include whether a general contractor's license will be needed; local building codes and permit requirements; and mandated state benefits. Even though the agency may be a nonprofit, well-intended provider, it must adhere to these laws and regulations, and there are costs associated with doing so.

AGENCY CULTURE

As a final point, the culture of the agency providing this service cannot be overlooked. Successful SSPOP agencies examined how they perceived their mission. The governing board and executive leadership must see the agency's mission in terms broad enough to encompass a radically new line of business. Defining the agency's purpose as "We provide home health care" is insufficient. Instead, successful participating organizations were fully comfortable with a concept such as "Our mission is to help seniors age in place and maintain independence in their own homes by organizing and delivering whatever services are necessary."

In addition, the positive attitude and active support of the agency staff is critical to success. For example, like the staff in other nonprofit agencies, some SSPOP agency staff were reluctant to charge for services, since "Everybody we see *needs* our services," whether or not they can afford them. Another variation on this belief is "Our mission is to serve low-income people, so we should not even consider charging them." Aversion to charging for services must be overcome. In addition, the agency staff need to view customers not as passive and subservient "patients" who have decisions made for them, but as "customers" who actively participate in the decision-making process. Only in this way will the staff be able to respond to the expressed demand of the clients and increase their freedom of choice.

CONCLUSIONS

A lack of providers available and willing to provide home repair and maintenance services implies that a naturally occurring market has not developed for these services. One reason may be the relatively small scale of many of the jobs that need to be done, a scale that is unattractive to most private contractors. To compound that problem, however, many seniors noted that they do not trust the contractors who are available. These market problems make the possibility of a minor home repair and home maintenance business appear to be a natural for a service-oriented community agency, such as a visiting nurse association or area agency on aging.

At the same time, developing such a business successfully calls for new skills and management techniques for many agencies. Perhaps even more critical, it calls for a market-driven philosophy of doing business, rather than a provider-driven philosophy of providing services. The latter belief system predominates in most community agencies, and changing to the former approach creates conflicts and tensions which must be addressed head-on.

While the motive behind their interest may have been to provide needed services, the successful agencies also recognized that implementing such a program is not simply a social services venture but an investment and a business proposition.

ACKNOWLEDGMENTS

Preparation of this chapter was assisted by a grant from the Robert Wood Johnson Foundation, Princeton, New Jersey. The views expressed in the chapter are solely those of the author, and official endorsement by the Foundation is not intended and should not be inferred.

REFERENCES

1. J. Pynoos, Toward a National Policy on Home Modification, *Technology and Disability, 2*:4, pp. 1-8, Fall 1993.
2. P. Porter, Facilitating Aging in Place through Home Repairs, *Long Term Care Advances: Topics in Research, Training, Service & Policy, 6*:2, 1994.
3. S. M. Golant and A. J. LaGreca, The Relative Deprivation of U.S. Elderly Households as Judged by Their Housing Problems, *Journal of Gerontology: Social Sciences, 50B*, pp. S13-S23, 1995.
4. P. Hare, Frail Elders and the Suburbs, *Generations, 16*:2, pp. 35-39, 1992.
5. L. W. Kaye and A. Monk, Congregate Housing for the Elderly: Its Need, Function, and Perspectives, in *Congregate Housing for the Elderly: Theoretical, Policy, and Programmatic Perspectives,* L. W. Kaye and A. Monk (eds.), Haworth Press, Binghamton, New York, pp. 5-20, 1991.
6. B. Fogel, Psychological Aspects of Staying at Home, *Generations, 16*:2, pp. 15-19, 1992.
7. M. P. La Plante, G. E. Hendershot, and A. J. Moss, Assistive Technology Devices and Home Accessibility Features: Prevalence, Payment, Needs, and Trends, in National Center for Health Statistics, *Advance Data, 217*, pp. 1-12, 1992.
8. R. Hudson, Capacity Building in an Intergovernmental Context: The Case of the Aging Network, in *Perspectives on Management Capacity Building,* B. W. Honadle and A. M. Howitt (eds.), State University of New York Press, Albany, pp. 312-333, 1986.
9. J. Pynoos, Strategies for Home Modification and Repair, *Generations, 16*:2, pp. 21-25, 1992.
10. M. Mikelsons and M. Turner, *Housing Conditions of the Elderly in the 1980s: A Data Book,* Urban Institute, Washington, D.C., 1991.

11. S. M. Golant and A. J. LaGreca, Housing Quality of U.S. Elderly Households: Does Aging in Place Matter? *The Gerontologist, 34*:6, pp. 803-814, 1994.
12. J. Overton, Resources for Home-Modification/Repair Programs, *Technology and Disability, 2*:4, pp. 80-88, Fall 1993.
13. L. M. Rickman, C. E. Soble, and J. M. Prescop, *A Comprehensive Approach to Retrofitting Homes for a Lifetime,* NAHB Research Center, Upper Marlboro, Maryland, 1991.
14. *The Directory of Accessible Building Products,* NAHB Research Center, Upper Marlboro, Maryland, 1991.
15. R. V. Olsen, E. Ehrenkrantz, and B. Hutchings, *Alzheimer's and Related Dementias: Homes that Help,* New Jersey Institute of Technology, Newark, New Jersey, 1993.
16. E. E. Malizia, R. C. Duncan, and J. D. Reagan, *Financing Home Accessibility Modifications,* Center for Accessible Housing, North Carolina State University, Raleigh, North Carolina, 1993.
17. Fannie Mae Customer Education Group, *Money from Home: A Consumer's Guide to Home Equity Conversion Mortgages,* #CT066L06/92, Washington, D.C., 1992.
18. J. Pynoos and E. Cohen, *The Perfect Fit: Creative Ideas for a Safe and Livable Home,* American Association of Retired Persons, #PF 4912 (992) D14823, Washington, D.C., 1992.

CHAPTER
11

Adapting Subsidized Housing: The Experience of the Supportive Services Program in Senior Housing

Susan C. Lanspery

This book properly emphasizes housing adaptations for and by elderly homeowners, the largest group of elders. It would be less than complete, however, if it overlooked adaptation considerations for the nearly two million older residents[1] of subsidized housing, who constitute over 6 percent of all people over sixty-two [1]. In addition to its size, this group deserves attention for four principal reasons:

- Residents of subsidized housing are often perceived to be relatively well-off: their rents are subsidized, their buildings usually meet minimum safety standards, and they are somewhat more protected than other renters from the whims of landlords. Yet while their housing may be better than some other poor elders' apartments or homes, these residents tend to have lower incomes, to be older, and to live alone more often than the elderly population as a whole [1-7]. In addition, it is estimated that about 24 percent of them are "frail"[2] compared to fewer than 18 percent of elderly not in government-assisted housing [1].

---

[1] Throughout this chapter, tenants of subsidized housing are referred to as "residents" or "consumers."

[2] The definition of frailty used in this estimate was "having at least two of twenty medical conditions (e.g., heart trouble, arthritis) or one of five difficulties with personal mobility (e.g., getting around outside, going up or down stairs)" [1].

• Another common perception is that senior housing buildings are already physically adapted for people with disabilities. Most apartments in subsidized senior housing, however, do not readily accommodate disabilities [8, 9]. Even designated wheelchair-accessible apartments have problems such as windows that only an able-bodied person can close or bathrooms with grab bars in the wrong places for some residents. Other building problems include lack of community or service delivery space and designs that don't promote security or socializing. Residents are unlikely to make needed modifications, due to their low income and lack of control over the property, and many private and public building owners lack the resources or the knowledge needed to make them. Older people who live in subsidized housing not specifically designated for seniors (family housing) face even greater challenges.

• Many people also assume that senior housing residents benefit from the nearness of neighbors and on-site assistance. In fact, however, most housing developments do not have service coordinators, managers are often encouraged to limit their work to managing the "bricks and mortar," and many residents don't even know their nearest neighbors [10, 11]. Again, the situation is often even worse for older people living in family housing.

• Even more than in other settings, residents' behavior and circumstances affect others intimately, including the manager, other site staff, and neighbors [9, 11, 12]. For example, in a neighborhood of single-family households, one worries less about a neighbor's insomnia, paranoia, or tendency to leave the oven on than when those problems are on the other side of one's wall.

In short, residents' needs may be significant but their options for meeting them are limited. At the same time, units in multi-unit housing developments tend to be more readily, and less expensively, adaptable than single-family homes. The fact that they are clustered also offers opportunities for cost-effective service delivery and for building a sense of community [11, 13, 14]. This chapter will illustrate how a national demonstration program, the Supportive Services Program in Senior Housing, took advantage of such opportunities. Before describing that program, however, a conceptual structure for the senior housing environment is suggested.

THE SENIOR HOUSING ENVIRONMENT

Adapting senior housing is a "special case" of home adaptation. When considering how to adapt the senior housing environment to suit its residents better, it is useful to think of the environment as the sum and interaction of many elements. This notion draws on decades of research and discussion about interactions between people and where they live [11, 15-25]. In this chapter, we will look at three interrelated elements: the physical, the organizational, and the social.

The *physical environment* is the building's interior, exterior, and setting. It includes individual apartment features as well as laundry rooms, sidewalks, steps, mailboxes, windows, security systems, community spaces, office space, and neighborhood characteristics. It influences the organizational environment by promoting or impeding service organization and delivery. For example, having a service coordinator's office and a medical exam room promotes confidential conversation with residents and private health screening. The physical environment also influences the social environment by encouraging or discouraging positive resident interaction. For example, a well-furnished, temperature-controlled community space promotes resident activity in that room. The physical environment is in turn influenced by the other dimensions.

The *organizational environment* includes management policies and procedures, on-site staff, and the nature of the service delivery system (services provided or coordinated; the type, costs, and eligibility requirements of state and local services; and the extent of its orientation to consumers). The organizational environment affects the physical and social environments in various ways. For example, housekeeping services may help residents maintain their apartments; meal services may help prevent burns or fires; a service coordinator may help to form or rejuvenate a residents' council; and clustering services may limit the number of service providers in the building, increasing familiarity and trust.

The *social environment* includes the residents' sense of belonging, neighborliness, interdependence, relationships, and quality of life. The social environment also influences the other two dimensions. For example, an active resident community may improve building security through more activity in common areas, a sense of personal investment in the building, buddy systems, neighborhood watch programs, and improved dealings with strangers at the door or in the building. On the other hand, a resident community characterized by inter-group tensions, isolation, and distrust may dissuade management from changing policies to encourage more resident participation.

THE SUPPORTIVE SERVICES PROGRAM IN SENIOR HOUSING

To illustrate the possibilities in modifying the physical, organizational, and social elements of senior housing, this chapter reports on the experience of the Supportive Services Program in Senior Housing (SSPSH). In the SSPSH, a three-year national Robert Wood Johnson Foundation demonstration, ten state housing finance agencies (HFAs) linked housing and supportive services for older residents of subsidized housing. Working in partnership with residents and the services network, SSPSH, HFAs, and housing owners and managers modified buildings and apartments, changed management policies and procedures, implemented or coordinated services, and took steps to enrich the residents' sense of community. The SSPSH participants' experiences may be helpful to other housing sponsors, service providers, residents, planners, and people living in or involved with naturally occurring retirement communities (NORCs)[3] who are interested in linking housing and services for older people.

The largest national project linking housing and services since the federal Congregate Housing and Services Program, the SSPSH made housekeeping, transportation, service coordination, and other services available to more than 35,000 residents in 275 housing developments. HFAs, the developments, and 10,000 residents put more than $4.5 million in new service monies into these services and building modifications. (A second program, No Place Like Home (NPLH), replicated the 1988-1991 SSPSH in eleven sites in 1992-1994. Since the SSPSH did not require formal records after 1991, and since the NPLH was not formally evaluated, this chapter reports the 1988-1991 figures. Informal reports suggest that over 700 housing developments now participate in the programs.) Tables 1 and 2 summarize key SSPSH participants and "vital statistics." The program's results were achieved by:

- relying on consumer choice: residents participated in market surveys, focus groups, and resident associations and "voted with their wallets" regarding specific services
- marketing the program effectively and providing training and technical assistance to owners, managers, residents, and service providers
- keeping service costs low by taking advantage of economies of scale, reorganizing existing services, developing cooperative arrangements with service providers, and creatively developing new services.

In market surveys, residents expressed interest in and willingness to pay for heavy and light housekeeping, transportation, and activities. Although the survey results confirmed that these residents are relatively old, poor, and isolated, and experience a relatively high level of difficulty with activities of daily living, they also convinced development owners and managers that residents would share in the costs of services, and that preferred services were congruent with property management goals of maintaining the building, supporting resident autonomy, and minimizing vacancy rates. The results helped participating developments plan which services to initiate.

The philosophy of consumer choice supports the program and affects its relationship with all three elements of the environment. Consumer choice promotes resident autonomy and control, reduces the stigma of service use and the fear of eviction because of service use, generates modest revenues,[4] enhances

---

[3] NORCs are defined as apartment buildings or neighborhoods not designed to be retirement communities but where most residents are nevertheless over sixty [6].

[4] Despite their low incomes, residents appear willing to help pay for services they *want*. In fact, some residents purchase SSPSH services because of superior quality or greater flexibility, even though they are eligible for similar, less expensive, non-SSPSH services.

Table 1. Participants in the SSPSH

Colorado Housing and Finance Authority
Illinois Housing Development Authority
Maine State Housing Authority
Massachusetts Housing Finance Agency
New Hampshire Housing Finance Authority
New Jersey Housing and Mortgage Finance Agency
Pennsylvania Housing Finance Agency
Rhode Island Housing and Mortgage Finance Corporation
Vermont Housing Finance Agency
Virginia Housing Development Authority

Heller School, Brandeis University:
National Program Office

Center for Health Policy Studies, Georgetown University:
Program Evaluation

National Council of State Housing Agencies:
Program Development and Support

Table 2. SSPSH Vital Statistics[a]

Program Dates: November 1, 1988–October 31, 1991

Developments participating in the SSPSH: 275
This represents 29,000 apartment units and 35,000 individuals who stand to benefit from the SSPSH

Services
Number of developments offering:[b]

Service coordination	200
Housekeeping (light, heavy)	90
Transportation and/or shopping assistance	60
Meals	40

Financial investment during three-year period:

Developments:	$3 million
Residents:	$500,000
HFAs:	$1 million
RWJF:	$3.6 million

[a]Figures approximate as of Fall 1991.
[b]Many developments offer more than one service.

quality assurance, makes service delivery more responsive, and reduces owner and management liability ([15, 26]; see also Chapter 2 in this book). Services are "marketed" as a wise purchase rather than an admission of frailty or need. Residents often pay a portion—in some cases, all—of the cost of the service. Most services developed in the SSPSH are available to all residents, not just those who are poor or frail. SSPSH services are continued if residents purchase them and if residents, managers, service coordinators, and HFA staff representatives consider their quality acceptable. Monitoring methods include surveys, focus groups, regular formal and informal communication, and looking at utilization (a measure of satisfaction). As in a business, declines in service use are analyzed, and changes made when necessary. Emphasizing consumer choice challenges and requires adjustments for all parties [15, 26], but SSPSH participants have generally found the approach both rewarding and effective.

The following composite of SSPSH experiences illustrates how the three environments interact:

> When a service coordinator joined the Greentree House staff, one of the first residents she visited was Mrs. G, a former resident leader. Although her apartment was in good repair at the last inspection, the manager had noticed how much less often Mrs. G left the building, joined other residents in the community room, and picked up her mail.
>
> The service coordinator found Mrs. G to be an interesting, alert woman who readily acknowledged that both her arthritis and vision were worsening. She had rearranged her apartment to help her function, including keeping items she needed in a strong light and within easy reach of her bed or her favorite chair. Still, she had trouble completing chores, and even opening her door was difficult. She missed going out as she used to, missed a neighbor who had died, and missed the building's heyday when activity was the norm.
>
> Not all residents were as articulate as Mrs. G, but many had similar concerns. Fortunately—when asked—she and other residents also had suggestions to address such concerns. As a result, management replaced doorknobs with lever handles; renovated the poorly-lit, drafty, and not entirely secure mailbox area; improved the light, heat, and ventilation in the community room; and established an affordable housekeeping service. The coordinator helped the residents to:
> • revive the residents' association and re-establish a buddy system
> • link up with community services such as accessible transportation
> • initiate activities to connect Greentree with the community
> • develop new activities, including a program on "Making Your Apartment Safer," an exercise class for people with arthritis, and a support group for people with visual impairments.

The next three sections discuss SSPSH participants' specific physical, organizational, and social adaptations.

SSPSH AND THE PHYSICAL ENVIRONMENT

Although building modifications were not an explicit SSPSH goal, HFA marketing and education efforts, as well as financial incentives, encouraged demonstration participants to make them. HFAs persuaded owners that, as capital improvements, modifications would enhance their investment as well as increase residents' safety, enable residents to remain independent longer, and make possible a higher quality of life. Some HFAs offer grants or low-interest loans for "accommodative" modifications, sometimes in return for owners' committing funds to subsidize supportive services.

Resident preferences and concerns along with owner resources and interests determine the modifications made. SSPSH modifications, ranging from modest to extensive, include:

- building roofs over sidewalks between garden apartment buildings so that residents can walk safely in bad weather to mailboxes, the laundry room, the community room, the bus stop, etc.
- building or renovating space for social and educational activities and day health programs; kitchens and dining rooms for meal services; offices for service providers, health screening, medical exams, and other services such as hairdressing; and space for additional on-site staff such as service coordinators, chore workers, and housekeepers
- renovating building entrances to enhance security, safety, and the ease of retrieving mail
- adding or replacing elevators or stair lifts
- renovating laundry rooms to make them more accessible, adding one or more new laundry rooms in more convenient locations, or adding additional machines to make "clustering" possible (see next section)
- installing visual monitors at entrances and exits
- building ramps and covering ramps and stairs with anti-slip materials
- installing emergency response systems
- lowering the temperature of the hot water
- choosing "user-friendly" variations when routinely replacing appliances and other equipment—for example, stoves with front controls and automatic shut-offs, doors with lever or push handles and lower peepholes, doors and windows that move and lock easily, rugs that enhance traction for people with mobility problems and absorb noise for people with hearing or cognitive impairments, bathroom fixtures with rounded edges and easy-to-use controls, and raised toilets
- improving lighting and color contrasts in common areas to assist residents with visual and cognitive impairments and to enhance safety and security for all residents

- purchasing equipment for services, such as vans or vacuum cleaners
- improving heating and cooling systems
- inviting local home adaptation, repair, and safety experts to speak to residents, management, and service coordinators to inspire new ideas for individual apartments as well as common areas

These modifications have helped to make life easier for all residents, especially those with disabilities, and they smooth the way for improvements in the organizational and social environments. Resident involvement in choosing and planning the modification project has helped to promote appreciation for and use of the modification as well as a sense of community and pride. Residents have chosen furniture, new appliances, equipment, color schemes, and locations of and designs for new service-related space. They have also prioritized modifications (e.g., ranking security measures over laundry room renovations).

SSPSH AND THE ORGANIZATIONAL ENVIRONMENT

The SSPSH reliance on consumer choice runs as a theme through the program's principal organizational modifications, from resident market surveys and focus groups to consumer-oriented procedural modifications and new services. An important goal of the SSPSH was to make services available to more residents while promoting resident choice and control. This represented a philosophical change for most developments. Participating HFAs offered all key parties—development owners, managers, service coordinators, other site staff, residents, and service providers—the information and assistance needed to increase the knowledge of all participants about aging, housing, and services, and to affirm the benefits of consumer choice and control. Peer support groups and other informal strategies often complement formal training. The need for and effectiveness of such efforts is well documented [11, 27, 28].

Changes in HFA and management policies and procedures were directly related to the educational process and central for the SSPSH. Prior to the SSPSH, the organizational environment was generally oriented to "bricks and mortar." For example, most owners and managers avoided any mention of supportive services in management policies because of fear of liability. They were not aware that a lack of service-related policies and guidelines tends to increase liability since many managers are involved in service by default: they often know residents well, care about them, and go to great lengths to help them avoid institutionalization. Through the SSPSH, most owners and managers established better, clearer communication about services, procedures, management and resident responsibilities, and grounds for eviction. This helped to reduce liability and showed respect for residents even as it helped them to make informed choices and feel more secure.

In many developments, service coordination is the organizational key to developing new services, expanding consumer control, and responding to consumer preferences. Usually funded by the development, it is typically performed by a development employee or an individual or agency with whom the development has contracted. Some developments have their own full- or part-time service coordinators; others share; and still others assign service coordination functions to on-site property managers.

Because of the SSPSH emphasis on consumer choice, SSPSH service coordinators help residents to obtain the services they want rather than telling them what services they should or must have. The coordinators:

- develop and oversee affordable or free on-site services and link residents with existing services
- increase residents' discretionary income to help them purchase services, if desired, through SSI, Medicaid, food stamps, and other programs, or discovering allowable deductions to income (which lowers their rents)
- work closely with resident groups, such as helping to organize social and educational events and promoting resident participation in the services program, including making decisions about modifications

Finally, a number of policy and procedure changes involve awareness and initiative more than time and money. They are often related to problems in the physical environment. Some examples are:

- Management actively seeks to relocate a resident who uses a wheelchair and lives on the third floor in a building without an elevator.
- Management works more closely with resident associations about service, community, security, and maintenance issues. In some cases, residents are trained to participate effectively in building and service management.
- Management invites residents to participate in maintenance activities, such as gardening and landscaping, to promote a feeling of ownership.
- Management initiates procedures similar to those for work or repair orders for residents to make complaints, suggestions, or requests for building modifications.
- Management formulates clear policies about modifications it will undertake, and makes it easy for residents to modify apartments at their own expense without red tape.
- Management establishes communication systems that reach residents with visual and hearing impairments.

These organizational modifications have positively affected the physical and social environments of senior housing residents at relatively low cost. The effects are not limited to residents. Many managers report increased trust between residents and themselves, find increasing enjoyment of their job, and say that they are pleasantly surprised at how much residents contribute, both financially and otherwise, to supportive services and building modifications. Moreover, with the housing sponsor as a partner and services based on consumer choice, service provider agencies are more likely to "cluster"[5] services, sometimes saving enough money to serve additional eligible residents. Agencies are also likely to be more creative about serving the development as a whole, rather than only individual residents, and to suggest mutually beneficial arrangements that make better use of resources and provide affordable services or opportunities, such as sharing a minibus or sponsoring community education programs at the development.

SSPSH AND THE SOCIAL ENVIRONMENT

Although the SSPSH did not set out specifically to improve the social environment in participating developments, frequent dramatic improvements have been so beneficial that efforts to improve resident communities became more and more intentional as the SSPSH progressed. Whether healthy or frail, residents thrive in a community where neighbors know and help each other, service use is not a cause for eviction, choices are possible, and autonomy is encouraged. Higher levels of activity—resulting from a more accommodating physical environment, the greater availability of supportive services, and increased opportunities for social interaction—create a livelier, more hopeful atmosphere.

The SSPSH HFAs emphasize the benefits of cooperation among managers, service coordinators, and residents. They train and sensitize service coordinators and managers to help resident organizations to identify and act on their service, social, building-modification, and other needs and ideas.

Managers, service coordinators, and others often assume that resident organizations are difficult to start, are time-consuming, will demand improvements the managers cannot provide, are unlikely to offer meaningful activities, and cannot succeed because of residents' increasing frailty. The experience of many SSPSH developments, however, challenges these assumptions. The right kind of assistance leads to a relatively "low-maintenance" residents' organization, reasonable negotiations between residents and management, and effective resident participation in building-related decisions such as accessibility, designs, and meaningful activities. Such assistance consists of:

---

[5] With clustering, fewer providers (or the same number but in fewer hours) accomplish the same tasks. For example, instead of several residents receiving homemaker services from several homemakers who also serve clients in other locations, the agency assigns one homemaker to the residents. Laundry, shopping, and other errands are done for two or more residents at a time, reducing the homemaker hours required without decreasing each resident's time with the homemaker. Homemakers benefit from a more regular job and less traveling, which may reduce turnover.

- an emphasis on democracy, fair play, and good communication
- teaching residents the skills they need—starting and maintaining organizations is not an innate human skill—in ways that respect their age and experience
- helping an organization to establish its own guidelines (such as writing bylaws)
- support for resident leaders, especially through the early stages when participation and interest may be low, or through difficult transitional stages when leaders become ill or die
- a willingness to support the creative ideas residents generate once they experience a sense of control

Some HFAs use professional facilitators to help guide resident organizations, or to help service coordinators and managers to do so. These facilitators use a range of techniques to increase residents' self-esteem, develop and support leaders, and enhance community-building and problem-solving skills. Such activities improve residents' morale, strengthen resident-staff relationships, and make resident organizations more effective and more representative. Residents become more active and more invested in their building, and help each other more. In the words of one program observer, "A dying building becomes a living building."

Several HFAs report that previously isolated residents have become happier, more independent, and more active as a result of the SSPSH. For example, countless residents with mobility impairments were able to retrieve their own mail, participate in activities, and do their own laundry because of common space modifications. A resident purchasing an hour of housekeeping assistance weekly resumed a leadership role in the resident association "because I feel so much better being able to keep up my home the way I used to." Another resident was "liberated" after months of what she had thought was incurable incontinence. Modifying her bathroom and the community room bathroom enabled her to participate in activities, develop a social life again, and overcome depression.

Residents can play meaningful roles in supportive services and in other management matters. For example, residents of some developments defined their expectations of a service coordinator prior to hiring, helped to write interview questions, and participated in interviews. In some developments, resident advisory groups meet regularly with the service coordinator about services and activities. Residents have also, after training and technical assistance, helped to plan modifications and renovations; worked with designers and contractors to make their buildings more accessible; chosen from among bidders to provide services (e.g., conducted "taste tests" for bidders for meal contracts); chosen furniture, colors, and equipment; conducted fund-raising activities to subsidize services or activities; and modified their own apartments or made them safer.

DISCUSSION

In the experience of the SSPSH, then, housing sponsors are among the potential resources available to older people. Moreover, nontargeted, consumer-driven services are viable and cost-effective in linking housing and services, and "enhanced" service coordination leverages resources and uses existing resources well. SSPSH success benefited from the experience of previous efforts (including the Congregate Housing and Services Program, numerous state and local initiatives, and many service-conscious Section 202 developments) and from increasing awareness of and interest in the importance of housing in long-term care discussions [8-10, 29-32].

Most of the initial "modifications" of the SSPSH were organizational—changes in the way the development operated, including adding new supportive services and service coordination and changing policies and procedures. Because of the SSPSH emphasis on consumer preference, however, HFAs tailored the program to each participating development. This flexibility, along with the interrelated nature of the environmental elements, expanded the organizational modifications into the physical and social spheres and enhanced the interactive effects.

ACKNOWLEDGMENTS

Preparation of this chapter was assisted by a grant from the Robert Wood Johnson Foundation, Princeton, New Jersey. The views expressed in the chapter are solely those of the author, and official endorsement by the Foundation is not intended and should not be inferred.

REFERENCES

1. R. Struyk, D. Page, S. Newman et al. *Providing Supportive Services to the Frail Elderly in Federally Assisted Housing,* Urban Institute Press, Washington, D.C., 1989.
2. S. Lanspery, *Building Bridges and Promoting Participation: A Study of Social Workers as Enablers in Senior Public Housing,* Charles M. Farnsworth Housing Corporation, Boston, 1989.
3. W. L. Holshouser, Jr., *Aging in Place: The Demographics and Service Needs of Elders in Urban Public Housing,* Citizens Housing and Planning Association, Boston, 1988.
4. P. Hansel, *Beyond Bricks and Mortar: Issues Facing Senior Housing in California,* California Senate Office of Research, Senate Publication No. 713-5, Sacramento, 1993.
5. K. S. Gayda and L. F. Heumann, *The 1988 National Survey of Section 202 Housing for the Elderly and Handicapped,* Publication # 101376, U.S. House Subcommittee on Housing and Consumer Interests, Select Committee on Aging, December 1, 1989.
6. American Association of Retired Persons, *Understanding Senior Housing for the 1990s,* #PF4522 (593) D 13899, Washington, D.C., 1993.

7. S. M. Golant, *Housing America's Elderly: Many Possibilities, Few Choices,* Sage Publications, Newbury Park, California, 1992.
8. J. Pynoos, Linking Federally Assisted Housing with Services for Frail Older Persons, *Journal of Aging and Social Policy, 4,* pp. 157-177, 1992.
9. S. C. Lanspery and J. Pynoos, *Pivotal Choices in Housing and Services Programs,* National Eldercare Institute on Housing and Supportive Services, Andrus Gerontology Center, University of Southern California, Los Angeles, 1994.
10. S. M. Golant, The Desirability of Housing Exclusively for Older Persons, in *Expanding Housing Choices for Older People: Conference Papers and Recommendations,* The American Association of Retired Persons, Washington, D.C., 1995.
11. N. Sheehan, *Successful Administration of Senior Housing: Working with Elderly Residents,* Sage Publications, Newbury Park, California, 1992.
12. A. R. Hochschild, *The Unexpected Community: Portrait of an Old Age Subculture,* University of California Press, Berkeley, 1973.
13. S. Lanspery, Supportive Services in Senior Housing: New Partnerships between Housing Sponsors and Residents, *Generations, 16:2,* pp. 57-60, 1992.
14. L. Heumann, The Housing and Support Costs of Elderly with Comparable Support Needs Living in Long-Term Care and Congregate Housing, in *Aging in Place: The Role of Housing and Social Supports,* L. A. Pastalan (ed.), Haworth Press, Binghamton, New York, pp. 45-72, 1990.
15. J. J. Callahan, Jr., S. C. Lanspery, R. M. Loew, and D. M. Hines, *Supportive Services Program in Senior Housing Implementation Manual,* Heller School, Policy Center on Aging, Brandeis University, Waltham, Massachusetts, 1992.
16. M. P. Lawton, *Planning and Managing Housing for the Elderly,* Wiley, New York, 1975.
17. L. Festinger, S. Schachter, and K. Back, *Social Pressures in Informal Groups: A Study of Human Factors in Housing,* Harper, New York, 1950.
18. V. Regnier and J. Pynoos, *Housing the Aged: Design Directives and Policy Considerations,* Elsevier, New York, 1987.
19. R. Moos, S. Lemke, and T. David, Priorities for Design and Management in Residential Settings for the Elderly, in *Housing the Aged: Design Directives and Policy Considerations,* V. Regnier and J. Pynoos (eds.), Elsevier, New York, pp. 179-206, 1987.
20. S. Lanspery, *Expanding the Role of Housing Providers in Supportive Services,* paper presented at annual meeting of the Gerontological Society of America, Boston, 1990.
21. S. Baggett, *Residential Care for the Elderly: Critical Issues in Public Policy,* Greenwood Press, Connecticut, 1989.
22. L. W. Kaye and A. Monk (eds.), *Congregate Housing for the Elderly: Theoretical, Policy, and Programmatic Perspectives,* Haworth Press, Binghamton, New York, 1991.
23. A. N. Schwartz, Planning Micro-Environments for the Aged, in *Aging: Scientific Perspectives and Social Issues,* D. S. Woodruff and J. E. Birren (eds.), Van Nostrand Reinhold, New York, 1975.
24. E. Steinfeld and S. Shea, Enabling Home Environments: Identifying Barriers to Independence, *Technology and Disability, 2:4,* pp. 69-79, Fall 1993.

25. R. A. Barr, Human Factors and Aging: The Operator-Task Dynamic, in *Quality of Life: Charting New Territories in Behavioral Sciences Research,* R. P. Abeles, H. C. Gift, and M. G. Ory (eds.), Springer, New York, 1994.

26. E. Feingold and E. Werby, Supporting the Independence of Elderly Residents through Control over their Environment, in *Aging in Place: The Role of Housing and Social Supports,* L. A. Pastalan (ed.), Haworth Press, Binghamton, New York, 1990.

27. J. T. Sykes, Living Independently with Neighbors Who Care: Strategies to Facilitate Aging in Place, in *Aging in Place: Supporting the Frail Elderly in Residential Environments,* D. Tilson (ed.), Scott, Foresman, Glenview, Illinois, pp. 53-74, 1990.

28. G. C. Brice and K. M. Gorey, Facilitating Federally Subsidized Housing Managerial Role Expansion: Beyond Bricks and Mortar to Lifespace Intervention with Vulnerable Older Tenants, *Journal of Applied Gerontology, 10*:4, pp. 486-498, 1991.

29. J. Pynoos, Public Policy and Aging in Place: Identifying the Problems and Potential Solutions, in *Aging in Place: Supporting the Frail Elderly in Residential Environments,* D. Tilson (ed.), Scott, Foresman, Glenview, Illinois, pp. 167-208, 1990.

30. D. L. Redfoot, Coordinating Housing and Services for the Elderly, *Caring,* pp. 44-56, May 1991.

31. V. Prosper, The Changing Role of Housing for the Older Population, *Saint Louis University Public Law Review, 10*:2, pp. 485-500, 1991.

32. S. C. Lanspery and J. J. Callahan, Jr. (eds.), *Supportive Services Programs in Senior Housing: Making Them Work,* Conference Proceedings, Policy Center on Aging, Heller School, Brandeis University, Waltham, Massachusetts, 1994.

PART IV

HOUSING ADAPTATION POLICY

Introduction

In the last few years, much has changed with respect to home adaptation. The Fair Housing Act and the Americans with Disabilities Act have been implemented, and Medicaid waivers to cover home adaptation have become more common. However, like much other social policy in this era, change has been slow. Achieving systematic—or even chaotic but steady—modification of this country's housing stock will require more of a policy initiative than permitting people who need changes in their homes to make those changes themselves. In the absence of significant government programs to jump-start the home modifications and adaptive technology industries, progress has been limited: new products have been slow to come onto the market, few companies or agencies that provide home adaptation-related services have opened their doors, and many existing programs have reduced their services or gone out of business.

These trends may be reversed in the coming decade. Health care reform discussions still often address community-based care, including home modification and adaptive products. However, the efforts of providers, consumer advocacy groups, and researchers with an interest in the field will be crucial to the expansion of home modification services. The information contained in this volume is available to assist those who provide, advocate for, and study home adaptation services. This section, in particular, lays the groundwork for the future, encouraging those in the field to work side-by-side to increase recognition for the field and to put systems in place for implementation and financing.

Chapter 12 gives an overview of federal laws pertaining to adaptation, with particular reference to the Americans with Disabilities Act, while Chapter 13 discusses the implications of the Fair Housing Act for the frail elderly. Chapter 14 provides a summary of the book in setting out the policy, research, and practice agendas for home adaptation. The Epilogue summarizes the proceedings of a conference hosted by the Adaptive Environments Center (described in Chapter 1), which brought together many of the themes explored in these pages.

CHAPTER
12

Fostering Adaptive Housing:
An Overview of Funding Sources,
Laws, and Policies

*Joan Hyde, Robin Talbert, and
Paul John Grayson*

No single federal law or program regulates comprehensively—or supports—the design and adaptation of housing specifically for people who are older or have disabilities. A patchwork of federal programs and funding mechanisms, however, supports the implementation of adaptation. And, in the past decade, two dynamic pieces of legislation have been signed into law and may lead to a comprehensive and more inclusive approach to housing for people who are older or have disabilities. These laws—the Fair Housing Amendments Act of 1988 (FHAA) and the Americans with Disabilities Act of 1990 (ADA)—will have a dramatic impact on the way we treat people with physical, sensory, cognitive, and communications impairments. Derived from the civil rights laws of the 1960s and 1970s, these laws cover many forms of discrimination against persons with disabilities, mandating accessibility in the workplace and in places of public accommodation as well as in multi-family housing. As summarized by Milstein and Hitov:

> Housing consumers with disabilities benefit in at least four ways from the dual coverage provided by the ADA and the FHAA: greater architectural accessibility in both existing and new construction, expanded procedural approaches, more clearly defined tenancy rights, and new bases for gaining access to integrated housing [1, pp. 138-139].

In this chapter, we will review existing programs for home adaptation, and then consider these two laws.

PROGRAMS SUPPORTING HOME ADAPTATIONS

Several programs currently provide support for home adaptation and adaptive products. Although the list is long, the total amount of financial support is very limited.[1] The list, included to give the reader a sense of the types of programs that might be tapped for this purpose, covers health care financing, social service agencies, and housing-related programs. (For additional information about programs, financing, and features, see Chapter 9 in this book and [3-11].)

Medicare and Medicaid

Medicare does not currently fund home adaptation, although it does provide support for "durable medical equipment" such as wheelchairs and walkers. Medicare may also reimburse older people for such devices as chairs that lift the user into a standing position, if they are prescribed by a physician for specific medical conditions. Under Medicaid, durable medical equipment generally is covered under guidelines similar to Medicare's. In addition, optional Medicaid waiver provisions in a growing number of states allow payment for home adaptations as long as they are shown to be cost-effective in reducing the need for a more restrictive or costly setting. A survey by the Adaptive Environments Center [12] identified eight states using the Medicaid Home and Community Based Waivers to support home modifications for eligible older people and people with physical disabilities in 1985. A later survey followed up on those identified state programs to determine the range of home adaptations provided as well as the eligibility criteria [13]. There was wide variation throughout; all programs covered the installation of grab bars, and some covered air conditioners (for those with respiratory problems), bathroom modifications, construction of ramps, or installation of lights. By 1993, twenty-six states allowed some Medicaid payments for home modifications [6].

Private Sources

Like Medicare, private insurance companies typically do not pay for home adaptation, but may do so if its "use is consistent with the insurer's obligation of maintaining/restoring a beneficiary's health and it is perceived to be cost-effective" [14].

---

[1] As noted in [2], "third party payments accounted for only one-fourth of home accessibility features" (p. 4) in a 1992 national study.

Some older homeowners might consider home equity loans to pay for adaptations to their homes. Reverse mortgages are another possibility for financing home repairs and modifications. Reverse mortgages allow older homeowners in need of additional income to tap the equity in their homes. The opposite of conventional mortgages, cash advances are paid to the homeowner monthly or a line of credit is set up that could be used as needed. Because of high up-front fees, an individual must carefully consider whether a reverse mortgage is right for his/her particular financial situation and needs.

Area Agencies on Aging and the Formal Network

Under the terms of the Older Americans Act (OAA), state and area agencies on aging provide some services (meals, transportation, companions, and occasionally homemakers) to support older people who reside in their own homes. Nationwide, of the many programs that use OAA funding supplemented with state, local, or foundation funding, some offer limited support for home adaptation. For example, in Massachusetts, older people who are eligible for home care services may receive up to $300 for repairs or adaptations for health and safety reasons.

Federal and State Housing Programs

Currently, the largest sources of funds that may be used for home adaptation are Community Development Block Grants (CDBGs) and tax-exempt bonds [14]. Farmers Home Administration and Section 8 certificate programs also provide some funding for home adaptation.

Community Development Block Grants

Federal CDBG funds are allocated through the Department of Housing and Urban Development (HUD) to states and local communities, which have considerable discretion, within broad guidelines, regarding their use. In many urban areas, Community Development Block Grants currently are being used to provide low-interest loans and grants for home adaptation to low-income residents. Extensive programs have been established in several cities, including New York City and Oakland, California. The usefulness of this source of funds for home adaptation is limited, however, because its main purpose—to reverse urban decay and to maintain the housing stock in disadvantaged neighborhoods—itself requires substantial funds.

Department of Housing and Urban Development

In another model, programs make low-interest deferred loans available to low-income homeowners to cover the costs of home repair and adaptation. For example, HUD has instituted a home equity conversion demonstration project, and several states have made loans available through state bonding agencies. Older people have shown willingness to use equity financing for home repair and adaptation if the arrangements are properly structured, and such government support can be beneficial.

State Housing Finance Agency Loan Funds

Similarly, state housing finance agencies, which issue bonds for housing production and other housing related purposes, may create revolving, low-interest loan funds for the purpose of home repair and adaptation. Availability, as well as individual and project eligibility, varies by state.

Section 8 Rental Subsidies

Another source of housing dollars to support adaptation of existing housing is the Section 8 program, which subsidizes rent payments for low-income families in both public and private housing, making up the difference between 30 percent of the renter's income and the cost basis or fair market rent for the unit. Under this program, a landlord may pass on to the Section 8 program some home adaptation costs, in the form of higher rents.

Farmers Home Administration

For qualifying rural or suburban homeowners over the age of sixty-five, the Farmers Home Administration can provide low-interest loans (up to $80,000) and grants (up to $5,000) for needed home adaptations.

The Veterans Administration

The Veterans Administration also offers home adaptation loans and grants to veterans who meet specific criteria. Grant funding programs are categorized by type of disability and whether it is service-related. Veterans Administration housing mortgage monies also may be made available as a home equity loan to eligible veterans for this use.

Energy Programs

The Department of Energy funds weatherization programs for low-income homeowners as well as renters. Weatherization can help lower utility bills and make homes safer and more comfortable. The federal weatherization program is administered by state and local agencies. Some utility companies, as well as nonprofit agencies, also offer weatherization and financial assistance programs. The federally sponsored Low Income Home Energy Assistance Program (LIHEAP) assists low-income individuals with heating and cooling bills; it gives priority assistance to older people and persons with disabilities.

Other Programs

Two federally sponsored programs can help low-income persons afford telephone service. Linkup helps with connection charges and Lifeline discounts monthly bills. Information on these programs is available from state public service (or utility) commissions. Other federal funding sources include Vocational Rehabilitation Programs, the Department of Education (through its special education programs for people who are blind or have other disabilities), and Social Services Block Grants. These programs provide either funding or services, including assistance with home adaptations for individuals with disabilities. Such programs may target primarily children or young adults with vocational goals, but the federal Age Discrimination Act of 1975 prohibits discrimination on the basis of age in any program receiving federal funds.

Another significant piece of legislation is The Technology-Related Assistance for Individuals with Disabilities Act of 1988. Known as "The Tech Act," its purpose is to promote consumer-responsive assistive technology devices and services. It actively involves people with disabilities and their caregivers in the development and administration of programs encouraging self-direction, independence, fuller participation in society, and greater access to the built environment, by providing product and funding resource information, model demonstration and innovation projects, and consumer awareness training programs.

Finally, two other federal branches—the Internal Revenue Service and the Rehabilitation Services Administration—may help people with disabilities to defray the cost of modification [6]. Some may be able to deduct costs as a medical expense for federal income tax purposes. Those who can show that modifications help them to meet vocational objectives may quality for state vocational rehabilitation service funding.

As this book goes to press, the future of many programs is uncertain. Federal funding may be severely curtailed; funds that *are* available to states and localities are more likely to be in the form of block grants, with more local control. Learning about state and local programs (see References and the Bibliography) and communicating with state and local decision-makers will help consumers to accomplish, or to advocate for assistance with, modifications.

THE FAIR HOUSING AMENDMENTS ACT

The FHAA, discussed in more detail in Chapter 13, sets minimum standards for accessibility in newly constructed multi-family dwelling units. This law considers a dwelling unit accessible if—and only if—a person using a wheelchair can access the building from the site, the parking areas and pathways, and main entrance, mail boxes, laundry, social areas, elevator and corridors, to the front door of the unit and into all the spaces of the dwelling (vestibule, living room, kitchen, closets, storage, electrical control boxes, bedroom, and bathroom). It also introduces some adaptability in bathrooms, to provide for future installation of grab bars. The law does not cover private single-family residences. Applying the law's requirements to the design of such residences, however, can help to enhance accessibility.

There are also significant implications for existing rental units. Under the FHAA, landlords are required to allow tenants with disabilities to make adaptations, at their own expense, that will enable them to fully use the unit.[2] (Buildings constructed after March 13, 1991, containing four or more dwelling units, must be built with future accessibility needs in mind, for example, wide doorways, and reinforced bathroom walls for later grab-bar installation.) The Massachusetts Housing Bill of Rights goes even further, requiring landlords, under certain circumstances, to pay for such adaptations themselves. Municipal housing authorities must make such adaptations "if funding is available."

THE AMERICANS WITH DISABILITIES ACT

The Americans with Disabilities Act of 1990 (ADA) prohibits discrimination against persons with disabilities in a range of settings. In addition to employment, it also covers accessibility to programs, activities, and services provided by state and local government,[3] businesses which serve the public, private business, and commercial buildings such as hotels and lodging houses. The law sets accessibility requirements for transportation and communications. Although the ADA was not intended to cover private residential settings, many of its basic physical and communications access standards are adaptable to housing needs for older persons. The ADA Accessibility Guidelines (ADAAG), providing minimum standards for physical and communications elements, can serve as a valuable reference checklist when working with the FHAA standards. Both the FHAA and the ADA build on the minimum design standards that first were established by the American National Standards Institute (ANSI). Many other codes and laws have used the ANSI standards.

The FHAA's and ADA's macro-level approach is especially interesting. These laws consider accessibility in the built environment as an inclusive right and, in so doing, advance public policy toward the notion of universal design, which aims to accommodate the needs of all and to create safe and barrier-free environments usable by people who are older or have disabilities. In the past, designers and developers considered creating accessible environments to be costly and bothersome. Today, these laws mandate accessibility in privately as well as publicly

---

[2] The FHAA also requires changes in policy to accommodate a person with a disability. This could involve allowing service dogs even in a building with a "no pets" rule.

[3] Federal buildings already comply with Section 504 of the Rehabilitation Act of 1973 and the Uniform Federal Accessibility Standards (UFAS) checklist.

owned buildings. Entities covered by the laws and their implementing regulations must provide access to persons with disabilities or face penalties for not meeting their obligations.

The ADA's Scope

The ADA combines the principles of universal accessibility with civil rights. It provides comprehensive civil rights protection to individuals with disabilities in the areas of employment, businesses which serve the public, state and local government services, and telecommunications. The ADA defines the term "disability" as follows:

1. A physical or mental impairment that substantially limits one or more of the major life activities (caring for oneself, performing manual tasks, walking, seeing, hearing, speaking, breathing, learning, and working);
2. A record of such impairment; or,
3. Being regarded as having such an impairment (regardless of whether the person actually has an impairment, the perception of others triggers coverage).

This three-part definition was first used in the Rehabilitation Act of 1973 which, among other things, prohibited discrimination by federally-assisted programs and activities.

There are five components of the Americans with Disabilities Act.

TITLE I relates to equal employment opportunities for qualified people with disabilities. It speaks to the responsibility of the employer to provide reasonable accommodations, so long as it is not an undue hardship to do so.

TITLE II extends the mandate of Section 504 of the Rehabilitation Act to state and local government activities, to the facilities and buildings in which they operate, and to public transportation (though not airlines, which are covered by a separate statute, the Air Carrier Access Act). It expands and clarifies requirements for effective communications.

TITLE III pertains to the private sector and privately operated places of business, public accommodations, services, and commercial facilities. It covers virtually all places which provide services to the public, but exempts religious institutions and private clubs.

TITLE IV addresses telecommunications, specifically telephone access, and also includes closed captioning of public service announcements.[4]

TITLE V has a wide range of miscellaneous provisions and states that:

---

[4] It mandates a national system of telephone relay services for people with hearing and speech impairments. Each state is required to establish a third-party service in which people who use TTYs can communicate with other telephone users.

- The ADA does not set a lesser standard than the Rehabilitation Act of 1973.
- The ADA does not invalidate or limit rights, remedies, or procedures of any state, federal, or local law that affords equal or greater protection.
- States are not immune from the Act's provisions.
- Congress and other legislative agencies are required to comply with the Act.
- Retaliation and coercion are prohibited.
- The Architectural Transportation and Barriers Compliance Board issues minimum guidelines for Titles II and III.
- Attorney's fees may be recovered.
- Technical assistance will be available.
- Alternative means of dispute resolution are encouraged.

Since the purpose of this chapter is to identify laws and policies that foster adaptive housing, we will review in greater detail pertinent elements of Titles III and IV.

Title III: Public Accommodations

The ADA is designed to complement the FHAA, which prohibits discrimination based on disability in most residential dwellings. While the ADA's Title III specifically addresses discrimination in commercial facilities and public accommodations, all or part of some residential facilities may be covered by both laws if they have commercial facilities or "places of public accommodation."

"Places of public accommodation" are facilities that affect commerce and fall into at least one of twelve categories specifically listed in the law. The categories most relevant to elderly housing are places of lodging, social service centers, and service establishments. Also included are hospitals, medical offices, pharmacies, restaurants, hotels, theaters, shopping centers and malls, retail stores, museums, libraries, parks, private schools, and day care centers ([16], 36.104).

For the first time there are requirements to try to remove barriers in existing buildings even when no construction is planned. Physical barriers in existing places of public accommodation must be removed if doing so is readily achievable, that is, easily accomplished and able to be carried out without much difficulty or expense. If not, alternative methods of providing services must be offered if those methods are readily achievable ([16], 36.304 and 36.305). It also requires making reasonable modifications in policies, practices, and procedures to make sure that no individual with a disability is excluded or treated differently than people who do not have disabilities, or providing auxiliary aids and services to assure effective communication for people with hearing, vision, speech, and cognitive disabilities. It may mean creating more accessible parking spaces, rearranging furniture, or widening doors. In addition, newly constructed places of public accommodation and commercial facilities (nonresidential facilities affecting commerce) first occupied after January 1993 must be accessible ([16], 36.401).

Alterations to existing places of public accommodation and commercial facilities must be done in a manner that results in an accessible environment. When alterations affect usability of or access to "primary function" areas of a facility, an accessible path of travel must be provided to the altered areas. In other words, a facility is more than just a single shop or lobby or office: it includes an entire site. Public restrooms, telephones, and even drinking fountains serving the site must be made accessible to the extent that added costs (for access) are not disproportionate to overall costs of the original alteration.

The American Association of Homes and Services for the Aged (AAHSA) has expressed concern that certain building codes used in conjunction with the ADA are not workable for older persons with disabilities. For example, dimensions for toilet placement for wheelchair users do not take into consideration that older wheelchair users often have their elbows projected, or may need another person in the stall for transfer assistance [17]. This suggests a need for special attention for buildings intended to house or serve older people.

Provision of Services

Even if a facility is covered under the Fair Housing Act, the provision of services to the public triggers ADA Title III coverage for those services. Services also must be provided in the most integrated fashion possible. Individuals with disabilities are entitled to participate to the same extent as those without disabilities, even if they cannot achieve the same result.

If an entity provides separate specialized services, a person with a disability cannot be denied access to the programs that are *not* separate or different. Moreover, such special programs or benefits are prohibited unless they are necessary to allow people with disabilities the same opportunity to participate as people without disabilities. Special restrooms and parking facilities would fall into this exception. Surcharges for costs of modifications or auxiliary aids are prohibited.

Eligibility criteria imposed for safety considerations must be based on actual risks, not on stereotypes or generalizations about persons with disabilities. A public accommodation may preclude a person with a disability from participating in a service or program only if the person poses a direct threat to the health or safety of others. The risk must be one which cannot be eliminated by a modification of policies, practices, or procedures, or by the provision of auxiliary aids or services. Higher insurance rates cannot be used as a barrier to the provision of services.

It is important to remember that the ADA covers those with mental disabilities—cognitive impairments as well as mental illness. Discrimination against such individuals in the provision of public accommodations is illegal under the Act. Designing accommodations for persons with mental impairments may require more creativity and flexibility than accommodating physical needs. For instance, making available an ombudsperson to provide individualized assistance, or an information assistant to help with communication issues, may be appropriate.

Title IV: Telecommunications

Title IV of the ADA requires that both local and long-distance telephone services provide around-the-clock relay operators. Relay services provide the link between people who have speech or hearing impairments and those who do not. The relay operator translates the written messages transmitted via telephone communications devices (TTYs or TDDs) into voice messages and vice versa. Such services had been available to a limited degree in the past but are now available at all times, providing an important connection between people who are deaf or speech-impaired and families, friends, and businesses. Such services can play a particularly important role for those wishing to age in place.

Implications for Elderly Housing Facilities

The precise extent to which the Americans with Disabilities Act covers types or components of elderly housing facilities is not completely clear, as uncertainty exists over what constitutes "public" activities and functions for current and prospective residents. What is clear is that in accessible transient lodging (including boarding houses and similar facilities), a specific percentage of the rooms (either new construction or modified through substantial alterations) must be accessible according to the ADA Accessibility Guidelines, published by the Department of Justice. It is also clear that substantial renovations to these facilities or portions thereof used for sleeping accommodations must include accessibility features specified in the guidelines. (All states, however, have at least some access standards which cover renovations and new construction, so this is not unique to the ADA.) Social service functions offered by the facility (transportation, meals, etc.) are covered by Title III, as are all other programs and services open to the public.

Whether Title III covers nursing homes depends on how they are characterized. If the totality of services is considered, they would appear to be covered. Residential facilities are excluded from ADA coverage, but the ADA and the Fair Housing Act cover places of lodging such as inns, hotels, and motels that do not have separate units for residential and short-term stays. Because nursing facilities often are like places of lodging, in that at least some of the residents stay for short periods of time, they may be covered under Title III.

This analysis is supported by the preamble to the regulations implementing Title III, which discuss single room occupancy hotels (SROs). SROs used only for long-term residency are subject only to the Fair Housing Act. ADA regulations would cover social services if they are provided. The regulations state that a similar analysis can be made for other facilities, including nursing facilities, that provide social services and whose residents vary in their length of tenure. Determinations are to be made on a case-by-case basis.

There are many implications for such coverage, beyond the most obvious ones of physical access. For example, if a public accommodation provides a customer, client, resident, patient, or participant the opportunity to make outgoing telephone calls on more than an incidental basis, text telephones must be provided for those with hearing impairments. Places of lodging that provide television sets in five or more guest rooms or hospitals that provide television sets for patient use must provide, upon request, a means for decoding captions for use by persons with hearing impairments. New standards under the ADA also cover signage—for example, Braille must be added to permanent room signs and overhead signs must meet specific size and other criteria. Aurally delivered materials must be made available to individuals with hearing impairments via qualified interpreters, computer-aided transcription, notetakers, assistive listening devices, captioning, or other means.

CONCLUSION

Many "gray areas" of the ADA and the Fair Housing Act are still being settled in the courts. One case filed soon after implementation of the Act tested the applicability of the new laws to group homes. In *Potomac Group Home v. Montgomery County,* a federal judge blocked the eviction of two women with Alzheimer's disease from a group home. The county had tried to evict the women because they could not vacate the home unassisted in the event of an emergency. The judge found that the county's actions unreasonably limited older persons with disabilities from living in the community of their choice.

These programs and laws are beginning to make an impact on the availability of suitable living environments for people who are older or have disabilities. In particular, the Americans with Disabilities Act has opened up many new possibilities and opportunities for creating more public and private spaces that will be accessible. It also has much to offer people who are older or have disabilities in how state and local governments, as well as health care and social service providers, deliver services. Furthermore, it will raise the consciousness of businesses and the general public about meeting the needs of persons with disabilities. Many implementation issues have yet to be answered. Experience in interpreting the regulations, legal action, and enforcement will continue to define the parameters of the law. But whether mandated by law or encouraged by public policy, the provision of housing that is adaptable, barrier-free, and safe just makes good sense. For service providers, accessible and adaptable housing will reduce the stress and strain of caregiving. For the user, it will enhance independence, aging-in-place, and the quality of one's life. For developers and designers, it will open up new marketing opportunities. Not only will this form of housing help satisfy the wants and needs of the elderly and those with disabilities, but it can also benefit the entire population.

As professionals and the general public become more aware of the long-term advantages of accessible and adaptable environments, such programs and laws as described in this chapter will become the foundation and the catalyst for developing Universal Design (see Chapter 4). Whether residential or workplace, environments that are accessible and usable, regardless of individual levels of ability, are a benefit to all.

REFERENCES

1. B. Milstein and S. Hitov, Housing and the ADA, in *Implementing the Americans with Disabilities Act: Rights and Responsibilities of all Americans,* L. O. Gostin and H. A. Beyer (eds.), Brookes Publishing, Baltimore, 1993.
2. J. Pynoos, Toward a National Policy on Home Modification, *Technology and Disability,* 2:4, pp. 1-8, Fall 1993.
3. L. M. Rickman, C. E. Soble, and J. M. Prescop, *A Comprehensive Approach to Retrofitting Homes for a Lifetime,* NAHB Research Center, Upper Marlboro, Maryland, 1991.
4. *The Directory of Accessible Building Products,* NAHB Research Center, Upper Marlboro, Maryland, 1991.
5. R. V. Olsen, E. Ehrenkrantz, and B. Hutchings, *Alzheimer's and Related Dementias: Homes that Help,* New Jersey Institute of Technology, Newark, New Jersey, 1993.
6. E. E. Malizia, R. C. Duncan, and J. D. Reagan, *Financing Home Accessibility Modifications,* Center for Accessible Housing, North Carolina State University, Raleigh, North Carolina, 1993.
7. Fannie Mae Customer Education Group, *Money from Home: A Consumer's Guide to Home Equity Conversion Mortgages,* #CT066L06/92, Washington, D.C., 1992.
8. J. Pynoos and E. Cohen, *The Perfect Fit: Creative Ideas for a Safe and Livable Home,* American Association of Retired Persons, #PF 4912 (992) D14823, Washington, D.C., 1992.
9. J. Overton, Resources for Home-Modification/Repair Programs, *Technology and Disability,* 2:4, pp. 80-88, Fall 1993.
10. National Resource and Policy Center on Housing and Long-Term Care, *Home Modifications Resource Guide,* Andrus Gerontology Center, University of Southern California, Los Angeles, 1994.
11. G. Gaberlavage and P. Forsythe, *Home Repair and Modification: A Survey of City Programs,* American Association of Retired Persons (#9504), Washington, D.C., 1995.
12. P. Dunn, *An Overview of Housing Adaptation Services Covered by Medicare and Medicaid in Massachusetts,* Adaptive Environments Center, Boston, Massachusetts, 1985.
13. E. Ostroff, *Survey of Home Adaptation Programs in Selected States,* Human Services Research Institute, Cambridge, Massachusetts, 1988.

14. M. Ellison, V. Bradley, J. Knoll, and K. Moore, *Financing Options for Home Care for Children with Chronic Illness and Severe Disability*, technical assistance manual, Human Services Research Institute, Cambridge, Massachusetts, 1989.
15. W. Mitchell, Financing Home Modifications for Accessibility, *Design for Independent Living*, Housing Accessibility Institute, Center for Accessible Housing, Washington, D.C., 1991.
16. 28 CFR Part 36, *Federal Register, Department of Justice: Nondiscrimination on the Basis of Disability by Public Accommodations and in Commercial Facilities: Final Rule*, ADA-Title III, 1991.
17. AAHA *Provider News*, September 1993.

BIBLIOGRAPHY

24 CFR Chapter 1, *Federal Register: Department of Housing and Urban Development Final Fair Housing Accessibility Guidelines* (FHAA), U.S. Department of Housing and Urban Development, Office of the Assistance Secretary for Fair Housing and Equal Opportunity, 1991.

24 CFR Part 14 et al., *Federal Register: Implementation of the Fair Housing Amendments Act of 1988; Final Rule* (FHAA), U.S. Department of Housing and Urban Development: Office of the Assistant Secretary for Fair Housing and Equal Opportunity, 1989.

28 CFR Part 35, *Federal Register, Department of Justice: Nondiscrimination on the Basis of Disability in State and Local Government Services: Final Rule* (ADA Title IV), 1991.

29 CFR 1630, *Federal Register, Equal Employment Opportunity Commission: Equal Employment Opportunities for Individuals with Disabilities: Final Rule* (ADA Title II), 1991.

ADA: Accessibility for Older Persons with Disabilities, American Association of Retired Persons, Washington, D.C., 1995.

ADA Accessibility Guidelines for Buildings and Facilities: Federal Register, Vol. 56, No. 144, Rules and Regulations, (ADAAG, Title III), 1991.

Barrier-Free Site Design, U.S. Department of Housing and Urban Development, Office of Policy Development and Research, American Society of Landscape Architects Foundation; distributed by U.S. Government Printing Office, Washington, D.C., 1975.

Designing Affordable Houses, U.S. Department of Housing and Urban Development, Office of Policy Development and Research; distributed by U.S. Government Printing Office, Washington, D.C., 1983.

Fair Housing: It's Your Right, U.S. Department of Housing and Urban Development, Office of Fair Housing and Equal Opportunity; distributed by U.S. Government Printing Office, Washington, D.C., 1992.

Opening the Doors to Older Persons: An ADA Accessibility Checklist, American Association of Retired Persons, Washington, D.C., 1995.

West, J. (ed.), *The Americans With Disabilities Act: From Policy to Practice*, Milbank Memorial Fund, New York, 1991.

CHAPTER
13

Implications of the 1988
Fair Housing Act for the Frail Elderly

Sandra J. Newman and Molli N. Mezrich

The Fair Housing Act[1] passed by Congress in September 1988 is a significant piece of legislation for individuals with functional impairments, including the frail elderly. Until passage of this Act, physically or mentally impaired individuals were excluded from explicit coverage by the housing discrimination provisions of Title VIII of the Civil Rights Act of 1968.[2] These provisions pertain to the sale or rental of a dwelling as well as a range of other real estate transactions (e.g., financing, building, appraising). The new Fair Housing legislation adds people with disabilities as a "protected class" and extends to them the principle of equal housing opportunity. With respect to this book's focus on housing modifications, the Act is also "by far the most far-reaching legislation encouraging accessible housing" [1, p. 7]. Summarizing elements important to our discussion, two other analysts have noted:

* The amendments to the Fair Housing law guaranteed the right to make home modifications in multi-family housing. This removed a legal barrier to serving the needs of low-income individuals [2, p. vi].

---

[1] Formally known as the Fair Housing Amendments Act of 1988.

[2] Title VIII is commonly known as the Fair Housing Act of 1968. Discriminatory housing practices that are illegal under this Act include such actions as the refusal to sell or rent a dwelling, or to negotiate to sell or rent a dwelling, advertise a dwelling for sale or rent with an explicitly stated preference for offerors of a particular race, religion, sex, or other covered characteristics, and failing to provide an individual in a real estate transaction with information regarding financing because of that individual's race, sex, etc.

- In the case of handicap or disability, discrimination includes a refusal to permit reasonable modifications to the premises, or to make reasonable accommodations in rules and procedures, to allow the tenant equal access to and enjoyment of the housing [3, p. 10].

In addition, the 1988 amendments restructure the enforcement provisions in a way that gives greater enforcement power both to the federal government and to private individuals.

This chapter reviews the potential effects of the Fair Housing Amendments Act of 1988 on the frail elderly—that is, elderly individuals who need assistance in carrying out the normal activities of daily living. Definitions and applications related to the statute continue to evolve as case law accumulates, but we are still in the early stages of anticipating its ultimate effects [3-5]. In the present case, because the Act does not single out the frail elderly in its designation of the handicapped, even the fundamental question of who among the frail elderly are considered part of this newly protected class is open to debate.

We begin our review by discussing the key provisions in the Act that pertain to protection for the handicapped, and suggest the relevance of these provisions for the frail elderly. Because even the best law in concept cannot achieve its goals without an effective enforcement mechanism, we then briefly describe and evaluate the enforcement procedures created by the Act. In the final section, we provide some rough estimates of the number of frail elderly individuals and dwelling units that may be affected by the Act, and offer some concluding remarks.

It should be noted that some of the actual and potential effects of the Act are linked with those of Section 504 of the Rehabilitation Act of 1973 and the Americans with Disabilities Act (ADA). Detailed discussion of these statutes is outside the scope of this chapter. See Chapter 12 in this book for more information on the ADA's implications with respect to home modifications.

PROTECTION FOR THE HANDICAPPED: "PEOPLE" AND "PLACES"

For simplicity, it is useful to distinguish between two types of provisions in the 1988 Act that pertain to the protection of the handicapped from housing discrimination: those that focus on people and those that are concerned with places. The first category includes the definition of handicapped status under the Act and is, therefore, of fundamental importance in establishing who among the frail elderly are likely to be afforded this new protection. The second category delineates which properties must abide by the new law and what actions property owners are required to undertake, or to allow, to make their properties accommodative to the handicapped. Each of these will be discussed, in turn.

"People" Provisions

The core of the Fair Housing Act's definition of "handicap" is "a physical or mental impairment which substantially limits one or more . . . major life activities" ([6, Sec. 5(b)].[3] The regulations provide further specification for the two key concepts in this definition, namely, "physical or mental impairment" and "major life activities" [7, Sec. 100-201(a)]. Physical impairments are interpreted to include diseases, disorders, or conditions that affect any body systems or organs (e.g., musculoskeletal, neurological, digestive, sensory organs). Interestingly, the regulations refer to the category "mental impairments" as "mental and psychological disorders," presumably to establish at the outset that a broad range of mental and emotional illnesses are included. And, in fact, both emotional and mental illness are specifically cited in the regulations. Other examples of impairments listed are organic brain syndrome (which includes Alzheimer's disease) and mental retardation.

"Major life activities," the second key concept in the definition of handicap, refers to "functions such as caring for one's self, performing manual tasks, walking, seeing, hearing, speaking, breathing, learning and working" [7, Sec. 100-201(b)]. For gerontologists who generally work with measures of functional impairment such as Activity of Daily Living (ADL) and Instrumental Activity of Daily Living (IADL) scales, the phrase "caring for one's self" raises the question of whether self-care is restricted to tasks such as toileting and bathing or includes a broader range of instrumental activities such as shopping, preparing meals, and managing money. The life activities listed in the regulations offer little guidance here since they include both very basic bodily functions, such as breathing, and such instrumental functions as walking or working. Thus, from the perspective of the frail elderly, it is unclear whether an individual limited in IADLs only is considered handicapped under the Fair Housing Act. Here, as elsewhere, a final determination will come with experience. But at least some observers believe that the definition of "handicap" in the regulation is extremely broad and all-encompassing,[4] which would suggest that IADL needs alone would qualify an individual as handicapped.

Although these observers were commenting on the regulation rather than the Act itself, a convincing argument could be made that one need look no further than the language of the Act to conclude that the intent of Congress was to provide broad coverage. In particular, it is not solely individuals who *have* physical or mental impairments which limit major life activities who are considered to be

---

[3] Individuals with current, illegal use of or addiction to a controlled substance are specifically excluded from this definition.

[4] See 24 CFR App. 1 Subch. A Sec. 100.201, 577 reporting on the group of commenters including the National Association of Home Builders and the National Association of Realtors. See also [4, p. 208].

handicapped, but also individuals who 1) have a *record* of having such an impairment or 2) are *regarded* as having such an impairment. According to the regulations, these additional criteria would extend the law's protection to individuals who may have been *wrongly* diagnosed as functionally impaired at some time in their lives, as well as individuals who may have no impairments but who are considered to be impaired by at least one other person. Including the attitudes of others as a criterion for determining handicapped status demonstrates the legislators' recognition that the perceptions and apprehensions of others can create obstacles to freedom of choice that are as great as those faced by individuals with actual, measurable impairments. Thus, for example, the regulations include "cosmetic disfigurement" in the list of examples of conditions and disorders that would qualify as physical impairments. But attitudes of others may also be relevant for determining whether subgroups of the elderly are covered by the Act. For example, a very old individual who has no physical or mental impairment would appear to qualify for the law's protection because others often view such individuals as "impaired." Arguably, then, the provision designed to prohibit housing discrimination on the basis of handicap may, when applied to the very old, actually have the effect of prohibiting discrimination by age. This is ironic, since age does *not* define a protected class in this law.

Despite the seemingly open-ended nature of these criteria and the absence of any guidance in the regulations (regarding how individuals would verify either their misclassification or the treatment or attitudes of others), these additional components of the definition were not the specific focus of comments received by HUD in response to the publication of regulations. Instead, the comments emphasized the prospect that housing providers would have to admit *any* person with a handicap, even if that individual did not meet standard tenant selection criteria applied to all potential tenants (e.g., past rental history, violation of rules, history of dangerous behavior). At first glance, this reaction is surprising since both the Act and the regulations explicitly state that individuals who pose "a direct threat to the health or safety" of others or "whose tenancy would result in substantial physical damage to the property of others" can be excluded [6; 7, Sec. 102.202(5)(d)]. But here, as elsewhere, the cause for concern is with implementing this provision, and particularly the restrictions that govern the tenant selection process. In fact, older residents, housing managers, advocates, and others attribute the increase in the number of nonelderly tenants with disabilities in many elderly housing developments, and an increase in community problems, to Fair Housing requirements [4].[5]

---

[5] In the original statute, which prohibits housing discrimination against families with children as well as against persons with disabilities, "Congress recognized the existence and virtues of housing exclusively for older persons and exempted this housing category from the familial provisions of FHAA if they met [certain] conditions" [4, p. 207]. Attempts to clarify these provisions have been controversial and are ongoing [4, 8, 9].

Because the cognitive impairments experienced by some elderly can raise concerns about safety and security issues, this provision is worth exploring. Of special interest is the kind of information sellers and landlords are legally allowed to collect in determining whether prospective buyers or tenants will pose a direct threat to the health and safety of others. This information is historical rather than projective, is limited to the applicant's past behavior as a housing resident, and cannot probe into underlying medical conditions.[6] The rationale for this approach is to avoid any presumption that individuals with handicaps pose greater safety threats than individuals without handicaps [7, App. 1 Subch. A Sec. 100.202, 580]. Thus, in the case of an elderly tenant applicant in the early stages of Alzheimer's disease, for example, landlords cannot speculate about possible future problems as a basis for denying tenancy. Taken one step further, this approach in the law implies that additional needs for support that tenants may experience at some point in the future in order to ensure both their safety and the safety of others are to be dealt with at that time. If those needs cannot be met adequately to assure the safety of the property, of other tenants, or of the handicapped tenant, then typical procedures for assuring security—presumably including eviction—could be pursued.

A final provision in the statute that is relevant to the frail elderly is the fact that it is not only the handicapped buyer[7] or renter himself or herself who is afforded the Act's protection from housing discrimination, but also any person "intending to reside" in the dwelling after it is sold or rented as well as any person associated with the buyer or renter. While the standards that will be used to measure "intent" are not spelled out, it is at least possible that frail older persons who intend to move in with their adult children would be among those covered under this component of the law.

Provisions Regarding "Places"

As noted earlier, the provisions in the Act pertaining to places fall into two categories: the definition of properties that are covered by the new law versus those that are exempt from it, and the actions that must be taken or allowed to accommodate residence by individuals with handicaps.

---

[6] However, landlords are allowed to ask whether the tenant applicant qualifies for a dwelling that is only available to the handicapped. This type of inquiry is allowed because it appears to be the only way to determine whether the tenant is eligible for special government housing programs for the handicapped or for housing units that are available exclusively to the handicapped [7, Sec. 100.202(c) Appl. 1 Subch. A Sec. 100.202, 579]. Even here, however, as noted in [3, p. 12], "documentation in support of a disability should be obtained in the manner which best protects the privacy of the applicant."

[7] In the case of discrimination against the handicapped, discrimination in selling a property is likely to refer to sales of condominiums in multifamily buildings. This interpretation has also been offered by Payne [10].

The Act sets forth a somewhat different set of requirements for newly constructed, as compared to existing, housing. Newly constructed housing must comply with three requirements governing: 1) common or public areas; 2) doors into and within the dwelling; and 3) adaptive design features within the dwelling. More specifically:

1. public use and common use portions of the dwellings must be readily accessible to, and useable by, handicapped persons. This has been interpreted to mean that at least one regular entrance to common areas must be accessible [11];
2. passage doorways—that is, access doors into these dwellings, and doors required for circulation inside these dwellings—must be wide enough for use by someone in a wheelchair;
3. adaptive design features inside these dwellings must include: an accessible route into and through the dwelling; light switches, thermostats, and other controls in accessible locations; reinforcements in bathroom walls to allow installation of grab bars; and kitchens and bathrooms that can be used by someone in a wheelchair.

"Covered" newly constructed housing is restricted to dwellings that are occupied for the first time after March 13, 1991[8] *and* are multifamily buildings with four or more units. If the building has four or more units but does not have an elevator, then the law applies to the ground floor units only.[9] A wide range of residential uses must comply with these requirements including boarding homes, single room occupancy (SRO) buildings, and shelters for the homeless. Exempt properties include newly constructed single-family as well as two- and three-family housing. The regulations further clarify that multi-story townhouses or rowhouses that are connected (and therefore constitute four or more dwellings in a building) would be covered only if each had an elevator.[10]

Also exempt are buildings constructed in locations with unusual terrain or other site characteristics that make it impractical to meet the accessibility requirement of the Act. Because the statute itself does not contain an explicit standard for measuring the concept of "impracticality," this aspect of the law has generated much debate and will likely continue to be a source of confusion until case law provides some clarification. To date, concern has focused on whether the emphasis of the Act is on "physical impracticality" or whether "economic impracticality" can also come into play. The gist of the argument for considering

---

[8] The regulations clarify that substantially rehabilitated properties would be exempt from coverage because it could not be argued that the premises had never before been used.

[9] The Act does not require the installation of elevators.

[10] Implicit in the reasoning behind this interpretation of the regulation is that even if the first floor of the townhouse were at ground level, the remainder of the dwelling would not be accessible without an elevator.

economic factors is that, given the advanced state of building technologies, there are only rare instances in which it is physically impossible to make virtually any site accessible, but many more instances in which doing so would threaten the economic feasibility of some housing development projects, or have a severe effect on the affordability of the resulting housing units. HUD's response to these concerns emphasizes the language of the House report on the Act, including its statement that the accessibility provisions of the Act should be met without imposing "unreasonable requirements" on homebuilders, landlords, and non-handicapped tenants [11, p. 27].

In contrast to the case of newly constructed multifamily buildings, in which the owner must be an active participant in making the property accessible and usable by the handicapped, the statute imposes a more passive role on owners of *existing* properties. These owners have two types of obligations under the Law. The first pertains to physical modifications. Under this feature of the Act, owners must allow residents with disabilities to make "reasonable modifications" that would enable these individuals to fully enjoy their housing. In private housing, modifications to the resident's own unit are to be made at the handicapped individual's expense. Also in private housing, residents with disabilities can request reasonable modifications to common interior or exterior areas at the landlord's expense [3]. "In public and federally subsidized housing (covered by Section 504 of the Rehabilitation Act of 1973), the provider pays for all reasonable modifications, both to the individual unit and to the common areas" [3, p. 19]. Examples cited in the regulations include the installation of grab bars in the bathroom, which may also require the installation of proper wall reinforcements, and the widening of passage doorways into, and within, the dwelling. In the case of rental property, the owner can require the tenant to restore the premises to their original condition where it is reasonable to do so. (It is worth noting here that modifications may increase property value [12, p. 20].) For example, in the case of grab bar installation that also requires the strengthening of walls, it would be reasonable to ask the tenant to remove the grab bars but unreasonable to also ask that the extra reinforcement in the walls be removed since the strengthened walls will not interfere with the future enjoyment of the dwelling. Although security deposits cannot be increased for handicapped tenants who plan to make building accommodations, owners can ask that an escrow account be set up in the approximate amount of the cost of the restoration. However, such escrow accounts are only allowed in instances deemed "reasonable." This reasonableness standard is interpreted to refer to instances in which the proposed modifications that are to be restored are extensive, the tenant's credit history is only "fair," and/or other factors suggest that the tenant would not be able to ensure that the restorations are completed [7, App. 1 Subch. A Sec. 100.203, p. 582]. Finally, owners may also require tenants to provide a description of the proposed modification and some assurance that the work will be done "in a workman-like fashion."

The second requirement imposed on owners of existing dwellings pertains to "reasonable accommodations." This aspect of the law shifts the focus from modifications of physical features to adjustments in rules, policies, practices, or services that have the effect of excluding the handicapped residents from full enjoyment of their housing. Examples of accommodations include allowing a blind individual with a seeing-eye dog to live in a building that doesn't allow pets, and assigning a reserved parking space adjacent to the main building entrance to a mobility-impaired tenant in a building that does not assign parking spaces for other tenants. Reactions to this section of the law have focused on the interpretation of explicit reference to services. The main question raised has been whether housing providers are now required to actually provide special services to tenants with disabilities. For example, if the only laundry facilities in a rental building are located in a basement that is inaccessible by a wheelchair, would a landlord be required to provide laundry services to a resident who uses a wheelchair? HUD's response seems to indicate that such service provision is not the intent of the statute. Housing providers are not obligated to provide any services that are not normally provided as part of the housing "package" offered to all tenants. As stated in the preamble to the regulations, "a housing provider is required to make modifications in order to enable a qualified applicant with handicaps to live in the housing, but is not required to offer housing of a fundamentally different nature" [13, p. 3249]. But if any services are provided to building residents, then owners or landlords must allow adjustments or accommodations in these services if such accommodations would allow tenants with disabilities to fully enjoy these services. In the case of the inaccessible laundry facility, for example, the landlord could be required to waive the rule that limits access to the laundry area to tenants only, thereby permitting the housekeeper of a tenant with disabilities to do the tenant's laundry. Alternatively, permission could be granted to install a washer and dryer in the tenant's apartment. Since this approach might also necessitate dwelling modifications, it would require the landlord's agreement to both reasonable modifications and reasonable accommodations.

ENFORCEMENT

As noted at the outset, even the most well-conceptualized law will be of little consequence if the mechanisms to ensure its proper enforcement are ineffective (although it should be noted that many accommodation issues are resolved positively without ever reaching the enforcement stage [3]). Therefore, it is important to review and evaluate the enforcement mechanisms put in place by the 1988 Act.

Procedures

Under the 1988 amendments, enforcement of fair housing law is triggered in one of two ways. First, an individual who claims to have been subject to housing discrimination either files a complaint with HUD or initiates a suit in federal court. Second, the HUD Secretary may initiate a complaint based on his or her own investigation of housing practices across the nation or in particular markets. Civil suits must be brought within two years from the time of the alleged discriminatory practice, while complaints to the Secretary of HUD must be filed within one year of the alleged violation.

A complaint filed with the Secretary of HUD initiates what is known as an administrative enforcement procedure.[11] Because the administrative procedure is the primary improvement in enforcement offered by the 1988 amendments, it is the main focus of our discussion. Under this enforcement approach, the Secretary has 100 days in which to investigate the complaint.[12] During this period, the Secretary is required to engage in a "conciliation" process, with the goal of negotiating a resolution of the dispute. This function is typically delegated to a local agency in the geographic area where the dispute arose as long as HUD considers the area's fair housing laws to be the "substantial equivalent" to the Federal Fair Housing Act. If the conciliation fails and the Secretary finds reasonable cause to issue a charge, then the administrative process begins. The parties appear before an Administrative Law Judge (ALJ), who is an individual appointed by a federal agency, paid by the federal Office of Personnel Management, and assigned by the appointing agency to administrative law cases on a rotating basis.[13] The administrative hearing is a formal adjudication procedure with many similarities to a civil trial. For example, each party to the complaint must file a brief which provides the basis for its position in the case, and all aspects of the pre-trial "discovery" process of information gathering are followed. If the ALJ finds that the law has been violated, the amendments allow access to the full range of legal remedies including the payment of civil penalties of up to $100,000 by the violator. Because it is recognized that considerable time may pass between the filing of a complaint with HUD and a decision by the ALJ, the HUD Secretary has the authority to require that the tenant applicant filing the complaint be provided with housing—or that the landlord be enjoined from renting the property to another—if HUD's investigation reveals that the complainant had reasonable

---

[11]Generally, when legislation provides for an administrative enforcement procedure, the administrative process must be exhausted *before* an individual can file a civil action. The 1988 Fair Housing Act, however, gives the individual the choice between the administrative procedure and civil trial.

[12]If it is impractical to either issue a charge or proceed with negotiations within the 100 days, the Secretary must state the reasons for the delay (see [14]).

[13]See [15]. Taken at face value, these features of the ALJ position should result in impartial judgments by individuals with expertise in particular substantive areas. For example, appointment by each agency should maximize expertise in a specific subject area, payment by the Office of Personnel Management should eliminate any conflict of interest between the ALJ and the appointing agency, and if the rotation of assignments approximates random assignment, it should reduce various sources of potential bias.

cause to file the complaint. HUD also bears the expense of the administrative mechanism.

Evaluation

One approach to evaluating the enforcement mechanisms established by the 1988 amendments is to compare them to the procedures that were followed before passage of these amendments. This "relative" approach suggests at least three ways in which the new amendments have strengthened the enforcement of fair housing legislation. First, prior to the 1988 Act, the only avenues of redress open to private individuals experiencing housing discrimination were filing a civil suit or submitting a complaint to HUD and agreeing to allow HUD to work with the parties toward conciliation [14]. Under the newly amended law, this individual now has the additional option of the administrative enforcement procedure. Second, the "statute of limitations" for taking action on an alleged incident of housing discrimination has been extended substantially, from 180 days under the pre-existing statute to two years for a civil suit or one year for the administrative procedure. Finally, the new amendments enable the Attorney General of the United States to intervene in housing discrimination cases that are particularly significant, including cases that involve chronic violators.[14]

To these pre-post comparisons, we can add the comparison between the design of the administrative enforcement approach of the fair housing amendments and that of other laws that also utilize an administrative approach. Perhaps the most prominent example here is the Social Security Act. Under the new fair housing amendments, the aggrieved party is given the option of either filing a complaint with HUD, thereby initiating the administrative enforcement mechanism, or bringing a civil lawsuit. In addition, if the administrative option is chosen, the ALJ's decision can be appealed in the Circuit Court. In contrast, in Social Security cases, such as complaints regarding denial of claims for Social Security benefits and termination of benefits, the aggrieved party *must* begin with the administrative approach first. The Fair Housing Amendments, then, offer the private individual greater choice in how to pursue the complaint.

Overall, the relative standard of evaluation suggests that the new mechanisms are an improvement over previous practice and offer more options for enforcement than exist in other social policies. But a more "absolute" standard demonstrates that each provision has both strengths and weaknesses. This second approach uses the more demanding standard of judging these provisions on their own merits.

---

[14]Defined as individuals with a "pattern or practice" of housing discrimination over the preceding five years.

Two particularly attractive features of the administrative enforcement process are the attempt in the statute to move the case through the system quickly and expeditiously, and HUD's ability to intervene to secure housing for the aggrieved individual while the administrative process is ongoing. Unfortunately, early estimates of the way the administrative mechanism actually worked when the amendments initially took effect suggest that the 100-day limit for the HUD Secretary's review was overly optimistic, at least in the early stages: as of April 1990, roughly 5,000 complaints were active on the HUD docket, and about half of them had already exceeded the 100-day limit [10].[15]

The administrative process also appears to be less formal than a trial in District Court, less adversarial, and less expensive—three factors that arguably reduce the burden on the individual filing the complaint. For example, the parties to the complaint need not engage lawyers. The responsibility for establishing a full record of the facts rests with the ALJ, who, unlike judges in other courts, takes an active role in the case. Realistically, however, a frail elderly individual may require a lawyer to handle the filing of the original complaint, respond to inquiries, and monitor the process of the case.

Another potentially attractive aspect of the administrative mechanism is the expertise of the Administrative Law Judge. Technical expertise could be especially important in cases involving claims of the "impracticality" of meeting the accessibility or reasonable accommodation requirements of the Act, since these cases raise complex technical questions of engineering, building technologies, and architecture. On the other hand, the usual jury trial system is routinely relied upon for cases involving extremely complex, technical issues.

Finally, although the administrative procedure allows the ALJ's decision to be appealed to Federal Circuit Court, the case is not re-litigated there. The appellate judges do not second-guess agency procedures, do not reevaluate the evidence, and do not redetermine the facts of the case. As long as the reviewing court finds that there is substantial evidence, based on the record as a whole, to support the agency's decision, the review is restricted to whether the rules of the administrative procedure were followed correctly. Given this circumscribed focus, the probability that the decision would be overturned based on the facts of the case seem slim. Additionally, it is worth noting that the Circuit Court of Appeals does not involve a jury trial; the review and decision making are carried out by judges.

The alternative of a civil suit also has benefits and costs. Claimants who choose to file a civil lawsuit get their "day in court," the right to be heard by a jury of their peers, and the possibility of being awarded punitive damages that are not limited

---

[15]HUD's first report to Congress indicates that as of the end of 1989, 53 percent of a pool of 4221 complaints had been open for 100 days or more [14]. Note that Payne's figure of total complaints filed with HUD differs from the considerably smaller figure of 3,758 cited by HUD. The source of discrepancy is likely to be the longer time period covered by Payne's research.

in amount. But civil procedures take energy, are expensive,[16] and are slow: delays of up to four years in having a case heard are not uncommon. In the interim, the aggrieved person may be forced to live in unsuitable housing.

The topic of the relative merits of a civil trial versus administrative proceedings is far beyond the scope of this chapter. But a reasonable hypothesis is that a primary motivation for creating the administrative enforcement mechanism for the Fair Housing Act was to offer a lower-cost, faster, and generally more efficient alternative to civil procedure.[17] To what extent have these goals been achieved? The evidence from the early years of the Act is not encouraging. As of April 1990, HUD has received 6,818 complaints. Only about one quarter of these had moved through the administrative process, leaving 5,000 remaining in the queue. As noted earlier, about half of these cases had exceeded the statutory 100-day limit for review by the Secretary of HUD [10, 14]. Whether HUD had not anticipated this deluge of cases, or whether resources have not been available to meet the need, is not entirely clear.[18] What is clear, however, is that the speed and efficiency goals of the administrative procedure were not being met in the initial years of implementation. Indirect evidence suggests that the situation has subsequently improved: of a total of 20,108 complaints filed with HUD between March 1989 and November 1992, only 2,659—or about 13 percent—were still pending at the end of the period [16]. But how many complaints exceeded the 100-day limit or were withdrawn is unknown.

At a more fundamental level, there is reason for concern that, realistically, the only way the amended statute will be enforced is if private individuals file complaints or bring suit. As noted earlier, many concerns are resolved informally; but where good will is lacking, problems will arise. Because the law does not require anyone—HUD, the states, or the localities—to conduct ongoing monitoring of housing market practices, it is unlikely that such monitoring will be undertaken, particularly in the current budgetary environment. Thus, the burden falls entirely on the individual. This reality of the enforcement process is particularly worrisome in the case of the frail elderly. While the statute does present a definite choice of enforcement, both choices require substantial energy, motivation, and at least some financial burden. Thus, whether the frail elderly will take action if they are discriminated against remains an open question.

---

[16]There are provisions for waiving court costs and providing legal representation to indigent individuals.

[17]Not adding to the already overburdened courts is also likely to have played some role.

[18]HUD's first report to Congress on the 1988 Act suggests that the Department *had* anticipated the increased workload and therefore requested a Fiscal Year 1989 supplemental appropriation from the Office of Management and Budget. After a several-month delay, this request was ultimately granted and enabled the enforcement staff to grow from 169 in 1988 to 309 in 1990 [14]. This substantial growth in staff occurred after the period covered in this chapter. Its effects on the more expeditious handling of complaints should be described in subsequent HUD reports to Congress on the Act.

CONCLUSIONS

Between March 1989, when the Fair Housing Amendments Act became effective, and November 1992, a total of 20,108 HUD complaints were filed.[19] Of these, 24 percent were complaints of discrimination because of handicap [16]. This represents a 5 percent increase in filings from the first nineteen months of the Act's implementation [14, 17]. The proportion of these complaints that were filed by the elderly is not available from published sources.

Most Fair Housing cases decided to date appear to concern complaints about discrimination against younger people with disabilities [18, p. 229]. Those that concern older people have focused on, inter alia:

- zoning and land use (e.g., location of group residences) [5; 18, pp. 229-230]
- clarifying the ability of public housing authorities to "ask applicants about their ability to live independently [or] require that applicants provide confidential medical records to confirm a statement that they can live independently" [3, p. 14]
- examining whether state and local health and safety regulations for group residences are "discriminatory [or] prohibit persons with disabilities from living in the housing of their choice" [18, p. 236]—i.e., whether such regulations serve to restrict location unreasonably or force eviction based on level of disability
- clarifying the "reasonable accommodations" requirement and non-discriminatory eviction procedures [5, 8].

The effect of the Fair Housing Amendments Act of 1988 on the frail elderly, or any other handicapped group, is difficult to predict. Part of the difficulty arises because many of the provisions of the Act and its regulations are open to multiple interpretations. Included here are even the most fundamental elements such as the definition of "handicap" and how it will be applied to the frail elderly, and other questions—for example:

> At what point does a requested accommodation cease to be reasonable? Who is responsible in the event of injury to the older person? What about the person whose capacity to make decisions is diminished? Do state and local regulations unlawfully interfere with the right of persons with disabilities to live where they choose? [18, p. 221].

Furthermore, those most directly affected by the law often lack knowledge about it:

[19]"HUD complaints" exclude complaints that are within the jurisdiction of state and local agencies [14].

[S]ome housing managers have been overly cautious and have hesitated even to take actions which are permitted. Others . . . have asked inappropriate questions or taken unlawful actions. Adding to the confusion, members of the aging network and consumers themselves are unclear as to the rights and responsibilities of landlords and tenants [3, p. 11].

This uncertainty obviously renders any attempt to estimate the number of individuals or dwellings that are likely to be affected by the Act little more than guesswork. With this caveat in mind, we provide some very rough figures simply to establish some orders-of-magnitude, given a set of assumptions about the Act's interpretation.

For example, if all community resident elderly with either ADL or IADL needs are assumed to be covered by the 1988 fair housing amendments, then roughly 6 million frail elderly individuals would be afforded this new protection,[20] or about 3.8 million households in which the owner or renter is sixty-five or older.[21] These numbers may underestimate the actual covered population if our earlier speculation regarding potentially broad coverage for the very old turns out to be correct.

A very rough estimate of the number of existing rental dwellings occupied by the frail elderly that might be affected by the law is in the range of about 1-1.2 million.[22] Estimating the number of covered newly constructed multifamily buildings is far more difficult because it involves the interpretation of the statute and regulations, as well as projections of new multifamily construction. In the absence of readily available projections, an acceptable alternative is to provide some order-of-magnitude estimates of the number of units that would have been affected had the law been in effect between 1982 and 1986.[23] During that four-year time period, roughly 1.6 to 1.7 million multifamily dwellings were built. Of these, nearly half—or about one million—were in buildings that did *not* have any apartments located on the same floor as the main entrance to the building. How many of these buildings could have been built with an accessible main entrance, or whether a second entrance was located on the same floor as at least some apartments, is not known.

[20]Derived by applying the incidence rate of ADL or IADL in the 1982 National Long-Term Care Survey screener (19%) to the community resident population sixty-five and older.

[21]This is the definition of "households in which the householder is 65 or older" that is used in the national American Housing Survey.

[22]Derived by applying the rental rate among the elderly (about 28%) to the number of elderly households in 1987 (19,744,000), and then applying the same incidence of frailty as in the total community resident elderly population.

[23]These estimates are based on the published tabulations from the 1987 national American Housing Survey. Note that the published tabs provide breakdowns for multifamily buildings with *five or more units,* rather than the four or more covered by the Act. This will result in an underestimation of the actual units that would have been covered.

Whether the 1988 Act will affect a broad spectrum of the frail elderly will primarily depend on two factors: how liberally the relevant provisions are interpreted, and how effectively the Act is enforced. If Congress's explicit concern for broad coverage under this Act is adhered to in implementation, then we should expect a liberal interpretation of protected subgroups that compose the handicapped class, including the frail elderly. With regard to enforcement, although there is an ongoing debate among legal scholars regarding administrative versus civil procedure for resolving legal disputes, the main concern in the case of the fair housing amendments is far more rudimentary and practical. Since enforcement will only be initiated if an aggrieved party complains, the question is whether the frail elderly are likely to initiate action. Based on our initial examination, we are more optimistic about broad coverage than about broad—and therefore effective—enforcement.

ACKNOWLEDGMENTS

This chapter was originally prepared for the annual meeting of the Gerontological Society of America, Boston, Massachusetts, November 17, 1990, and revised in December 1991 and November 1992. Whenever possible, numerical estimates were subsequently updated. The authors acknowledge the generosity of Don Redfoot and Katrinka Smith Sloan of the American Association of Retired Persons for sharing thoughts and materials

REFERENCES

1. J. Pynoos, Toward a National Policy on Home Modification, *Technology and Disability, 2*:4, pp. 1-8, Fall 1993.
2. E. Steinfeld, Introduction, *Technology and Disability, 2*:4, pp. vi-viii, Fall 1993.
3. S. Edelstein, *Federal Antidiscrimination Law and Housing for Frail Older Renters,* National Eldercare Institute on Housing and Supportive Services, Andrus Gerontology Center, University of Southern California, Los Angeles, 1994.
4. S. M. Golant, The Desirability of Housing Exclusively for Older Persons, in *Expanding Housing Choices for Older People: Conference Papers and Recommendations,* The American Association of Retired Persons, #LR5309 (495) D15819, Washington, D.C., pp. 181-217, 1995.
5. B. Milstein and S. Hitov, Housing and the ADA, in *Implementing the Americans with Disabilities Act,* L. O. Gostin and H. A. Beyer (eds.), Brookes Publishing, Baltimore, pp. 137-153, 1993.
6. Pub. L. No. 100-430 (1988).
7. 24 CFR 100.1-100.205 (1988).
8. CD Publications, When The Government Comes Knocking: Following the Letter of the Fair Housing Law, *Housing the Elderly Report,* #95-8, pp. 1-3, August 1995.
9. American Association of Retired Persons Public Policy Institute, *Implementation of the Housing for Older Persons Exemptions to the Fair Housing Amendments Act of 1988,* Washington, D.C., 1995.

10. J. Payne, Enforcing the New Fair Housing Act, *Real Estate Law Journal, 19,* pp. 151-157, 1990.
11. House Report 100-711 (1988).
12. S. Edelstein, Addressing Major Legal Issues, *Summary Report: Aging and Housing Linkages Conference,* Administration on Aging, U.S. Department of Health and Human Services, Washington, D.C., pp. 18-20, 1995.
13. *Federal Register, 54*:13, January 23, 1989.
14. *The State of Fair Housing: Report to the Congress Pursuant to Section 808(e)(2) of the Fair Housing Act,* U.S. Department of Housing and Urban Development, Washington, D.C., 1990.
15. Administrative Procedure Act Sec. 3105, 1966.
16. Office of Fair Housing, U.S. Department of Housing and Urban Development, phone interviews with A. Chud and A. Mundy, 1992.
17. *Annual Report to Congress: Civil Rights Data on HUD Program Applicants and Beneficiaries,* U.S. Department of Housing and Urban Development, Washington, D.C., 1989.
18. S. Edelstein, Fair Housing Laws and Group Residences for Frail Older Persons, in *Expanding Housing Choices for Older People: Conference Papers and Recommendations,* The American Association of Retired Persons, #LR5309 (495) D15819, Washington, D.C., pp. 219-238, 1995.

SUGGESTED READING

American Association of Homes and Services for the Aging, *Senior Housing Management: Guidelines to Developing Admissions and Occupancy Policies,* Washington, D.C., 1994.

National Association of Home Builders, *Fair Housing Compliance Guide,* Washington, D.C., 1994.

CHAPTER
14

Research, Policy, and Practice in Housing Adaptation: Future Directions

Katrinka Smith Sloan, Joan Hyde, and Susan Lanspery

The nice young man at the elderly agency asked me to look over this book. At first I said, why would anybody want to write a whole book on home adaptation? After all, it's just a fancy name for fixing up your house the way you want it, only now it's how you want it because of your arthritis or something.

But from reading all those charts and tables I see I'm not the only one who's got troubles with their house and troubles fixing it up so I can still get around in it. Really, somebody should do something about all this.

For the last fifteen years, experts, including many of the authors in this book, have been making a strong and cogent case for home adaptation and universal design in the United States. As documented throughout this book, the great majority of elderly and disabled individuals desire, and manage, to remain in their homes until their final illness. It is clear (see especially Chapters 1, 2, and 4) that home adaptation and adaptive products are integral parts of long-term care: they provide support for individuals with disabilities and chronic health problems in ways that replace or complement home health aides and other supportive services.

There is some good news. The incidence of home adaptation is increasing even without much government or industry support—53 percent of older people surveyed in 1992 [1] had made at least minor home modifications. Laws eliminating legal barriers to and encouraging better accessibility now exist—the Fair Housing

Amendments Act of 1988 and the Americans with Disabilities Act (see Chapters 12 and 13)—although lack of funding and fragmented service delivery inhibit their implementation. Research documents not only how improvements in medical care (such as hip replacement and control of heart disease and stroke), but also how the use of assistive devices and home modifications, have actually reduced the incidence of disability [2]. Finally, the increased availability of mechanisms for older people to use the equity in their homes for various purposes, including home repair and adaptation, gives consumers more choices [3].

Still, as we conclude this first book dedicated to the issue of home adaptation, we must ask why there is so little progress toward making residential environments more accessible. The public has not begun to clamor for home adaptation services. Providers have failed to rush in to develop and operate home adaptation programs. Manufacturers have not made dramatic progress in new products. During a near-final review, an outside editor who is not an expert in home adaptation sent back several chapters with the comment "Needs update: things must have changed since this chapter was written." The editors dutifully sent the chapters back to the authors, who promptly returned them with the confirmation that, alas, nothing had changed.

Many factors affect this slow progress. Pynoos notes three important ones: "the [low] level of awareness of persons concerning problems in the home environment, affordability of home modifications, and the adequacy of the service delivery system" [3, p. 3] which he described as "fragmented, full of gaps, and inadequately funded" [3, p. 1]. Influencing this policy and funding fragmentation in turn is the fact that "home modification needs . . . are generally invisible to most policymakers [because the available data] do not provide information on the specific actions necessary to alleviate problems" [4, p. viii]. Other considerations inhibit progress in this area, including:

- stereotypical assumptions about the competence and potential contributions of older people and people with disabilities
- medicalized strategies that focus on diagnoses and ignore environmental modifications
- the overwhelming degree to which the built environment must be adapted to make it accessible
- the need to consider repairs and maintenance in conjunction with adaptations [5, 6].

The purpose of this chapter is to give an overview of the chapters that have come before, help the reader assess where we stand today, and discuss the steps needed in research, practice, and public policy that will allow us to move forward into a world where our homes can better support us to live full and fulfilling lives throughout our lifespan. We are still some twenty-five years from the demographic crest of demand for home adaptation to meet the needs of the growing population of older people and people with disabilities. It is important that we use those years wisely to understand how adaptation works for individuals, and how to create systems to assess, implement, and pay for the home adaptations that our changing population requires.

THE RESEARCH AGENDA

The 1992 American Association of Retired Persons study [1] of consumer preferences and needs underscores the importance of research concerning adaptation. Consistent with their stated desire to "age in place," an increasing number (28%) of older Americans had lived in their current residence for over thirty years; another 19 percent had been in their homes for twenty-one to thirty years. These figures suggest great attachment and familiarity as well as an association between older people and older homes. Importantly, while 84 percent of persons age fifty-five and over express a preference for staying in their current home for the rest of their lives, few have made plans for their future housing needs, including plans to adapt their homes.

We may see changes in planning or adaptation behavior as baby boomers grow older: many will have had first-hand experience as caregivers for their parents and other elderly family members. This group may be no more likely to move as they age, but they may be more interested in adapting their homes. Research can assist them to learn more about others' experiences, what's possible, and how to plan. It can also show us how to effectively convey information that will make home adaptation easier, and guide policymakers and program developers.

While no one chapter in this book focuses on the research agenda, research issues surface throughout. The book presents original research, reviews others' research, and discusses research paradigms. Research is comparatively thorough concerning which groups, among those with physical limitations, have unmet needs for home adaptation. As Mutschler (Chapter 8) and others [6, 7] have documented, it is most often widows, renters, those with low income, and the oldest old who require adaptation.[1]

Two teams, Ohta and Ohta (Chapter 5) and Connell and Sanford (Chapter 7), have developed different methodologies for investigating how older and disabled people make choices about the adaptations they use and how they use them. Ohta and Ohta's paradigm hypothesizes that older and disabled people make rational decisions about the use of adaptations, relying on their understanding of the seriousness and likelihood of potential problems they may encounter in performing activities without such adaptations, the likelihood that the adaptation will be

---

[1] In an analysis focusing on repair and maintenance, Golant and LaGreca found similarly that "certain longtime homeowners—the very poor, blacks, men living alone—are less able to maintain their homes" [8, p. 812].

helpful, and their analysis of the social, behavioral, and financial costs of the adaptations. Connell and Sanford focus on evaluating and understanding the ways in which people perform a range of tasks. They have developed a methodology that incorporates task breakdowns as well as analysis of the features of the physical environment that are germane to understanding how adaptations may be helpful. In addition to developing a usable research methodology, Connell and Sanford have developed a systematic way of categorizing both the tasks and the aspects of the environment that may require modification. Both approaches emphasize the individuality of adaptations, a point underscored in other research (e.g., Chapter 6 of this book, [9] and [10]).

Additionally, as noted by Pynoos et al. in Chapter 9, the field of occupational therapy has amassed considerable information on how people complete tasks and how prosthetic devices and adaptations can assist them. This body of knowledge, obtained primarily with the younger disabled population, needs to be expanded, specifically applied to home adaptations for frail elders, and disseminated much more widely (see also [11]).

These rich research veins need to be tapped to learn more about how people with disabilities use adaptations, and how adaptations change their ability to carry out activities independently, increase quality of life, reduce the need for paid or informal assistance, increase safety, and decrease medical costs. Information on how adaptations and universal design affect home values and real estate sales needs to be collected and added to the decision-making process. We also have much to learn from past, present, and future pilot projects and successful service delivery models in home adaptation.

One impediment to research is the lack of a common language and understanding of the cross-cutting issues among those in the field with respect to both the adaptation and behavioral outcomes. A consistent use of terminology, such as that proposed in Chapter 3 by Pynoos and Regnier, and systematic environmental categories such as those used by Grayson in Chapter 4, would help move research forward. A more important impediment, the lack of funding, is addressed in the policy section below.

THE PRACTICE AGENDA

One hundred years from now, when people look at twentieth-century building design, they will likely be amazed at how primitive our approach has been. Building immutable structures for an "average" user, instead of employing universal design—ever-changing buildings for users with disparate and ever-changing needs—will seem strange and shortsighted. Because our housing stock is replaced slowly, however, most houses and workplaces in use today will still be in use when the baby boom generation reaches advanced old age in the mid-twenty-first century. As it is doubtful that future cohorts of elderly will be significantly more prone to move than the current ones, millions of adaptations will most likely occur, despite cost and difficulty, and millions of adjustments will be made, although they may compromise health, safety, and autonomy [3].

In Chapters 9 and 10, the authors report on the practices of agencies providing home adaptation services. Housing, health, and other professionals are not always knowledgeable about home adaptation, and often do not refer consumers to, or coordinate services with, agencies that provide home adaptation services. Both the funding and delivery of home adaptation are unsystematic. As home adaptation is usually a secondary service, and as there is no recognized protocol for assessing the need for adaptation, the type and quality of such services vary widely. Most modifications are done privately by tradespeople with no special training in this area. Professional in-home assessments that review the need for adaptations are not even available in most communities. The training of the assessors is uneven, and many focus only on health and safety issues rather than on supporting independent functioning. Less commonly, such agencies may assist clients who choose to undertake recommended adaptations, including referral to reliable agencies (or to providers of home adaptation products and construction services) and assistance with locating grants, loans, or third-party reimbursement for which the client is eligible. Home repair agencies may also provide similar types of assistance to those who wish to undertake adaptations.

Case managers, visiting nurses, and others in the community long-term care network should be trained to assess the need for adaptation. By adding an adaptation section to existing assessment forms, the system's ability to serve frail elders would increase significantly. Home assessment would be part of the client assessment protocols used for all types of community-based supportive services. The home assessment could at a minimum be tied to measures of need for assistance in activities of daily living used for eligibility for other types of services.

The delivery of home adaptation services is complicated by the individual requirements of each job. Staff in agencies performing adaptations need special training to match the adaptations to each user's strengths and preferences, and to customize adaptations according to the user's housing, medical, social, and motivational situation.

Specialized agency-driven assessments and services are not enough, however. Even the best practices will fall short without meaningful consumer (including caregiver) involvement (see especially Chapters 2, 5, 6, and 11). Educating the public about the importance of and possibilities for home adaptation and repair is a crucial part of the practice agenda.

In addition to these education, assessment, and service delivery imperatives, products should be made more available and contractors better informed; as noted in Chapter 4, more assistive devices and adaptation techniques are available abroad than in the United States. Consumer and producer education should help to increase both demand and supply. Strategies such as those described at the end of Chapter 1 will increase public awareness and acceptance and help us to use the next quarter-century wisely to prepare for the baby boom generation's adaptation requirements. Additional useful information about programs can be found in the Epilogue of this book, in [3, 5, 12-14], and through several organizations such as the Center for Accessible Housing at North Carolina State University and the National Resource and Policy Center on Housing and Long-Term Care at the University of Southern California's Andrus Gerontology Center.

THE POLICY AGENDA

Funding

An underlying assumption of this book is that the widespread modification of the housing stock, to meet the needs of our aging population, is a social good that public action and funding should support in a variety of ways. In Chapter 8, Mutschler documents what we know intuitively: people with low incomes are much more likely than those with higher incomes to have an unmet need for assistive devices and home modifications, mainly because they cannot afford to pay for them. Similarly, a National Center for Health Statistics study found that affordability is a major barrier to consumers' use of assistive devices [15]. At the same time, consumers at all income levels are paying for most modifications [3] and economic resources alone do not appear to determine whether modifications are made [16].

While numerous programs pay for adaptations (see Chapter 12), the available funds are inadequate to the need. Moreover, as described in Chapters 9 and 12, the funds available are limited and governed by disparate sets of rules, making it difficult for consumers to access those funds in a way that corresponds to their needs.

The funds are generally not even earmarked specifically for housing adaptation and are located in diverse systems, including: housing and community development (Department of Housing and Urban Development, Community Development Block Grants), tax (federal income tax deductions), health care (health insurance, Medicaid, Medicare), and community-based long-term care (state aging and home care programs and federal Older Americans Act). Consumers themselves, however, pay for most adaptations—or bear the brunt of adjusting to disabling environments [3].

Given so many programs, with separate goals and requirements, and so many gaps in coverage, many people who cannot afford to make adaptations either cannot find or cannot qualify for funding. This problem is complicated by the individual nature of adaptations. The same disabling condition may require different adaptive responses depending on the user's housing, social, physical, and motivational situations; conversely, different disabilities may call for identical adaptations. Because of the variations, these otherwise similar situations may or may not be covered by the same funding source. Assisting mobility-impaired people to purchase wheelchairs, without helping them to modify their homes so that they can use the wheelchairs, does not maximize their independence.

This dilemma begs for a public policy response. To accomplish the systematic adaptation of our housing stock to meet the needs of our aging population requires national policy changes. These changes in turn require coordinating both financing and service delivery in private and public housing, in health, and in long-term care programs. Advocates at the state and local level should utilize HUD's consolidated planning process to encourage assessment of modification needs.

For example, HUD should modify regulations for the HOME program to promote home repair and adaptation for low-income and disabled homeowners. HUD should also encourage the development of home repair programs in low-income and multi-cultural communities where the need is especially great.

For more costly adaptations, either the health care or housing systems or both could provide financial support. For example, in one scenario, elders with high incomes, sufficient liquid assets, or both would not be eligible for any financial assistance, but could receive technical assistance in arranging for adaptations. Low- to moderate-income older homeowners with disabilities would be eligible for low-interest loans to pay for adaptations. Repayment of these loans could be deferred until the sale of the home. Loans and grants for low- income homeowners could be administered and funded through the federal housing programs (such as the Community Development Block Grant or HOME programs), through state housing finance agencies, or through a program modeled after the weatherization programs. The nucleus of such a program already exists in many localities [14].

Medicare, Medicaid, and private acute and long-term care insurance programs could, at minimum, cover adaptations that are shown to be cost-effective and to reduce the need for other covered services, including those provided in more restrictive or costly settings. Such funding would parallel and expand that which currently exists in the Medicaid Home and Community Based Waiver Program.

Lastly, there is a critical need for more research funding. A National Institute of Health or philanthropic initiative in this area, with a combination of funds for university research, small business innovations, and demonstration project grants, could be used to increase knowledge and support the development of programs and devices that assist people who are older or have disabilities to remain in their homes.

Coordination

As with the funding of home adaptation, the coordination of delivery is uneven. As already noted, while increasing numbers of home care and home health agencies are beginning to assess clients' need for adaptations, the training of the assessors is uneven, and many focus on health and safety issues rather than supporting independent functioning. Less commonly, such agencies may also provide referrals to reliable agencies (or to providers of home adaptation products and construction services) and/or assistance with locating grants, loans, or third-party reimbursements for which the client is eligible. Similarly, home repair and adaptation agencies may refer clients to home care agencies and/or offer financing information. We need, however, public policy that supports the type of comprehensive coordination described earlier, as well as support for developing materials and training programs, conducting research, "best practices" demonstration projects, and conferences and other dissemination activities.

CONCLUSION

This is an exciting time to be involved with home adaptation. Although pioneers—many of whom are among this book's authors—have begun to lay a groundwork, much is still in flux. Relatively small contributions, such as a successful state funding program, a particularly good training curriculum, a well-designed research project, or a useful assessment tool, can have a disproportionately large effect on the directions this field can take. Consumers, health and housing providers, design and construction professionals, advocates, and those involved in public policy have begun to work together.

Consumers are a particularly central element. When older people and those with disabilities demand homes that foster independence, then more manufacturers will design more useful products, more home builders will build and renovate homes appropriately, more service agencies will offer assessments and other assistance, and public policy will support (or at least not hinder) these activities.

Unfortunately, consumers rarely ask for products they do not think exist. In a recent survey, consumers with disabilities named several products they would use "if they existed," without realizing that such products are currently available. Much more consumer education is needed. This includes educating referral sources, such as hospital discharge planners, local councils on aging, physicians, and religious leaders. It also means educating families, especially the large numbers of adult children who would also benefit from their parents' increased safety and independence. Governmental actions fostering demand could pay off in several ways, including expanding and improving housing options for older people and people with disabilities as well as jump-starting the housing adaptations industry, with associated positive effects on the construction industry as a whole.

Readers from all backgrounds are invited to take the initiative, participate in adapting an aging housing stock to meet the needs of an aging population, and help to develop new ways of looking at the issues raised throughout the book. Only when enough of us do so will we able to meet the challenge of change.

REFERENCES

1. American Association of Retired Persons, *Understanding Senior Housing for the 1990s*, AARP, #PF 4522 (593) D 13899, Washington, D.C., 1993.

2. K. Manton, L. Corder, and E. Stallard, Changes in the Use of Personal Assistance and Special Equipment from 1982 to 1989: Results for the 1982 and 1989 NLTCS, *The Gerontologist, 33*:2, pp. 168-176, 1993.

3. J. Pynoos, Toward a National Policy on Home Modification, *Technology and Disability,* 2:4, pp. 1-8, Fall 1993.

4. E. Steinfeld, Introduction, *Technology and Disability,* 2:4, pp. vi-viii, Fall 1993.

5. P. Porter, Facilitating Aging in Place through Home Repairs, *Long Term Care Advances: Topics in Research, Training, Service & Policy, 6*:2, 1994.

6. B. J. Soldo and C. F. Longino, Jr., Social and Physical Environments in the Vulnerable Aged, in *The Social and Built Environment in an Older Society,* Institute of Medicine and National Research Council, Committee on an Aging Society, National Academy Press, Washington, D.C., pp. 103-133, 1988.

7. United States General Accounting Office, *Elderly Americans: Health, Housing, and Nutrition Gaps Between the Poor and Nonpoor,* GAO/PEMD-92-29, 1992.

8. S. M. Golant and A. J. LaGreca, Housing Quality of U.S. Elderly Households: Does Aging in Place Matter? *The Gerontologist, 34*:6, pp. 803-814, 1994.

9. E. Steinfeld and S. Shea, Enabling Home Environments: Identifying Barriers to Independence, *Technology and Disability,* 2:4, pp. 69-79, Fall 1993.

10. R. V. Olsen, E. Ehrenkrantz, and B. Hutchings, Creating Supportive Environments for People with Dementia and Their Caregivers Through Home Modifications, *Technology and Disability,* 2:4, pp. 47-57, Fall 1993.

11. Aging Design Research Program, *Design for Aging: Strategies for Collaboration Between Architects and Occupational Therapists,* AIA/ACSA Council on Architectural Research, ISBN 0-935502-07-6, Washington, D.C., 1993.

12. H. D. Kiewel, Serving Community Needs for Home-Accessibility Modifications, *Technology and Disability,* 2:4, pp. 40-46, Fall 1993.

13. J. Overton, Resources for Home-Modification/Repair Programs, *Technology and Disability,* 2:4, pp. 80-88, Fall 1993.

14. G. Gaberlavage and P. Forsythe, *Home Repair and Modification: A Survey of City Programs,* American Association of Retired Persons (#9504), Washington, D.C., 1995.

15. M. P. La Plante, G. E. Hendershot, and A. J. Moss, Assistive Technology Devices and Home Accessibility Features: Prevalence, Payment, Needs, and Trends, in National Center for Health Statistics, *Advance Data, 217,* pp. 1-12, 1992.

16. J. E. K. Norburn, S. Bernard, T. Konrad, A. Woomert, G. H. DeFriese, W. D. Kalsbeek, G. G. Koch, and M. G. Ory, Self-Care and Assistance from Others in Coping with Functional Limitations Among a National Sample of Older Adults, *Journal of Gerontology: Social Sciences, 50B*:2, pp. S101-S109, 1995.

EPILOGUE

Report on the First National Invitational Conference on Home Modification

Mary Ann Wilner

Friday, November 5, 1993 was a historic day in the history of home adaptation. As this first book on the subject was taking shape, sixty experts representing virtually every aspect of the field met in Baltimore for an invitational conference. The Center for Accessible Housing at the North Carolina State University School of Design and the nonprofit Adaptive Environments Center in Boston planned the conference at the recommendation of the National Institute of Disability and Rehabilitation Research to "bring together people who can help shape needed home modification policies."

And bring together people they did: home builders and remodelers, younger and older consumers with disabilities, manufacturers of assistive devices, architects and designers, the American Occupational Therapy Association, financial lenders, national foundations, the U.S. Departments of Housing and Urban Development (HUD), Education, and Health and Human Services (HHS), state housing finance agencies, state and area agencies on aging, the National Association of Remodelers, National Association of Home Builders, home adaptation provider groups, the American Association of Retired Persons (AARP), and researchers from leading universities and research centers involved in the study of home adaptation. Never before has such a diverse group attacked this important topic.

ISSUES RAISED DURING THE CONFERENCE

Paralleling this book, the conference stressed the importance of and great need for adaptation. Participants noted in particular the complexity of the problem: not everyone has the same level or type of need, each person's needs and abilities may change over time, and each house or apartment is different. Conference attendees also discussed the lack of a single, comprehensive system of financing and delivery by which vulnerable people who need home modifications or repairs can make changes in order to remain in their own home. The home modifications field, a hybrid of the housing and social services domains, has been noticeably absent from most policy discussions at the federal level and from most policy discussions at the state and local levels. Although representatives of the housing and building trades were present at the conference, the "bricks and mortar people" in these trades have not generally embraced home adaptation, even though adding a wheelchair ramp, lowering kitchen cabinets, and installing bathroom grab bars are changes to structures. Social services providers have also been slow to bring home modifications into their realm, although home modifications could help many agencies fulfill their service missions and could reduce the need for certain kinds of personal, at-home assistance.

This gap is reflected in significant problems in funding home adaptations. Too often, both HUD and state and local housing departments on the one hand and social service agencies on the other view home adaptations as outside their mission. These distinctions are exacerbated by recent housing and social service funding cutbacks. Agencies that do provide home modification and repair services must seek funding from a complex variety of sources and compete with other important needs.

Yet, successful home modifications are a key factor in supporting aging in place and independent living. They make it possible for an individual with disabilities to develop or maintain important social relations with peers, a community, and the workplace. With the assistance of structural changes to her house, a teenager in a wheelchair can independently enter and exit from it; an older adult with hearing difficulties can remain in contact with friends by seeing a blinking light when the telephone rings or a neighbor comes to the door; a frail older woman can safely bathe herself with the use of handrail supports. Investments in home modification can save service dollars, make caregiving easier, and forestall or even prevent institutionalization. The guiding philosophy of home modification stresses the rights of individuals across the spectrum of age and functional disability to live in their own homes and arrange for both the support services and the environmental adaptations that will enhance their health, safety, independence, and quality of life.

With appropriate modifications, the home environment complements individuals' abilities instead of exacerbating their disabilities. For many people home modifications replace or reduce the need for personal care attendants or home health supports because the environmental adaptations enable the person to manage on his/her own. This is especially important as we approach the twenty-first century, when the labor force availability of personal care attendants and home health assistants is not expected to keep pace with the increase in the numbers of older and younger people with disabilities.

This conference sought to identify the barriers that prevent a successful home modifications system, to describe the solutions that exist, and more importantly, to forge communication networks so the information can be widely disseminated and easily accessed.

Several themes echoed throughout the day deserve significant attention by federal, state, and local policymakers, financial lenders, builders and remodelers, and the various health care, design, and social service professionals who serve older and young consumers with disabilities.

- Although small programs exist across the country, the funding and delivery systems are fragmented, and, with few exceptions, funding for both public- and private-sector initiatives has been minimal.
- Low-tech and low-cost solutions are available now for adapting homes to enhance consumers' independence, but information about them is not readily available. Consumers, families, service professionals, designers, and builders too often waste time and money reinventing the wheel, or make costly mistakes; or they opt out of making home modifications because training and professional or consumer education programs are not available. Builders and remodelers frequently have preconceived notions about the cost and construction involved in home modification and steer clear of this potential market, or they sell themselves as experts when they have not been adequately trained. Knowledgeable subcontractors with experience in this area are difficult to locate.
- Government programs and funding have been inadequate, inflexible, and unaccommodating to the consumers' or the remodelers' needs. Waiting lists for the small available pots of money outpace significantly the numbers of consumers who can be served. Funding authorizations, client eligibility criteria, per capita funding limits, and service delivery methods vary across programs, states, departments, and federal funding sources, further inhibiting program effectiveness. Most people in need of home modifications go unserved—even though solutions are often simple, low-cost, and low-tech in nature.
- Traditional coalitions among financial lenders, government loan programs, and the building industry have been noticeably absent in this growing field. Some builders feel that government programs encroach on a potentially profitable market for home modifications for middle- and upper-income customers. In truth, there is more than enough work to be done in this area,

but tax incentives, loans, and other private-market financial vehicles are not easily available to consumers or contractors. The lack of such incentives contributes to a lack of enthusiasm and to misconceptions about modifications, accessibility, and universal design.

- Certain states, on their own or assisted with federal funds, have crafted workable, flexible programs to make housing accessible for consumers of all ages who live with physical disabilities. Minnesota's Housing Finance Agency, for example, has made loans and grants available for home adaptations. Pennsylvania distributes state lottery proceeds through the area agencies on aging for home adaptations. These models and the Maryland program are described in a later section. However, programs like these are few and often limited in scope, and in some cases funds are shrinking due to the fiscal problems facing so many states.

- As a result of these system problems, while the need for home adaptations is great, in a classic "catch-22" situation, the expressed demand for these services has historically been modest, because consumers don't know what's possible, or because they do know that adaptations are unaffordable or unavailable.

IDENTIFYING BARRIERS
AND PROPOSING SOLUTIONS

The conference identified barriers and proposed solutions in the areas of effective service delivery, information and technology dissemination, and financing. They are summarized here. A fuller review of these barriers and solutions is available in the conference proceedings. Although implementing the proposed solutions presents many challenges, it is encouraging that, for the first time, considerable consensus exists about what needs to be done.

Barriers and Solutions to Effective Service Delivery

The lack of coordination between housing and health services provision was cited as the major barrier to providing home adaptation services. This barrier is at the heart of the lack of availability of agencies and knowledgeable personnel who are able to assess need, help make the adaptations, and help obtain funding for them. Proposed solutions include:

- Mandating, at a federal level, coordination across agencies to ease and enhance consumers' ability to access home modification services
- Ensuring that services are directed by consumers
- Making service coordinators available
- Developing and disseminating quality standards or guidelines

- Studying outcomes of home modification
- Making available financing for home adaptation
- Developing new models of service delivery

Barriers and Solutions to Widespread Information and Technology Dissemination

Both consumers and providers may be unaware of existing technology and best practices, or even the availability of home adaptation services. In one study cited, 400 people with disabilities were asked to imagine what kinds of devices would be helpful to them; every device they described was already available. Another barrier is that insufficient numbers of appropriately trained people exist to assess the needs and make modifications. A third barrier is that many adaptive devices or environmental modifications have had an institutional appearance in the past, and consumers may view them as stigmatizing, especially if they are unaware of trends toward more unobtrusive and attractive designs. Proposed solutions to these problems include:

- Developing a directory of existing programs, devices, and successful models
- Forming coalitions of consumers, professionals, and service providers to lobby for home modification policies
- Incorporating information about home adaptation into the initial and ongoing training of all physical design, health, and social service professionals
- Creating marketing and public relations initiatives to educate the public, potential consumers, manufacturers, designers, and lenders
- Developing government- and foundation-sponsored research and demonstration projects and dissemination
- Encouraging universal design in new construction

Barriers and Solutions to Problems of Financing Home Adaptations

Probably the single greatest barrier to the widespread use of home adaptation is the lack of readily available funding. Consumers with disabilities often have limited incomes, and third-party payers, such as federal or local governments or health insurance, cover modifications only in limited and sporadic cases; even then, such funds often cover only the "hard" costs, not the crucial assessment and coordination services that make it possible for people to begin the adaptation process. Information regarding eligibility is confusing and difficult to obtain. Private homes, where three-quarters of the elderly (including many low-income elders) live, are not covered by HUD funds, except occasionally through locally controlled Community Development Block Grants; and Medicare coverage is limited to medically oriented assistive devices. Some of the funds available are restricted to services purchased through government-related agencies, thus proving a disincentive to the private market to develop home adaptation capabilities.

The proposed solutions focus on expanding access to funding:

- Developing a federal clearinghouse for information on funding sources
- Allocating more funds on the federal and local levels, including a commitment by HUD to fund adaptation in its own properties
- Making IRS home modification deduction allowances more generous, for both homeowners and renters; and allowing for a longer amortization period if taxpayers choose to amortize rather than deduct the entire expense
- Promoting a range of state policies and banking industry practices to make it easier to access home equity funds for modification
- Encouraging homebuilders, private insurance companies, and other industry groups to develop financial products and policies which finance home adaptation
- Promoting the incorporation of home adaptations in health care reform

MODEL STATE PROGRAMS

Most encouraging is the example of programs which overcome the difficulties in establishing home adaptation systems. The conference featured three such programs. Each of these state programs addresses service delivery, information dissemination, and financing issues differently.

Pennsylvania

The Philadelphia Corporation for Aging (PCA) has various ways to provide and finance home adaptations for younger and older individuals with disabilities. For most of its programs, the PCA hires and trains its own staff to assure their sensitivity to working with people who are older or have disabilities. The state lottery, the proceeds of which are targeted exclusively to Pennsylvania's older citizens, finances two of their programs. The Senior Housing Assistance Repair Program (SHARP), begun in 1980, provides minor repairs and adaptations that older people can no longer do for themselves. Typical adaptations are changing doors, locks, and faucets and installing smoke alarms, grab bars, and railings. Although SHARP services are available to all Philadelphians over sixty who have low incomes, are owner-occupants, and live in structurally sound dwellings, they are targeted to those over seventy-five who live alone, have incomes at 130 percent of poverty, have mobility limitations, and are at significant risks for safety and health problems. The program, funded at $1 million per year through the lottery and Community Development Block Grants (CDBG), provides up to

$1,600 of work per client. No client contribution is required. While many are served, the demand is great: 1,900 individuals applied for this program in 1993 and over 600 remain on the waiting list.

The Adaptive Modifications Program (AMP) is targeted at increasing the independence of people with disabilities and has $300,000 available per year from CDBG funds. This program provides up to $12,000 per client in major adaptations such as wheelchair lifts, first floor bathrooms, ramps, and kitchens. Funds are available first-come, first-served to clients who have a permanent disability and are owner-occupants with moderate incomes as defined by Section 8 eligibility. At this point no co-pay is required. For this program, the PCA relies on subcontractors, not in-house staff.

Minnesota

Minnesota's comprehensive set of programs incorporates both financing and technical assistance for constructing home modifications. Borrowed funds, including tax-exempt bonds, taxable bonds, and discretionary grant funds, are available through the Minnesota Housing Finance Agency (MHFA). The key to the program's success is its flexibility.

The MHFA Accessibility Loan Program, funded with appropriations from the Minnesota Legislature, has a current biannual budget of $600,000. Since 1979, appropriations have totaled about $4,600,000. Loan maximum is $10,000 with up to five years for payback, after which time it becomes a grant.

To be eligible, individuals must have a long-term physical condition that substantially affects functioning in the home, and must be either the homeowner or a relative. Household adjusted income cannot exceed $18,000 in the metropolitan area or $15,000 in other areas, with a total value of assets not exceeding $25,000. Single- and two-family homes, mobile homes, and manufactured housing are eligible. Work must be directly related to the priority needs of the resident with disabilities. Entering, exiting, and using the bathroom are top priorities. Neither temporary modifications nor portable equipment are eligible. Critical, basic repairs may be completed in addition to the access work, to assure that the home is decent, safe, and energy-efficient.

MHFA's cluster of modest-income homeowner repair programs, the Rehabilitation Loan Program, includes the following, besides the Accessibility Program:

- The Deferred Loan Program has $7.6 million in state appropriated funds and offers loans up to $10,000 with a ten-year repayment lien for households with $10,000 adjusted income and $25,000 in assets.
- The HOME Loan Program offers $1 million of federally funded "deferred" loans for general repairs.
- The Revolving Loan Program, backed by state appropriations and bond proceeds, offers $10,000 loans for general repairs, with fifteen-year

paybacks, to households with up to $18,000 in adjusted income and $25,000 in assets.

- Minnesota's Fix-Up Plan uses proceeds from sales of tax-exempt bonds to provide home improvement loans at reduced interest rates, on a sliding scale basis, to homeowners who need to finance home modifications. As of early 1994, this program had processed five thousand loans using four hundred lenders.

- The Fix-Up Fund Access Program stretches available funds from Medicaid waiver programs to fund room additions or other modifications needed to assist low- and moderate-income households with a family member with a disability. Minnesota has obtained six different Medicaid waivers which enhance its flexible use of state and federal dollars.

Lending decisions for all parts of the Rehab Loan Program are based on MHFA guidelines, not on such conventional real estate lending standards as the home's appraised value relative to the borrower's indebtedness and equity, or the borrower's "economic viability." For revolving loans, a household must be ineligible for conventional financing. Total household expenses and income are evaluated to determine affordable monthly payments.

The Rehab Loan Program is administered by sixty-five housing and redevelopment authorities and community action programs. Many of these agencies also administer weatherization, general repair, and energy assistance programs in addition to access modifications. They use Community Development Block Grants, Farmers' Home Administration Home Repair, Housing Preservation Grant Programs, the MHFA's Home Improvement Loan Program, county or locally funded repair programs, and social-service-based funds, such as Medicaid waivers for home- and community-based support. Many access projects are funded with a mix of these resources. The success of these programs lies in each agency or housing authority's ability to manage its pool of funds very flexibly to meet each consumer's needs for the "highest and best use."

In addition to securing funding, housing authority or agency staff provide technical assistance throughout the home modification process. The MHFA staff assists the housing and redevelopment authority and community action program administrators at all stages of operations.

Maryland

In Maryland, the response to meeting home adaptation and repair needs has expanded. It now focuses on maintaining the highest possible level of functional independence by addressing barriers to the accessibility, safety, security, and comfort of a senior's living environment. Several initiatives are part of this expansion.

The Maryland State Office on Aging recently received a Medicaid waiver to enhance the services provided in its Senior Assisted Housing Programs. Recipients of this funding are low-income residents of small group homes which provide housing and services to people who may be at risk of institutionalization. Eligible residents receive subsidies from the Maryland Office on Aging. The new Medicaid waiver enables the state to enrich the service package to serve more residents who may otherwise have required a more restrictive living environment. Services now covered by the waiver include: an occupational therapist's functional assessment of the individual resident; an environmental assessment of the home; assistive devices up to $1,000; and home modifications up to $3,000.

The Senior Care program has provided case-managed in-home services to people in their own homes since 1982. Senior Care funds have been used to construct access ramps for individuals who have difficulty getting in and out of their homes.

As part of its effort to explore alternative home repair and modification resources for seniors, the Maryland Office on Aging facilitated a partnership with the local home builders' association and Hechinger's, a building supply company, to provide volunteer labor and materials for improvements and repairs for low-income elderly in metropolitan Baltimore area homes. This special project, completed in 1992, demonstrated the need for home modification and repair efforts, and the effectiveness of local approaches using a variety of resources. It is expected to add new participants as part of a major state inter-agency information and education initiative on retrofit.

Maryland has also offered grants to local organizations, including area agencies on aging, for minor repairs and maintenance of properties occupied by low-income individuals who are elderly or have disabilities. Their experience has shown that older homeowners are reluctant to take out a loan for repairs or modifications because of worries about new debt, future money needs, having a lien on a home which is already mortgage-free, or inheritance concerns.

Loans, however, remain an important resource for home modifications and repairs. The Department of Housing and Community Development (DHCD) administers several loan programs, including low-interest and deferred-payment loans, which seniors can use to finance needed work for their homes.

SUMMARY AND CONCLUSIONS

The strength of this conference was its bringing together consumers, professional and provider groups, researchers, and funding sources to forge a consensus on key elements in achieving home modifications. These can be summarized as follows:

- Build upon the wealth of information and experience that currently exists about home modifications, assistive devices, and portable equipment.

- Facilitate the widespread dissemination of this knowledge base to consumers, lenders, policymakers, designers, builders, product manufacturers, and medical professionals.

- Assure plentiful, multiple, and flexible streams of funding to accommodate the hundreds of thousands of individuals with disabilities living in homes that limit safe and independent functioning. Meeting this goal will require changing restrictive eligibility requirements in existing public programs and providing incentives for the private sector to become more actively involved in financing, constructing, and insuring home modifications.

- Assure that services are directed by the consumer and customized to meet individual needs.

- Assure that high-quality services are provided to consumers.

- Advocate for federal action. Assure that programs are better coordinated through mechanisms such as legislative mandates or the creation of a national home modification program.

- Promote universal design in new construction and substantial rehabilitation.

Although the direction of federal policy discussions has shifted since 1993-94, there is still hope that interest and activity in home modifications may increase. If the discussion proceeds on the scope of health care reform, if the Departments of Health and Human Services and Housing and Urban Development increase their coordination, and if the Fair Housing and Americans with Disabilities Acts begin to have an impact on the way Americans think about the built environment, home adaptation may, for the first time, rank with access to telephones and televisions as a basic criterion for a decent standard of living.

A full summary and a white paper with recommendations which came out of the conference are available through the Center for Accessible Housing of North Carolina State University.

Contributors

JAMES J. CALLAHAN, JR., PH.D., is a Research Professor and Director of the Policy Center on Aging at the Heller School at Brandeis University. He directed the Robert Wood Johnson Foundation national demonstrations on linking housing and services, "No Place Like Home" and "Supportive Services in Senior Housing." He has served in Massachusetts as Commissioner of Mental Health and Secretary of Elder Affairs. He has published widely in aging and social welfare journals on supportive services, delivery systems, and long-term care for the elderly. His book, *Reforming the Long-Term Care System,* is a classic in the field. He recently received the Maxwell Pollack Award for demonstrated excellence in bridging the worlds of research and practice and the Health Care Finance Administration's Regional Administrators Award for leadership.

EMILY CALVERT, MSG/MPA, earned her dual degree master's in Gerontology and Public Administration from the University of Southern California (USC) in 1992. After working as a research assistant for USC's National Eldercare Institute on Housing and Supportive Services during graduate school, she was hired by the Evanston, Illinois Living At Home Program. Her main responsibility has been to develop and coordinate the Money Management Program (MMP) serving the southside of Chicago, which links volunteers one-on-one with older adults for assistance with monthly bill paying.

BETTYE ROSE CONNELL, PH.D., is the Director of Research and Design Development at the Center for Accessible Housing (CAH) at North Carolina State University, and a Research Architect and Chief of the Environmental Section at the Rehab R&D Center, Veterans Administration (VA) Medical Center, Atlanta. She is involved in several of CAH's ongoing projects to characterize the capabilities and housing needs of disabled people of all ages, and to describe and evaluate their housing. At the VA, she is conducting studies on architectural contributions to naturally occurring falls in elderly people, and on the effect of building design and staffing patterns on safety of nursing home residents with Alzheimer's disease.

PAUL JOHN GRAYSON, AIA, M.Arch. (Harvard, 1956), Principal, Environments for Living, advises private and public entities on universal design and strategic planning for housing, health care facilities, and supportive services. He also assists owners and architects in modifying existing and designing new housing that supports self-help and encourages independent living for the elderly and persons with disabilities. Mr. Grayson is co-editor of the book, *Life Care: A Long Term Solution?* and wrote a chapter for *Design Intervention: Toward a More Humane Architecture.* A 1987 Harvard Graduate School of Design Wheelwright Fellow and a 1991 Fellow of the World Rehabilitation Fund's *International Exchange of Experts and Information in Rehabilitation,* he has written numerous articles and has lectured extensively in the United States, Europe, and Japan.

RUSSELL HEREFORD, PH.D., is Project Leader in the Office of Evaluation and Inspection in the Office of the Inspector General at the Department of Health and Human Services (Region I) in Boston. He was the Deputy Director of the Supportive Services Program for Older Persons, a four-year Robert Wood Johnson Foundation demonstration program with several grantee agencies that developed housing adaptation projects. He has published several articles and made numerous presentations in this area. He received his Ph.D. in Social Welfare from Brandeis University's Heller School in 1986.

JOAN HYDE, PH.D., is Senior Policy Analyst in the Gerontology Institute of the University of Massachusetts in Boston, where her work focuses on home and community settings for people with dementia. Her home adaptation work includes training seniors as peer educators, policy research for the Pepper Commission, and the research reported in Chapter 6 of this book. The former Executive Director of the Massachusetts Alzheimer's Association and Principal Investigator of the Administration on Aging-funded Partnerships for Community-Based Alzheimer's Services Project, Dr. Hyde co-founded Hearthstone Alzheimer Care, where she does research and development and operates assisted living facilities for people with dementia. Her degree is in Literature and Psychology, SUNY Buffalo, 1979.

SUSAN LANSPERY, PH.D., a Senior Research Associate at Brandeis University's Heller School, is Co-Director of The Robert Wood Johnson Foundation No Place Like Home program, Co-Principal Investigator of a national study on supportive services in naturally occurring retirement communities, evaluator of the Connecticut Housing Ombudsman Program, and on the staff of the National Resource and Policy Center on Housing and Long-Term Care. A frequent speaker at American Society on Aging, Gerontological Society of America, American Association of Homes and Services for the Aging, and other meetings, she earned her doctorate in social welfare from the Heller School in 1989.

M. POWELL LAWTON, PH.D., was Director of Research at the Philadelphia Geriatric Center for thirty years and is now Senior Research Scientist. His doctorate was in clinical psychology from Teachers College, Columbia University, 1952. He has done research in the environmental psychology of later life, assessment of the aged, the psychological well-being and quality of life for older people, and caregiving stress, and has evaluated programs for the aged and for the mentally ill. He was a member of the technical committee on housing for the 1971

White House Conference on Aging. Among his extensive writings are his books *Environment and Aging* and *Planning and Managing Housing for the Elderly.*

PHOEBE LIEBIG, PH.D., holds a joint faculty appointment in USC's Schools of Public Administration and Gerontology. She consults frequently with state units and area agencies on aging, providing critical information on federal housing legislation and aging network efforts in housing, and is active in national aging organizations. She has written numerous book chapters and articles on long-term care and elderly housing. A fellow of the Gerontological Society of America and a former senior policy analyst with the American Association of Retired Persons' Public Policy Institute, she serves on the editorial board of the *Journal of Aging & Social Policy.*

MOLLI N. MEZRICH, BA, JD, is an attorney practicing in Princeton, New Jersey.

JUDITH RAE MILLER, MPH, PH.D., was the Manager of Project Assist for the Rhode Island Department of Health until her untimely death in December 1994 (see Acknowledgments). Her contributions to this book grew out of her dissertation research—"Disabled elderly homeowners who modify their homes, and the effects of modifications on remaining in those homes"—and her earlier work on a report on senior housing for the Hartford Foundation. A dedicated public health educator, practitioner, and researcher, she played leadership roles in the American Public Health Association (APHA) and other national and local public health organizations. In recognition of her commitment and achievements, the APHA's Public Health Education and Health Promotion section has elected to make an award yearly in her name at the annual meeting. She received her Ph.D. in Social Welfare in 1994 from the Heller School at Brandeis University.

PHYLLIS H. MUTSCHLER, PH.D., Associate Research Professor at the Heller School at Brandeis University, is currently Director of the National Resource and Policy Center on Women and Aging. Her housing adaptation work includes senior authorship of a report for the Hartford Foundation and two Gerontological Society of America presentations. She has also written and presented papers on community-based long-term care, caregiving, and retirement decisions. She received her Ph.D. in Social Welfare in 1985 from the Heller School at Brandeis University.

SANDRA J. NEWMAN, PH.D., is the Associate Director for Research at the Johns Hopkins University Institute for Policy Studies and Research Professor in the Department of Geography and Environmental Engineering. Her research focuses on the housing needs of vulnerable populations, including the frail elderly, and on housing and long-term care policy. She has published extensively in these areas and is a frequent keynote speaker and invited presenter. She holds a Ph.D. from New York University in urban planning.

BRENDA OHTA, MSD, MSW, is presently a partner with Southwest Geriatric Consultation Services in Phoenix and Director of Social Services for Sun Health Corporation in Sun City, Arizona. She holds a Master of Science in Gerontology from the Andrus Gerontology Center at the University of Southern California

(USC), and a Master of Social Work also from USC. Her professional areas of interest include health behaviors of older adults, hospital- and community-based health care delivery, and services to older adults.

RUSSELL J. OHTA, PH.D., a psychologist specializing in the environment and aging, is a partner with Southwest Geriatric Consultation Services in Phoenix, and is a faculty member at Arizona State University West. While on the faculty at the Andrus Gerontology Center at the University of Southern California, he was Project Director of a home modification project for the Center's Program in Policy and Services Research. He has published extensively on the subject of aging and the environment. Dr. Ohta's areas of interest include factors affecting health-related behaviors in older adults, the impact of the environment on the elderly, and in-home and institutional care of dementia patients.

JULIE OVERTON, MSG, MPH, is the Program Coordinator of the National Resource and Policy Center on Housing and Long-Term Care. She has co-authored several reports and monographs on home modifications and repairs and has served as an editor for two newsletters: *Linkages* and *Supportive Housing Options*. As Assistant Director for Dissemination of the National Eldercare Institute on Housing and Supportive Services (1990-1992), she oversaw training, technical assistance, and information dissemination.

JON PYNOOS, PH.D., is Director of the National Resource and Policy Center on Housing and Long-Term Care at the University of Southern California (USC) and Associate Professor of Gerontology and Urban Planning at USC's Andrus Gerontology Center where he heads the Division of Policy and Services Research. He has directed numerous national studies and programs and has authored several books on senior housing and long-term care. His articles appear frequently in major policy and aging journals. He is currently working on several projects in home adaptation.

VICTOR REGNIER, FAIA, is the Dean of the School of Architecture at USC. He has written over forty articles and monographs on elderly housing and has overseen several projects on assisted living and single room occupancy housing. He is a frequent speaker at conferences and consultant to more than eighty nonprofit and proprietary housing projects. A Fulbright Scholar and a fellow of the American Institute of Architects and GSA, he has received awards for his work from such organizations as *Progress Architecture* and *The American Planning Association*.

JON A. SANFORD, M.Arch., is the Coordinator of the Housing Evaluation Program, Center for Accessible Housing at North Carolina State University, and a Research Architect at the Rehab R&D Center, Atlanta Veterans' Administration (VA) Medical Center. Mr. Sanford is involved in several studies to document and evaluate the appropriateness of the living environments of people with impaired mobility, vision, and hearing as well as community residents diagnosed with early-stage Alzheimer's disease. Research projects at the VA include an assessment of the role of architectural contributions to wayfinding and spatial orientation of elderly people, as well as the effects of building design and staffing patterns on safety of Alzheimer's patients in nursing home settings.

NINA M. SILVERSTEIN, PH.D., is a research scientist at the Gerontology Institute at the University of Massachusetts in Boston and an adjunct associate professor of social work at Simmons College, where she has been leading community-based research seminars for graduate social work students since 1984. Recent research has focused on the needs of people with Alzheimer's disease and their families. She has worked closely with the Alzheimer's Association of Eastern Massachusetts on respite care, helpline, support groups, and home adaptation. She also serves on the Needham Council on Aging board. In addition to her training as a social worker, Dr. Silverstein earned a doctorate in 1980 in Social Welfare from the Heller School, Brandeis University.

KATRINKA SMITH SLOAN, MS, is the Manager of Consumer Affairs for the American Association of Retired Persons (AARP). Her responsibilities include: managing the Association's programmatic activities in housing, consumer protection, and consumer finances; overseeing public benefits outreach activities and a financial education program for mid-life and older women; and guiding other consumer education projects in housing and finances. Prior to joining AARP in 1984, she worked on long-term care issues for the American Association of Homes for the Aging. She has a master's degree from George Washington University in Public Policy. Sloan has co-authored a reference book published by ABC-CLIO called *Housing Options and Services for Older Adults* and has written numerous articles for professional journals.

ROBIN TALBERT, BA, JD, is the Assistant Manager of Consumer Affairs for the American Association of Retired Persons (AARP). Her responsibilities include monitoring the impact of the Americans with Disabilities Act on older persons. Prior to joining AARP, Talbert was an attorney with Land of Lincoln Legal Assistance Foundation in Illinois. She holds a BA degree from the University of North Carolina and a JD degree from Washington University School of Law. She co-authored "The Future of the Americans with Disabilities Act," published in the October 1992 *Clearinghouse Review,* and is a frequent speaker on the ADA.

MARY ANN WILNER, PH.D., has worked with providers and consumers of long-term care services for the past fifteen years. Her work has focused on teaching, consulting, and policy research addressing external forces affecting these organizations and strengthening the internal structures of these groups. Located in Brooklyn, New York, she currently has a consulting practice that provides nonprofit organizations with a range of services including strategic planning, agency assessments, program evaluation, and board and staff development and training. Her most recent research, funded by the National Institutes of Health, concerned reducing stress and turnover among nursing assistants through their participation in staff support groups. She received her Ph.D. in 1986 from the Heller School at Brandeis University.

IRVING KENNETH ZOLA, PH.D., was the Mortimer Gryzmish Professor of Human Relations in the Sociology Department at Brandeis University until his sudden death in December 1994 (see Acknowledgments). He was a founding member of Greenhouse, a free-standing mental health clinic; the Boston Self Help Center, an advocacy and counseling center for people with disabilities; the Society of Disability Studies, an academic and professional society; and Community Works, a Greater Boston progressive alternative to the United Way. Since 1981, he had been publisher, editor, and a regular contributor of the *Disability Studies Quarterly.* He was the author of a dozen books and nearly two hundred other publications and the recipient of countless awards and honors. Dr. Zola earned his doctorate from Harvard University in 1962 in Sociology.

Index

Accessory apartments, 10, 51, 72
Activities of daily living, 6-13, 26-28,
    34, 55-56, 66-69, 76, 87, 95-103,
    113-133, 150-154, 173, 180,
    193-194, 210, 238-239, 250, 257
Adaptive Environments Center, 17-18,
    222-224, 263
Administration on Aging (AoA) (*see*
    U.S. Administration on Aging)
Advocacy, 2-3, 11-17, 28, 85-87, 186,
    221, 227, 240, 259-260, 272
American Association of Homes and
    Services for the Aged (AAHSA),
    231
American Association of Retired
    Persons (AARP), 5, 7, 151-152,
    251, 255, 263
American Society on Aging, 7
Americans with Disabilities Act (ADA)
    8-9, 15-17, 28-32, 72, 221,
    223-233, 238, 254, 272
Andrus Gerontology Center, 93, 258
Appearance, 7, 46, 86, 97, 102-106,
    267
Appliances, 2, 16, 46-50, 55-66, 71, 108,
    116-128, 151, 213-214
Area agencies on aging (AAAs), 9,
    171-176, 184-186, 203, 225, 263,
    266, 271
Architects, iv, 10-11, 18, 29-30, 42, 52,
    263
Arthritis, 17, 28, 48, 80, 129, 158, 207,
    212
Assessment, 12-18, 46-51, 80, 87,
    92-110, 115-122, 169, 171-174,
    180-189, 255-260, 266-271
Assisted living, 10, 143

Assistive technology, iii-v, 3-19, 23,
    29-34, 46-50, 55-72, 76, 80,
    92-94, 119-129, 137, 150-154,
    164-165, 171, 187-189, 196-198,
    221-227, 232-233, 253-271
Autonomy, 8-11, 19, 28-31, 45-48, 58,
    210, 216, 257

Barriers, 3, 8, 27-29, 70, 228, 230, 233
Bathrooms, 2, 10, 16, 30-32, 44-52,
    57-70, 80, 107, 113-119, 125-129,
    135-143, 189, 208, 213, 217,
    224-228, 242-243, 264, 269
Bedrooms, 10, 16, 44-45, 57-58, 63-67,
    115, 131, 137, 212, 227
Behavioral issues, 5, 11-16, 41-51,
    75-87, 93-109, 114-116, 152-153,
    208, 240-241, 255-256
Block grants (*see* Community Develop-
    ment or Social Services Block
    Grants)
Brandeis University, 211
Burns, 47, 57, 60, 66, 209

California, 7, 225, 258
Caregiving, iv, 1-12, 32-33, 48, 56-67,
    76, 91-110, 140, 149, 160, 165,
    171, 189, 227, 233, 255-257, 264
Case management, 15, 18, 177-182,
    186-189, 194, 257, 271
Center for Accessible Housing, 115,
    143, 258, 263, 272
Chair lift, 16, 269
Chore services, 10, 46, 152, 171, 179,
    183, 193, 197, 212-213

Chronic conditions, 9, 25-34, 48, 66, 150-158, 165, 253

Clutter, 26, 46, 48, 80, 85, 95

Codes, building and safety, 5, 51-52, 115, 178, 203, 228, 231

Cognitive ability, iv, 8, 12, 34-35, 46-47, 56, 76, 91-110, 129, 213, 223, 230-233, 239-241

Colorado, 211

Communication impairments, 13, 34, 56-64, 71, 116, 125, 215, 223, 228-232

Community Development Block Grants (CDBG), 173-176, 183, 189, 225, 258-259, 267-270

Congregate housing, 10, 210, 218

Consumer Decision Model, 12, 80-87, 97

Consumer education, 7-18, 47-51, 76-87, 108-109, 143, 179, 186-187, 213-214, 227, 257-272

Decision making, 11-13, 28, 34, 58, 71-88, 92-110, 115, 150, 203, 215, 249, 255-256

Delaware, 195

Demographics, 6-7, 25, 33, 254

Depression, 45, 49, 124, 135, 137, 143, 217

Diabetes, 26-28

Discrimination, 158, 223, 227-231, 237-241, 245-249

Doors, 4-5, 11, 16, 30, 42, 47-49, 59-68, 94-96, 102, 114, 119, 125-141, 153, 165, 182, 195, 212-213, 227-230, 242-243, 268

Elder cottage housing opportunities, 10

Eligibility, 10-12, 16, 34, 169, 177, 209-210, 216, 224-231, 241, 257-259, 265-272

Emergency communications, 5, 59-64, 106, 125, 213

Environmental controls (HVAC), 13, 47-50, 57-64, 113-116, 123-138, 182, 212-214, 226, 242

Environmental Press, 4, 114-116, 119, 121

Environment-behavior (E-B), 41-43, 51, 94-95, 109

Europe, 32, 56

Eviction, 210, 214-216, 233, 241, 249

Fair Housing Amendments Act (FHAA), 15-18, 51, 72, 153, 189, 221-233, 237-251, 253, 272

Falling, 15, 31-32, 47-51, 58-62, 68-70, 138-143, 189, 213

Familiarity, importance of, 7, 30, 51, 57, 123, 129, 149, 209, 255

Farmers' Home Administration, 225-226, 270

Financing, 2, 8-18, 24, 30-32, 50-51, 56-58, 72, 75-77, 83-87, 93, 106-109, 143, 152, 158, 165-166, 169-178, 182-189, 194-197, 212-216, 221-234, 243, 254-260, 264-272

Flexibility, importance of, 2, 25, 32-35, 50-51, 61, 72, 210, 232, 265-272

France, 31

Functional ability, 3-4, 9, 48, 56, 79-80, 113-141, 151-153, 158, 165, 174, 180-182, 188, 237-240, 264, 270-271

Georgetown University, 211

Grab bars, 3-5, 12, 16-17, 29-32, 46-52, 59, 67-69, 76, 80, 94, 114-128, 135-143, 152-154, 165, 173, 177, 183, 189, 195, 208, 224, 228, 242-243, 264, 268

Health Belief Model, 80-81

Hearing, 6, 26, 45, 49, 56, 95, 121-128, 213-215, 229-233, 239, 264

Heart conditions, 26, 80, 151, 207, 254

Heller School, 211

Home care (see Supportive services)

Home equity, 2, 7, 16, 149, 153, 158, 165, 225-226, 254, 268-270

Home sharing, 10, 33, 44
Homeowners, iii-iv, 4-18, 32, 43, 51-52,
    76, 114, 124, 129, 135, 149-165,
    173-174, 182, 188-194, 207-208,
    225-228, 243, 250, 255, 259,
    268-271
Housekeeping, 9-10, 16, 123, 209-217,
    225, 244
Housing finance agencies, 14, 18, 176,
    209-217, 226, 259, 263-270
HUD (*see* U.S. Department of Housing
    and Urban Development)

Illinois, 211
Incentives encouraging adaptation, 16,
    32, 186, 213, 266, 268, 272
Independent Living Movement, 23, 33,
    34
Individualizing, 2, 12-13, 46, 77,
    115-123, 180-182, 232

Japan, 56-57, 71

Kitchens, 46, 48, 51, 60, 63-64, 71, 135,
    227, 242, 264, 269

Landlords, 153, 207, 226-228, 241-245,
    250
Lavatory, 58, 63-69, 119, 129, 141,
    143
Legal issues, iii-v, 14, 56, 179, 196-199,
    212-214, 223-253
Levers, 5, 16, 61, 62, 66, 76, 114, 119,
    189, 195, 212-213
Lighting, 5, 13, 24, 30, 45-50, 58-71,
    107, 114, 116, 119, 133, 212-213,
    224, 242
Low-Income Home Energy Assistance
    Program (LIHEAP), 175, 226

Maine, 195, 211
Maryland, 176, 266, 270-271

Massachusetts, 17-18, 97, 108, 211, 225,
    228
Meal services, 3, 9-10, 34, 64, 116, 125,
    131, 137, 209, 213, 217, 225, 232,
    239
Medicaid, 9, 12, 16-17, 180, 189, 215,
    221, 224, 258-259, 270-271
Medicare, 9, 16, 150, 189, 224, 258-259,
    267
Mental disabilities, 8, 46, 135, 229, 231,
    237, 239
Michigan, 195
Minnesota, 31, 176, 266, 269-270
Mobility, 3-5, 11, 17, 26, 29, 34, 48-49,
    56-66, 80, 114-138, 151-154, 174,
    189, 207, 212-213, 217, 244, 258,
    268
Monitoring systems, in-home, 29, 34,
    45, 60-66, 213
Multiple sclerosis, 26-27
Multi-unit housing, 3-4, 29-30, 51, 125,
    149, 207-217, 223, 227, 237-244,
    250, 264
Musculoskeletal problems, 26-27, 48,
    113, 239

National Affordable Housing Act, 189
National Association of Home Builders,
    7, 172, 239, 263
National Association of Remodelers, 264
National Council on the Aging, 7
National Institute on Disability and
    Rehabilitation Research, 144, 263
National Invitational Conference on
    Home Modifications Policy, 7,
    172, 263-272
National Long Term Care Surveys, 76,
    150-153, 165, 250
National Resource and Policy Center on
    Housing and Long-Term Care,
    258
New construction, iii, 3, 6-7, 16-19, 29,
    172, 223, 232, 267, 272
New Hampshire, 211
New Jersey, 195, 211
New York City, 195

New Zealand, 32
No Place Like Home Program, 210
North Carolina State University, 115,
   143, 258, 263, 272
Nursing, 13, 97, 102-110, 180-182, 195,
   199-203, 257

Occupational therapy, 10, 16, 180-189,
   256, 263, 271
Ohio, 176
Older Americans Act, 9, 14, 173-177,
   225, 258
Orientation and way finding, 46-47, 51,
   95, 129, 135
Orthopedic impairments, 124-128

Paraplegia, 26, 115
Pennsylvania, 211, 266, 268
Philadelphia Corporation for Aging,
   268-269
Physicians, 15, 84-85, 189, 224, 260
Planners, 5, 41-42, 52, 184, 209
Polio, 27, 81
Privacy, 11, 42-45, 55, 241
Private sector, 15-18, 32, 172-175,
   186-188, 194, 203, 208, 224,
   228-229, 257, 265-266, 272
Psychological issues, v, 11, 41-45, 79,
   87, 239
Public policy, iv-vi, 2-7, 14-19, 23-35,
   42-56, 77, 92-94, 149, 165-175,
   182-190, 193, 221-272

Quadriplegia, 26
Quality assurance, 14, 178, 184, 196,
   201, 210-212, 257, 266, 272
Quality of life, 2, 41-45, 51-58, 70-72,
   209-213, 233, 256, 264

Railings, 2, 5, 15-17, 29-30, 46-52, 62,
   75, 94, 119, 135-143, 152, 173,
   183, 264, 268

Ramps, 5, 12, 16, 29-32, 47-51, 60, 114,
   125, 135-143, 152-153, 165, 173,
   183, 195, 213, 224, 264, 269-271
Reasonable accommodation, 229-230,
   238, 243-249
Rehabilitation
   health and functional, 27, 57-58,
      114-116, 122, 129-131, 227-228
   housing, 8, 173, 184, 242, 269-272
Rehabilitation Act (Section 504),
   228-230, 238, 243
Remodelers, 7, 16, 19, 172, 188-189,
   194, 263-265, 271
Renters, 10, 13, 76, 149, 151-157, 174,
   207-218, 226-228, 237-245, 250,
   255, 268
Repairs, 1-9, 13-18, 30, 49, 151-157,
   165, 169-203, 214-215, 225-226,
   254-260, 264-271
Respiratory problems, 3, 17, 26, 224
Reverse mortgages, 16, 24, 188, 225
Rhode Island, 176, 211
Robert Wood Johnson Foundation, iv,
   4, 14, 152, 170, 194, 209

Safety and security, 1-5, 9-16, 26, 30-35,
   41-52, 55-71, 93-109, 129, 143,
   173-189, 193, 207-209, 213-215,
   225, 231, 240-241, 249, 256-260,
   264-270
Secondary disabilities, 9, 27
Senior housing, iii, 13-14, 76, 149, 154,
   170, 207-218, 225-226, 230, 232,
   240, 268-271
Sensory functioning, 35, 47-49, 55-64,
   113-116, 124-128, 223, 239
Service coordination, 14, 49, 208-218,
   257-259, 266-267
Showers, 16, 32, 45-47, 52, 59-60,
   67-71, 80, 116, 124-131, 137-141,
   177
Signs, 47, 108, 233
Single room occupancy hotels, 232, 242
Social costs, 82, 83, 256
Social interaction, 6-11, 14, 23, 27,
   42-45, 50, 82, 95, 208-218, 257,
   264

Social Security, 28, 246
Social Services Block Grants, 175, 227
Social workers, 103, 106, 110, 180-182, 199, 202, 267
Spina bifida, 25, 27
Spinal cord injury, 26, 27
Stairs, 3-5, 12, 32, 48-52, 62, 71, 75, 95, 125-132, 138, 151, 180, 207, 213
State units on aging, 9, 172, 176, 184, 186
Stigma, 16-18, 47, 57, 96, 210, 267
Stimulation, 45, 48-49, 86
Stroke, 135, 254
Supplemental Security Income, 215
Supportive services, v, 2-5, 8-19, 23-35, 42, 46, 51, 56, 66, 71, 108-109, 123, 149-152, 170, 184-189, 193-203, 207-218, 225-227, 231, 244, 253-260, 264-266, 270-271
Supportive Services Program for Older Persons, 14, 194-203
Supportive Services Program in Senior Housing, 14, 207-218
Sweden, 3, 31

Tax incentives, 16, 30, 32, 225-227, 258, 266, 269-270
Technology-Related Assistance for Individuals with Disabilities Act (Tech Act), 227
Telephone, 16, 44-50, 59, 64, 106, 116, 124-137, 227-233, 264, 272
Texas, 195
The Netherlands, 32
Toileting, 30-32, 44, 60, 66-69, 80, 87, 114, 119, 129-131, 135-143, 153, 165, 189, 213, 231, 239
Training,
  professionals, v, 16, 51, 169-182, 186-189, 210, 214-216, 257, 260, 265-268
  consumers, 18, 114, 131, 135, 210, 215-217, 227, 265
Transferring, 34, 58-62, 66-70, 80, 119, 123-129, 135-141, 189

Transportation, 9, 29, 60, 123, 184, 210-212, 225, 228-232

Universal design, 11, 18, 24, 51, 56-72, 143-144, 187-189, 228, 234, 253, 256, 266-267, 272
University of Massachusetts, 18
University of Southern California, 258
U.S. Administration on Aging, 176, 190
U.S. Department of Education, 227
U.S. Department of Energy, 173, 175-177, 226
U.S. Department of Health and Human Services, vi, 6, 150, 190, 263, 272
U.S. Department of Housing and Urban Development, vi, 6-8, 172, 225, 240-249, 258-272

Vermont, 211
Veterans Administration, 226
Virginia, 211
Visual impairment, 4, 17, 26-27, 45-50, 56-57, 62-64, 80, 95, 108, 119-131, 151, 212-215, 230
Vocational Rehabilitation Programs, 227
Volunteers, 14, 24, 169, 174, 177, 179, 185-186, 271

Washington, 195
Weatherization, 16, 171-177, 180-184, 187-188, 226, 259, 270
Wheelchairs, 4, 30, 45, 50-51, 58-71, 119-121, 128, 135-143, 174, 189, 195, 208, 215, 224-227, 231, 242-244, 258, 264, 269
Windows, 17, 45, 47-50, 60-64, 119-121, 131-133, 138, 173, 183, 193, 208-209, 213
World Institute on Disability, 34

Zoning, 51, 72, 249

Other Titles in the

SOCIETY AND AGING SERIES

Jon Hendricks, Series Editor

**Health & Economic Status of Older Women:
Research Issues and Data Sources**
A. Regula Herzog, Karen C. Holden, and Mildred M. Seltzer

Special Research Methods for Gerontology
M. Powell Lawton and A. Regula Herzog

Aging Public Policy: Bonding the Generations
Theodore H. Koff and Richard W. Park

Defining Acts: Aging as Drama
Robert Kastenbaum

Dorian Graying: Is Youth the Only Thing Worth Having?
Robert Kastenbaum

**The Old Age Challenge to the Biomedical Model:
Paradigm Strain and Health Policy**
Charles F. Longino, Jr. and John W. Murphy

Surviving Dependence: Voices of African American Elders
May M. Ball and Frank J. Whittington